Sociology of Education Series

Gary Natriello, SERIES EDITOR

ADVISORY BOARD: Jomills Braddock, Sanford Dornbusch,
Adam Gamoran, Marlaine Lockheed, Hugh Mehan,
Mary Metz, Aaron Pallas, Richard Rubinson

Mandating Academic Excellence:
High School Responses to State Curriculum Reform
Bruce L. Wilson and Gretchen B. Rossman

Mandating Academic Excellence

High School Responses to State Curriculum Reform

Bruce L. Wilson

Gretchen B. Rossman

TEACHERS COLLEGE PRESS

Teachers College, Columbia University
New York and London

This publication is based upon work performed by Research for Better Schools, Inc., under a contract from the Office of Educational Research and Improvement, U.S. Department of Education. However, the opinions expressed herein do not necessarily reflect the position or policy of the Office of Educational Research and Improvement and no official endorsement thereof shall be inferred.

Published by Teachers College Press, 1234 Amsterdam Avenue, New York, N.Y. 10027

Library of Congress Cataloging-in-Publication Data

Wilson, Bruce L.
   Mandating academic excellence: high school responses to state curriculum reform/Bruce L. Wilson, Gretchen B. Rossman.
     p.   cm.—(Sociology of education series)
   Includes bibliographical references (p.) and index.
   ISBN 0-8077-3264-8 (alk. paper).—ISBN 0-8077-3263-X (pbk.: alk. paper)
   1. High schools—United States—Curricula. 2. High schools—Maryland—Curricula—Case studies. 3. High schools—United States—Graduation requirements. 4. High schools—Maryland—Graduation requirements—Case studies. 5. Academic achievement—United States. 6. Academic achievement—Maryland—Case studies. 7. Curriculum change—United States. 8. Curriculum change—United States—Case studies. I. Rossman, Gretchen B. II. Title. III. Series:
Sociology of education series (New York, N.Y.)
LB1628.5W55 1993
373.19'0973—dc20   92-45749

ISBN 0-8077-3264-8
ISBN 0-8077-3263-X (pbk)

Printed on acid-free paper
Manufactured in the United States of America
99 98 97 96 95 94 93 8 7 6 5 4 3 2 1

Contents

Acknowledgments

A study of this magnitude would not have been possible without the assistance of a wide number of people and organizations. First, we would like to thank the Maryland State Department of Education for collaborating with us. Without the interest and commitment of Janice Earle, this study would never have been conceived, and without the department's continued support, this report would most certainly never have been produced. In particular, Maurice Howard and Eileen Oickle of the Division of Instruction were instrumental in paving our way to the schools, helping in the data collection, and being constructive critics of our work throughout the study.

A special vote of gratitude goes to the students and staff at the high schools. They endured repeated visits and interruptions to their daily routines with nary a complaint. They must remain anonymous for the purpose of this research. However, their candor, insightfulness, and humor were very real to us and made each of our visits a real pleasure.

Several colleagues offered valuable design advice during the research. In particular, we want to thank Gary Natriello, Mike Garet, and Bill Cooley. The work and words of Jeannie Oakes have also been sources of encouragement.

Our colleagues at Research for Better Schools were invaluable. Dick Corbett worked alongside us throughout the entire project and, as always, offered advice and a sense of perspective that greatly enriched our work. Lynne Adduci ensured that the research design was implemented as planned and offered valuable insights during the data analysis and report-writing stages. More than half the professional staff conducted interviews or transcribed student records. Nadine Fernandez, Joe D'Amico, Arlene Large, and Shannon Cahill contributed more than could be expected. The analysis of student transcripts was a daunting task made easier by the contributions of Marge Connelly, Peter Batschlet, and Larry Bullock. Finally, Rhonda Mordecai endured the messiest job of data entry, word processing, and electronic file transfers with patience and understanding. Editorial assistance by Keith Kershner and Ullik Rouk made our early drafts much more coherent.

   We also wish to acknowledge the assistance of two anonymous reviewers who raised a number of key questions that helped strengthen our arguments immeasurably. Finally, we are indebted to our editor at Teachers College Press, Brian Ellerbeck, who not only handled the mechanics of the process with competence and humor but also made valuable substantive contributions.

From the Series Editor

The current volume by Wilson and Rossman launches the Teachers College Press Series in the Sociology of Education. The series will publish high-quality studies in the field of sociology that are particularly relevant to educational researchers and practitioners. Volumes in the series will include works at the macrolevel dealing with key issues of the relationship of education to American and other societies, at the middle range dealing with the operation and organization of schools and other educational organizations, and at the microlevel dealing with social and interpersonal dimensions of the educational process in classrooms and other learning environments.

The study reported here illustrates some of the contributions that contemporary work in the sociology of education can make to analyses of educational practices and issues. Wilson and Rossman take as the subject of their study a common state policy reform of the 1980s, the adoption of additional high school course requirements for graduation. Examining such new requirements in a single state, Maryland, they focus much of their attention on the reaction to such state-mandated changes at the level of the local school. They study five high schools located in different kinds of communities and serving different kinds of student bodies. Their work exemplifies five strengths that studies in the sociology of education can bring to examinations of educational policies.

First, Wilson and Rossman build into the design of their work an explicit concern with the local social context in which the state-mandated reforms must operate. The contrasts in local circumstances built into the selection of schools enable Wilson and Rossman to consider the complexities of implementing statewide reforms in quite different local social contexts.

Second, the study considers key features of the social and organizational structure of schools as important variables in examining the effects of the new requirements. The fourth chapter of the book is devoted to an analysis of the impact of the graduation requirements on the tracking of students within each of the five high schools. Tracking systems that stratify curricular knowledge and the students granted access to such knowledge have long been a focus of study for sociologists of education. Wilson and Rossman rely on recent work on tracking systems as a framework for considering the impact of the new requirements on the tracks that operate to stratify knowledge and students in the five high schools.

A third strength of the current work further develops the general concern with the access of students to academic resources. In the fifth chapter, Wilson and Rossman consider the effects of the change in graduation requirements on those students most at risk of school failure: minority-group students, female students, and lower ability students. This interest in those students least well served by schools continues a long-standing tradition in the sociology of education.

Examination of the chain of events from the development of the new policy through the implementation of the policy in the five high schools, to assessments of the policy by staff in the schools and post-secondary educators and employers, represents a fourth defining strength of the current volume. Wilson and Rossman take the original intentions of the policy framers seriously enough to inquire as to whether the intended effects were realized. This kind of examination, although necessary if we are to learn from policy initiatives, is all too rare in the realm of educational policy making and implementation.

Finally, Wilson and Rossman make use of a variety of both qualitative and quantitative data from sources at multiple levels in the educational system and the larger environment to provide a complex portrait of the new requirements in operation. This kind of inquiry is becoming more common in contemporary work in the sociology of education and promises to strengthen studies as it has done in the current case.

In sum, this book makes use of theoretical perspectives and methodological tools developed by sociologists of educational reform initiative of the 1980s. As such, it represents the application of the sociological approach to educational phenomena that will also characterize further volumes in this series.

Gary Natriello

Foreword

Someone once told me that policy-making is an art of making wise decisions within a time frame that is shorter than desired, with less information than one needs and with less resources than one should have. With the advent of education reform, state education policymakers have assumed awesome responsibilities. Their actions affect the lives of our children and set in order the future of our public education enterprise.

In the 1980s, state policymakers initiated unprecedented action to improve the quality of education for America's youth. Universally, states increased graduation requirements and strengthened the core curriculum within schools. These stronger graduation requirements emerged as the key tools that states used to leverage education improvement in schools and districts.

And reform marched on. Policymakers continued to take action, often without the benefit of a dialogue about the effects of the early reform. Today, school reform is still at center stage. As they take action, state policymakers need to know much more about the effects and consequences of their early actions. They need to learn as many lessons as possible from schools that are impacted by their decisions. They need to have rich information presented in a meaningful format to establish future policies that are most beneficial to our children and youth and helpful to dedicated professionals within our schools.

Within this dynamic environment, policymakers yearn for well-researched and thoughtful analyses of our actions. We gravitate toward those who can offer assistance as we chart new directions for public education under this broad banner we call restructuring.

This book is must reading for state and local policymakers. In it, Wilson and Rossman provide us with an increased understanding of our early reform efforts by analyzing the responses of five schools to Maryland's increased course requirements. But more helpful are their insights into these local actions and their thorough analysis of the emerging themes that will drive future restructuring efforts. Most of us engaged in restructuring have given lip service to the importance of the local school. Wilson and Rossman move this dimension to a new plateau by placing the issue of local variation and circumstance at the center of their research. They note vast differences in the ways in which school districts responded to state action. They help us to understand the influence of previous practice, school conditions, tracking, school demography, and tradition on a school's ability and willingness to respond to state challenges. Their work helps us to understand the consequences of our actions on the most vulnerable students, on schools and schooling, and on the conditions of teaching and the practice of teachers. While recognizing and supporting an increased state role in education, Wilson and Rossman help us to see the constraints of policy made from afar. They provide advice about how we can focus and realign our energies to build local capacity, increase learning for students, and improve practice by teachers.

This book is a fresh reminder and a reaffirmation that our work is still undone for students of color, undone for students who perform below expectations, undone for many urban and rural schools that we serve, and undone in terms of ways to engage teachers in the improvement of practice and the development of policy.

This book is a case study of one state, but it is a source of guidance for all states. I ask policymakers to pay particular attention to Chapter 8, "Educational Reform: Retrospect and Prospect," in which Wilson and Rossman strike a match between the current reform challenges and the earlier education reform initiatives. Their challenges for schools and state policymakers provide a valuable context for organizing statewide restructuring efforts in the future. This book provides a glimpse of what the future could hold if we move to affect the technical core of schools. Wilson and Rossman advocate that we move beyond simple definitions of restructuring to a rethinking of the basic purposes and functions of schools. Their plea to state policymakers to set a clear vision to empower and support those close to students; to encourage experimentation, risk taking, and innovation around our visions and goals; and to transform the way we use information systems could very well provide a basis for strategic planning at the state level.

Wilson and Rossman do not answer all of your questions in this book. In fact, your questions will be more complex and you will desire additional information. But this book will provide you with a greater understanding of our past actions, a bridge to understanding new ways to build local capacity, and new frameworks for organizing our future actions.

Gene Wilhoit

Foreword

One of the most popular reforms of the 1980s was to increase high school graduation requirements. At least 45 states modified these rules in the 1980s, usually to increase the number of courses mandated overall and specifically in science and mathematics. Such changes had a surface logic to them. They were something that states could do. The legal authority was clear, and districts could easily be inspected for compliance. Such reforms were popular; they showed that states were "getting tough" with students and schools that were widely perceived to be sloughing off. Moreover, it seemed fairly obvious (and there was research to support the conclusion) that students would learn more if more was expected of them. There was even hope that tougher requirements would increase educational equity by ensuring that historically low achievers were introduced to more demanding academic content.

Wilson and Rossman provide a rich analysis of the implementation and effects of changes in graduation requirements in one state. It is an extremely positive example of how "academic" policy analysis—i.e., analysis that does not rush to judgment and that has the opportunity to raise questions that might not have been central to the original policy makers—can enlighten the policy process by ensuring that difficult questions are not overlooked. It is a useful example for national attention because Maryland, the state in question, was fairly thoughtful in designing its requirements. If such simple changes were to have broadly beneficial results, Maryland was a likely place for them to appear.

Wilson and Rossman's analysis is rich in several senses. First, it shows the subtle and complex pattern of effects that a simple policy brought about. Increasing high school graduation requirements did increase students' access to academic content, but only for some students and for some content. Some students, usually those who were not college bound, did take more mathematics, science, and a few other subjects, but at the expense of some vocational courses. In fact, it suggests that the changes resulting from this policy shift were hardly noticed by the employers of high school graduates.

Second, it raises one of the major value issues of the last decade: how to resolve the tension between excellence, improving the cognitive capacity of American youth in general, with equity, the effort to ensure that children of all ethnicities, classes,and genders have equal access to schooling. It does so by examining what happens when state mandates intersect with some of the most deeply embedded institutions in the American educational system. In this case, the effects of graduation requirements were filtered by pre-existing systems for tracking and scheduling students. Minority students are found disproportionately in lower tracks and have access to less challenging instructional content. While the state policy reduced some of the differences between tracks, particularly in mathematics, these differences continue to be profound and largely untouched by simple changes in graduation requirements.

Third, it points to the limits of policy as a way of improving education. This is not only done by showing how such entrenched institutions as tracking constrain the effects of new initiatives. A further contribution is made by showing that state policy is just one factor affecting local decisions about what to teach to whom. In spite of central efforts to rationalize and standardize, there is great variation in how schools carry out policy. The five schools (and their districts) differed in the attention they gave to this change in state policy as well as the interpretation of it. These differences reflected a difficult-to-specify mix of variation in student clientele and external community support, as well as administrative interest. The result was that the same policy had a very different impacts from school to school. Equity was achieved more in some schools than in others.

Finally, Wilson and Rossman debunk some of the (contradictory) myths about the policy in question. If they show that the expectations that tough standards would equalize access to education were not met, they also provide evidence that fears that increased graduation requirements would raise the dropout rate were equally unfounded. Both expectations were contradicted by larger social forces. Tracking undermined efforts to equalize access to content; and a wide variety of out-of-school factors had a concerted effect on students' decisions to complete their education than did graduation requirements.

Beyond this analysis of policy impacts, Wilson and Rossman offer important lessons for future policy—namely, that simple policy modifications do not lead to big changes in what students learn. To really increase the learning of all students, modified graduation requirements must be part of a larger effort that meets five criteria. It must:

- Be systemic, combining changes in curriculum, teaching strategies, organizational structures, and professional relations
  among other things;
- Be grounded in a constructivist view of students as active
  learners;
- Change relations between students and teachers;
- Modify and broaden conceptions of what should be learned in
  school and how learning should be assessed; and
- Emphasize inclusion and caring for children rather than exclusion and sorting.

In sum, this book provides important information for teachers, administrators, counselors, and policy makers about how to address some of the most significant educational issues of our time and what role state and local government can play in the improvement process. At the same time, it provides a model of careful and complex analysis that should be followed by those who seek to examine the effects of future reforms.

William A. Firestone

Mandating Academic Excellence

High School Responses to State Curriculum Reform

1

INTRODUCTION

Americans have a curious fascination with schooling as a powerful lever of social reform. Although there is often criticism of our schools, there is also eternal optimism that reforms in schools will right many of society's ills. The history of American education has been replete with such reform initiatives, many of which have focused specifically on the high school (Cuban, 1990; Passow, 1984). These date back before the turn of the century. For example, the Committee on Secondary School Studies (1893), composed of a group of university presidents, focused their attention on standardizing high school curricula with a concentration on precollegiate education. In 1918, the National Education Association's *Cardinal Principles of Secondary Education* (Commission on the Reorganization of Secondary Education, 1918) pushed for broadened goals for the American high school, with an emphasis on citizenship and ethical behavior. More recently, the post-Sputnik reforms in the early 1960s encouraged significant changes in mathematics and science curricula, with associated reform in teacher training and staff development (Atkin & House, 1981).

The 1980s brought yet another wave of what have been many attempts to reform our educational system, with particular attention being paid to the high school curriculum. This reform wave, with increased requirements for high school graduation as its centerpiece, has been driven by concern that our economic standing is eroding in the international marketplace, largely as a function of the inadequate training of our labor force.

What is significant about this latest round of reform initiatives is the active role of states in designing new policies to reform America's high schools. Although there is justified caution about the potential for rational, mandated reform to truly affect what happens in schools and classrooms (Cuban, 1990), that has not dampened the enthusiasm of policymakers for promoting such reform efforts. Despite states' intent to significantly improve student standards with new requirements, little is known about how local schools and districts responded. What have been the effects of this recent reform? This book attempts to answer that question by offering a systematic, empirical look at the most widely adopted policy reform strategy of the decade: changes in high school graduation requirements.

We use Maryland as a case study to illustrate the complexity of using state-initiated policy as a reform tool. Those local effects are described and interpreted in this book through a focus on the local perspective. The research incorporates both qualitative and quantitative methods to capture the full range of effects through the experiences of staff and students in five diverse high school settings. These findings from 1980s' policy reform are then linked to the current dialogue about reform. We conclude the book by offering challenges to practitioners and policymakers that encourage analysis of policy reform by focusing on technical, political, cultural, and moral issues simultaneously.

The results of our research suggest that the state-initiated policy reform of graduation requirements had only modest effects on local school organization and students' educational experiences. We found vast differences across the five high schools in response to the reform initiative, with this variation being a function of local capacity, will, and attention. Students also responded differentially to the changes. Tracks continued to play a significant role in explaining student opportunities, as did race and academic performance. We also noted a vacuum in key actors' efforts to influence the policy arena. Most of the individuals at various levels of the system felt powerless to shape policy-making or its implementation. Finally, when we talked to the consumers of the product of increased requirements—local employers and institutions of higher education—they were unimpressed with changes in students as a result of the reform. They were largely unaware of the tightened requirements and reported no increase in student preparedness.

PERSPECTIVE

Certainly, there has been plenty of speculation in the literature about what one might expect from state reform initiatives. Wise (1979) labels the process of state reform by policy mandate as "hyperrationalization"—that is, the application of excessively rationalistic, bureaucratic procedures to complex social phenomena like schooling. From his perspective, the proposed effects (better students) are far too ambitious for the means (increases in course and credit requirements) and are therefore unachievable. Others, like Resnick and Resnick (1985) and Serow (1986), argue that even if the proposed effects were more modest, there would still be little chance of achieving them. Historically, state-initiated graduation reforms have simply had little, if any, impact. State initiatives are often blunted or diverted as they trickle down to local education agencies (Elmore, 1980; Rossman, Corbett, & Dawson, 1986). Indeed, the most visible effects would likely be unintended or even unexpected (Merton, 1968). For example, stricter graduation requirements are seen as (1) alternatively raising (Glatthorn, 1986; McDill, Natriello, & Pallas, 1986) or lowering the dropout rate (Hamilton, 1986); (2) causing large-scale, costly alterations in the school day and the school year (Toch, 1984); (3) affecting the curriculum in terms of fewer courses offered, more basic—rather than accelerated—courses, and diminished curriculum articulation (Bickel, 1986); and (4) possibly eroding teacher morale (Cross, 1987).

Our research focused on the extent to which the new graduation requirements improved opportunities for students to have a more meaningful high school educational experience and the extent to which the reform altered the way schools went about their work. More specifically, five key questions drove the research. These five questions emerged from a combination of issues raised by previous policy research, the implicit philosophy undergirding the discussions that preceded the specific policy change in the state, and the concerns raised by practitioners in the field during the early stages of implementation. The five questions and a brief rationale for each are as follows:

1. *What is the local variation in response to the policy change?* Early research on planned change assumed fidelity in the implementation process. But more recent research has revealed the complexity of school change. The most compelling finding is the power of local context to shape or redefine mandated reforms. That is, local schools and districts vary enormously in their

responses to state-initiated policy reforms. Rather than being surprised by that finding, this question anticipates and makes use of it in interpreting the effects of the reform on local schools.

2. *How has the policy affected tracks and tracking systems as a form of access to resources?* An enduring feature of American schools is the way they sort students and the way those sorting mechanisms support or constrain students' access to educational opportunities. The research literature is replete with accounts of the deleterious effects of formal and informal tracking systems on student opportunity. Although the intent of the policy change was to encourage a wider range of students to take more challenging courses, interviews with students and teachers early in the implementation process suggested that intent may not always be fulfilled.

3. *What impact has the policy had on students and teachers at risk?* Tracking systems are not the only mechanisms by which winners and losers are identified in schools. Inequities by gender, race, and academic performance are also key themes in the literature on educational resources. A clearly underattended question is the degree to which policy reforms affect those that have traditionally been most at risk. Even before the new graduation policy took effect, local educators voiced concerns about potentially damaging consequences for some students. The concerns even extended to some groups of teachers.

4. *How has the policy altered educators' perceptions of their influence over their work?* The research literature suggests that those charged with daily implementation of a policy have more direct influence over the scope and fidelity of implementation. Thus, as one moves down the organizational hierarchy from the state to the schoolhouse, we should detect an increased sense of influence over the new policy change. Yet early conversations, even at the state level, revealed a policy vacuum where others (usually at a higher level) were viewed as having more influence. Everyone seemed to be saying that someone else had more influence to use the policy to make a difference in students' lives.

5. *What was the intent of the policy, and how well has that been met as perceived by those outside the secondary education community?* The implicit, intuitive causal model that drove policymakers to enact graduation requirement reforms was that more focus in course choices would better prepare students for their postsecondary experiences. Although that model was confirmed both by analysis of available documents and by interviews with key policymakers, it still left open whether the model worked. Was the

policy intent realized? Most of the analysis addressing the first four questions involved data taken from within the educational community. This final question broadened the issue by forcing an outside test—with consumers in colleges and universities as well as in industry.

To answer these questions, our research team observed how five different high schools responded to the reform over time. The assumption was that implementation would not be uniform across schools; indeed, the most interesting story is local variability and how that variability met local needs. Only about 10% of any desired change, in fact, is accounted for by a preferred strategy (e.g., increased course requirements for graduation); the remainder is dependent on implementation (Allison, 1971). Thus, observing local schools' behavior is the key to understanding the impact of a state reform.

Elmore (1980) describes a strategy of "backward mapping" for understanding local-level policy ramifications. Backward mapping questions whether policymakers control the organizational, political, and technological processes that impact implementation and whether their explicit directives, clear statements of administrative responsibilities, and well-defined outcomes really increase the probability that the policy will be successfully implemented. Backward mapping concentrates instead on behaviors at the target level of the implementation process (i.e., the behavior of students and professionals in schools). Much of the research energy in this study was directed toward local schools rather than toward the designers of the strategy.

The shift from the state's perspective to one that values local contextual variation has been driven in part by a growing awareness that "local knowledge" (Geertz, 1983) matters and that an organizational perspective may powerfully illuminate local responses. This "new" local perspective suggests to analysts that schools and districts are as significant in the policy process as the state (Fuhrman & Elmore, 1990; Timar & Kirp, 1989). State-local relations are no longer viewed as a zero-sum game in which control is the dominant variable; those relations are much more complex, driven as much by local as by the state's capacity and initiative:

> Districts often leverage state policies by using local influence networks to reinforce local political agendas and to engage in local policy entrepreneurship. The result is often that the local effects of state policy are greater than those one would predict on the basis of state capacity and that localities often gain influence as a result of state policymaking rather than lose it. (Fuhrman & Elmore, 1990, p. 94)

In addition to contributing to the literature on policy implementation, this research adds to the ongoing discourse about high schools, much of which has been critical of the patterns of inequities inherent in high school structures. Specifically, it extends the tradition of work that has examined how resources are differentially allocated in high schools and how adolescents of poverty and color and, at times, girls are denied that access. Within this tradition, for example, high school curricula are critiqued for reproducing the subordination and dependency of lower-class girls (Valli, 1988), while at times challenging forms of patriarchy, but only marginally (Weiss, 1988). Children of poverty, those often more disaffected from the structured middle-class forms of high schools, drop in and out of school with some regularity (Fine, 1991), and students of color become "invisible" (Rist, 1978; but see Stanlaw & Peshkin, 1988).

More globally, U.S. high schools encourage a "bargain" between teachers and students in which teachers agree not to challenge students too directly in exchange for reasonably decent classroom behavior (Cusick, 1983; Sizer, 1984). The mid-1980s curriculum reflected this bargain by offering a panoply of courses designed to interest students but, again, not challenge them too fiercely (Powell, Farrar, & Cohen, 1985).

In this book, we focus on resources that are high powered and of high status—the sorts of experiences that grant one entree into the world of postsecondary education. In so doing, we extend the notion, articulated by Hargreaves (1982) over a decade ago, that the sociologist's concern is often with "the differential allocation and distribution of . . . valued goods [occupation, social position, income, property, and power]" and with "the *differential opportunities of access to these valued goods*" (p. 11, emphasis added).

The sorting function of schools in general and of high schools in particular has been well documented in the literature (DiMaggio, 1977). Historically, the diploma was believed to represent the mastery of certain knowledge and skills and to certify that mastery to the larger society. Although that may have been true through mid-century, it is no longer the case (Sedlak, Wheeler, Pullin, & Cusick, 1986). Much of the recent critique of high schools may be attributed to an increasing sense of dissonance between the diploma and the knowledge and skills offered by its possessors—the graduates. The standards-raising movement—the wave of reform begun in the mid-1980s with strong elements alive and well today, one aspect of which this research has examined—may be viewed as "strong pressure to re-establish the high school credential as a comprehensive, meritocratic, academic sorting mechanism based upon content" (Sedlak, Wheeler, Pullin, & Cusick, 1986, p. 22).

We look beneath the generic diploma, however, to better understand how one aspect of that standards-raising movement—increased graduation requirements and differential diplomas—affected the high school careers of students generally. Increased access to high-status courses, those that promote entree to postsecondary education, was the intent of much of the graduation requirements reform. This reform, however, may well be "a crueler form of screening and pushing people out of educational opportunities" (Sedlak, Wheeler, Pullin, & Cusick, 1986, p. 23) should it not fulfill its promise of increasing access to educational opportunities. Our research in part confirms this dark prediction: that students who have historically been denied access to high-status courses continue to be excluded. Although the reform studied showed modest effects in terms of increased participation in academic and advanced courses, the patterns of exclusion persist.

Our research also adds to the research tradition that has focused on tracks and tracking in secondary schools (Garet & DeLany, 1988; Oakes, 1985; Page, 1987; Rosenbaum, 1976). Specifically, we have examined how a standards-raising reform—increased graduation requirements—has shaped the course-taking patterns of high school students. Understanding that one intent of this reform was to "beef up" the content represented by the high school diploma, we undertook an investigation of how students of various often-at-risk descriptions—students of color, girls, low performers, and those in the lower tracks—responded. We have tried to unpack some of the more informal processes in high schools—those in which students are subtly categorized and sorted into lower statuses—which result (at least in part) in course choices. Although the results describe aspects of high schools generally, they address more specifically this aspect of the standards-raising movement, judging it in large part a failure without the systemic change called for by today's reformists.

RESEARCH STRATEGY

The focus on the local response to state-mandated reform requires an in-depth look at changes over a significant period of time. We chose five high schools that were broadly representative of the Maryland high school experience and spent 4 years documenting the changes in those sites. System and building administrators, guidance counselors, teachers, and students were all interviewed, and 850 interviews were conducted. In addition, we analyzed almost 2,000 student transcripts from the five high schools, comparing course-taking patterns between the class of 1986, which was not affected by the new requirements, and the classes of 1989 and 1990, the first two classes to graduate under the new requirements. Researchers also examined course catalogs, master schedules, and brochures. Finally, we interviewed several Maryland High School Commission members (the group charged in 1982 with recommending changes in the nature and character of high schools) and staff from the Maryland State Department of Education (MSDE) who were responsible for implementation. Appendix A contains a full description of the research methods used in the study. Readers interested in all the research protocols are referred to the technical report (Wilson, Rossman, & Adduci, 1991).

RESEARCH SITES

This section briefly describes each of the five high schools and their larger district context. Pseudonyms are used to protect the confidentiality of respondents. The pseudonyms were chosen to be broadly descriptive of the character of each high school. The five schools are Fast Track, United Nations, Urban, Middle Class, and Rural.

Fast Track High School

Fast Track High School is located in a rapidly growing suburb of Baltimore. Once a quiet, self-contained community surrounded by farmland, Fast Track has become a bedroom community for the nearby city. New housing developments have brought an increasingly upwardly mobile population. The average household income across the county increased by 13% from 1980 to 1990, holding constant the value of the dollar. In the schools, there is high parental pressure for students to succeed and to enroll in college preparatory classes.

Fast Track enrolls nearly 1,100 students in grades 9 through 12. Over the past 6 years, enrollments have increased just under 10%. Students are predominantly white. The school offers students a menu of over 160 year-long courses. A strong emphasis on academics encourages students to take a rigorous program of studies. This emphasis is illustrated by a teacher initiative to create a cross-disciplinary humanities course (art, social sciences, and history) that qualified under the state's new fine arts requirement and was eligible for the Certificate of

Merit, a new certificate that recognizes effort and achievement beyond the minimum (see the "The New Requirements" section and Table 1.2 later in this chapter).

Parents often apply more pressure on students than does the school. Students spoke of being placed in Certificate of Merit courses because their parents insisted on it, and students felt intense pressure to remain there even when they performed poorly. Both the school and the district have clearly embraced academic rigor to the point that, at least informally, the school has two tracks: one with students who are working toward the Certificate of Merit and one with students who are not.

The county has not required credits or courses beyond the state minimum of 20 for graduation, with the exception of a half credit in health. However, it has been proactive in responding to the new graduation requirements. Committees with representation across staff roles developed curriculum plans with a strong emphasis on the Certificate of Merit option and modified courses to encourage higher order thinking skills. In the words of one administrator, the curriculum is "more challenging, and there is a more coherent set of curriculum guides." The district has also moved to a seven-period day to help students fit additional state requirements into their schedules.

United Nations High School

Located just outside Washington, D.C., United Nations High School is part of a large, wealthy school district. The school is located in an area of the county that includes both high- and low-income housing. It serves a student population of about 2,100 in grades 9 to 12. A significant percentage of students are non-native English-speaking children. The school's racial composition is one-third African-American, one-third white, one-sixth Hispanic, and one-sixth Asian. Enrollment has been increasing from a low of 1,850 and is projected to peak at 2,800. Unique to United Nations are its racially and ethnically diverse student population and its variety of special programs.

Students choose from more than 430 courses each semester. Special offerings include magnet, vocational, and ESOL programs. The magnet program, which draws students from across the county, focuses on mathematics, computer science, and science and graduated its first class in 1989. Initial enrollments in the program were low, but student demand and enthusiasm for the program are growing. Enrollment has steadily increased: In 1989, there were 72 graduates; by 1992, over 100 are expected. The magnet program offers students a different sequence of courses than in the regular curriculum, at an accelerated pace and with interdisciplinary breadth. A special research and experimentation seminar explores the interrelatedness of academic disciplines. Magnet students take eight subjects a semester instead of the more typical seven.

The magnet program dominates the culture of United Nations and sets a tone of elitism among its teachers and students. Teachers and students alike are tracked into this special-admissions, high-powered program so much so that they often have no knowledge of lower-achieving students, special needs students, or other at-risk students at the school. Nonmagnet students reported being denied access to some magnet courses and feeling excluded.

United Nations is also one of six high schools in the district designated as a vocational minicenter. It offers a variety of vocational programs (e.g., cooperative office education, automotive mechanics, and cosmetology) and has, in addition, a vocational support services team to work with special needs students.

The ESOL program is also growing. The program currently enrolls approximately 330 students, more than double the enrollment 7 years ago. At the time of the graduation requirements reform, the district had in place a set of graduation requirements stricter than those promulgated by the state; the district required 22 credits for graduation rather than the state's 20 credits. The district did not stipulate the subject matter areas for the additional two credits, leaving them as electives for students.

Urban High School

Urban High School is located in a large city. A comprehensive high school with grades 9 through 12 located in the heart of the metropolitan area, the school's African-American population has steadily increased over the past decade and is currently just under 50%. The balance of the population is white. There are just over 1,500 students enrolled at Urban, a significant drop from 2,400 students enrolled 10 years ago. Enrollment has bottomed out and is expected to rise again by 1992. Students enroll in a college preparatory, vocational, or general program of studies, choosing from more than 130 year-long course offerings. Most students enroll in the general and vocational programs and take six subjects a year.

The overall school budget has suffered cutbacks in recent years. The school has also had to deal with corresponding cuts in staff. Last year, the principal was forced to declare seven teaching positions "surplus," and four of these teachers (social studies, science, home economics, and physical education) were moved to district middle and elementary schools. Later in the school year, an additional two business education teachers were moved from the high school. The teacher loss also necessitated rescheduling 600 students, many of whom were placed in second semester classes unrelated to courses they took during the first semester. The average class size at Urban is between 30 and 35 students.

Urban is plagued by low attendance, teenage pregnancy, drugs and alcohol, and high dropout rates. In 1989–1990, the district reported a dropout rate of 31%. These factors contribute to an environment where doing enough to "get by" is acceptable and often encouraged. In fact, getting by has become the ultimate goal for staff and students in a school where half of the students who started ninth grade do not graduate.

Urban had a Certificate of Merit–type special diploma prior to the state's initiative. Students who graduate with 24 credits, having passed all six credits they are required to take each year, receive a special diploma. This diploma was often mistaken for the Certificate of Merit during interviews because it is more well known.

The city system has other requirements that go beyond state minimums. First, the state requires one U.S. history and two other unspecified social studies credits, but the city requires one credit of U.S. history, one credit in American government/urban growth, and one credit in world history. Second, the city requires that students earn three science credits instead of the two required by the state. These requirements were put into effect the year before the new state requirements. Finally, the city system requires that students earn one foreign language credit, except for students in business, vocational, and special education programs.

Middle Class High School

Middle Class High School is situated in a campuslike setting with a complex of schools: an elementary school, a middle school, a special education school, and a technical school. Middle Class serves grades 9 through 12 and has a student population of approximately 1,150. Over the last 6 years, enrollments have declined by 18%. The minority population in the school is predominantly African-American but accounts for only 8% of the total student body.

Middle Class offers more than 400 courses per semester in college preparation, business, general, vocational education, and special education programs. Each student takes six subjects per semester. Each course has a track or "phase" designation, numbered 0 through 4. Courses designated as phase 0 are not differentiated by degree of difficulty (e.g., language arts, music, art, and physical education). Phase 1 courses are intended for students who have difficulty with reading and/or writing, phase 2 courses are designed for students reading at grade level, phase 3 courses are college preparatory in nature, and phase 4 courses are advanced placement.

The district requires students to earn 22 credits to graduate. The district prides itself on anticipating requirements set by the state and often sets requirements in advance of the state that go beyond the state minimums. In addition, students can earn one of four Certificates of Program Achievement, but to do so, they must complete 24 credits. Unlike the state's Certificate of Merit, the Certificates of Program Achievement require no specified grade point average. There are four Certificates of Program Achievement: (1) the Advanced Academic Certificate, which requires students to earn two credits in advanced placement courses and three credits in the same foreign language, is designed for the student interested in pursuing a well-balanced, rigorous program of academic study; (2) the Academic Certificate, which requires that two credits be earned in the same foreign language and advanced placement courses be included in the student's planned program where possible, is designed for the student interested in pursuing a well-designed program of academic study; (3) the Specialized Certificate is designed to offer maximal program flexibility for the student with unique post–high school goals and/or specialized interests in art, music, or physical education and health (the student must complete a planned program with a minimum of five credits in the major subject area); and (4) the Vocational-Technical Certificate is designed for the student interested in training for a specific career or preparing for specialized vocational-technical training beyond high school.

Rural High School

Rural High School sits on the eastern shore of the Chesapeake Bay, in a small, picturesque historic community well known by tourists and water sport enthusiasts. The county's population of almost 30,000 represents a mix of wealthy residents who view the bay as an attractive resource for hobbies and much poorer residents who inescapably rely on the bay—and the concomitant influx of tourists and hunters—for their livelihood. This mix of residents has led to the passage of a property tax cap that places severe limits on the ability of schools to adopt and implement new curricular and instructional programs.

Rural High School is small, with enrollment leveled off at 222 in 1990–1991 after an enrollment high of 292 in 1985. Three quarters of the students at Rural are white, and the remainder are African-American. The community is fiercely proud of and loyal to its school and has successfully fought off several consolidation efforts. Students can choose from approximately 150 course titles and typically take seven full-year courses a year. Courses in the four major academic areas are grouped into three tracks: general, business, and college preparation. The school also has programs for both vocational and special education students.

The key to understanding curriculum in this tiny school is that almost every course is a "singleton," as one administrator put it. Few electives are taught. Thus, changing graduation requirements and distinguishing between courses (as with the Certificate of Merit) essentially meant increasing the number of courses offered (particularly in math and fine arts), which in turn meant increasing the number of course preparations for teachers. Additionally, the new requirements solidified curriculum tracking rather than making it more fluid; advanced students taking Certificate of Merit courses stay together the whole day because there is only one Certificate of Merit section in each subject. Interestingly, when the state dropped contemporary issues as a graduation requirement, this county kept the course as a requirement. The county has no additional requirements beyond the state minimum.

SETTING THE STAGE: DEVELOPMENT OF THE POLICY

A complete understanding of policy reform requires not only an explication of its local effects but also insight into why the initiative was proposed in the first place and an explanation of the process of policy development. This section puts the initiative into context by discussing what was happening in the state prior to the formation of the Commission on Secondary Education (the group responsible for recommending changes in graduation requirements to the State Board of Education) and by discussing commission members' varied perspectives on the commission's formation and operation. In other words, this discussion sets the stage.

The State Context Prior to the Commission

The formation of the Commission on Secondary Education followed considerable discussion in the state of Maryland about the role of the public high school. Some highlights of the many independent efforts throughout the state that eventually brought about the formation of the commission are summarized in the following.

In the fall of 1980, local assistant superintendents of instruction formed a committee on secondary school concerns. After several preliminary meetings, in December of 1980 they met to identify the most pressing of these problems, prioritize them, and begin to identify strategies for addressing them. Local superintendents identified similar concerns. At a retreat in April 1981, they devoted 2 days to discussion of four issues: (1) goals for high schools in the state, (2) the kind and content of learning that occur in high school, (3) administrative and organizational structures that best produce learning in high school, and (4) methods to maintain standards of quality in high school programs.

In the fall of 1981, MSDE staff met with a committee of the Maryland Association of Secondary School Principals that was formed to examine their concerns. They discussed five major areas: (1) the need to reexamine the credit/4-year requirements for graduation, (2) the need to ensure standards for curricular programs, (3) the need for consensus on the mission of the state's secondary schools, (4) the need to review alternative methods for delivering curriculum, and (5) the need for a regular 5-year follow-up study of selected Maryland high school students.

To promote continuation of the dialogue, MSDE staff generated a draft table of contents for a revised *Maryland High School Administrative Handbook*. The handbook was to replace a set of manuals and policies from the early 1960s. In the fall of 1981, both the committees of the assistant superintendents for instruction and the principals offered suggestions to MSDE on the proposed administrative handbook.

In the spring of 1982, the state colleges and universities issued recommendations that included a listing of secondary school courses that students must complete to be considered for admission to these higher education institutions. These recommendations had the potential of profoundly affecting the courses that college-bound high school students took.

With that background in mind and input from a variety of local groups, the State Board of Education asked the State Superintendent in March 1982 to appoint the Commission on Secondary Education. The commission's charge was to initiate a 3-year examination of the nature and character of secondary education in the state of Maryland.

Perspectives on the Impetus for the Commission

Discussions with key policymakers associated with the commission's work presented a complex portrait of the influences that pushed the state toward more aggressive state-initiated reform. One informant acknowledged the larger, national environment, with states taking a more active role in reform even before the formation of the National Commission on Excellence, as being an important influence:

> Various states had decided to take more hand in the operation of schools, and Maryland was one of those. There was general dissatisfaction with high schools. The U.S. Department of Education's *Condition of Education in 1980* had gone into great detail about dropping test scores and other indicators of the problem; there was a general concern about quality and the environment in high schools. It wasn't just that kids were dumb or lazy or not working hard or that the curriculum wasn't strong. There was also something organizationally amiss.

At the same time, others pointed out that the state leadership was strongly committed to reevaluating the organizational structure of Maryland's high schools and even acknowledged that the status quo had been allowed to continue without question for too long:

> The impetus to our work . . . came from the long-standing concern that I had and others on the staff had that there was a persistent need to make sure the organization of the schools and the curriculum of the schools were being reviewed systematically on a periodic basis, just to take into account the changing needs of kids, teachers' issues, and so on. Also, when we realized the testing program for Project Basic was going to make an impact on the schools, we thought it was pretty important to take a more comprehensive view of the organization.
>
> It was our feeling that the nature and character of secondary education had not been examined for a very long time. . . . A manual written about 30 years ago captured the description of how secondary education ought to be in Maryland, and for years it was sort of the Bible, and since that moment it has not been revisited. We went about this not with the intention of raising graduation requirements. In fact, I think the charge referred to the nature and character of secondary education, and the use of words "nature" and "character" were very deliberate. It was not the commission for high school graduation; it was the commission for the nature and character of secondary education.

Another informant was not able to pinpoint the impetus for reform but was quick to point out that the larger national concern with education added legitimacy to Maryland's effort and made it easier to get the necessary support. Rather than spending a lot of time arguing about what the problem was, policymakers could focus their energies on finding solutions:

> I suppose my first reaction is that I'm not sure which was the chicken
> and which was the egg. I think that all the publicity that was coming
> out with respect to the negatives of public education certainly allowed
> the commission, gave it direction. . . . The state was taking the posi-
> tion that there should be direction given and gave it an environment
> that allowed it to happen. All the other stuff kept it moving forward.

On a more local note, a superintendent talked about the positive
state environment in which the reform debate took place. According to
this superintendent, the structure of educational delivery in Maryland,
with its small number of districts, made building initial consensus a
manageable process:

> I think we have an advantage in Maryland, with 24 school districts and
> 24 superintendents. We meet monthly, and we pride ourselves on antic-
> ipating the governor, anticipating the legislatures, and anticipating local
> fiscal authority. . . . Hornbeck [state superintendent] did a good job of
> having superintendent retreats and having Boyer, Sizer, and Goodlad.
> We said, these guys all have a point.

THE COMMISSION AND ITS WORK

In the spring of 1982, at the request of the Maryland State Board of
Education, the State Superintendent of Education formed the Maryland Commission on Secondary Education to "initiate a major study on
the nature and character of secondary education in Maryland." He
appointed a central steering committee with 23 representatives (9 central office administrators, 4 teachers, 4 university/business representatives, 3 school board members, 2 principals, and 1 MSDE staff), charg-
ing them with "examining the philosophy, programs, principles, and
standards which provide direction for the Maryland public high
schools and making recommendations to me." The commission had
three major tasks.

First, the commission was charged with developing a mission statement for Maryland high schools that reflected the best available thinking about the goals of secondary education. A number of forums were
established to facilitate this process. Second, the commission was asked
to oversee the work of a series of task forces designed to examine critical issues in secondary education. Initially assigned 10 key issues,
these task forces were eventually charged with reporting to the full
commission on the following five issues: (1) graduation require-

ments/diploma, (2) curriculum, (3) student services and activities, (4) instruction/instructional support services, and (5) school administration/climate. Third, the commission was to structure a process by which exemplary secondary school programs could be identified. The original charge had a 3-year time line according to which the commission was to complete its work and issue a final report.

Early deliberations centered on building agreement among commission members about the purpose of Maryland public high schools. Eleven assumptions emerged from these discussions and guided the thinking of the commission and its task forces. The assumptions were grouped around three main themes: the public high school as an institution, the adolescent, and the place of the public high school in the education of students. These are detailed in Table 1.1.

After a series of meetings held over several months' time, the commission came to a consensus on a mission statement for Maryland's high schools:

> The mission of the public high school is to challenge and help students to grow intellectually, personally and socially. Graduates should be able and willing to take the first steps into their chosen field of work or study, to act responsibly as citizens, and to enjoy a productive life. (Maryland State Board of Education, 1985)

The majority of the commission's work was accomplished through its five task forces. The first task force impaneled had responsibility for graduation requirements/diploma This task force was charged in November of 1982 with five tasks: (1) to examine the requirements and standards (e.g., enrollment, credits, and competencies) for graduating from a Maryland public high school; (2) to examine the diplomas awarded by MSDE; (3) to investigate modifications that local systems could make to graduation requirements; (4) to examine student grading and reporting practices in the state; and (5) to examine the procedures that govern the transfer of students into Maryland public high schools.

The goal was to have each task force contribute equally to reform deliberations prior to the passage of new bylaws. Thus, the total high school system would have been reviewed. In reality, only the graduation requirements/diploma task force received full consideration by the Maryland State Board of Education. The original broad conception of a "major study of the nature and character of secondary education in Maryland" took a narrower focus on course and credit requirements.

The task force began its deliberations in December of 1982 and recommended changes to the full commission in September 1983. The full

---

TABLE 1.1.
ASSUMPTIONS THAT GUIDED THE
MARYLAND COMMISSION ON SECONDARY EDUCATION

The Public High School as an Institution:

1. Needs reaffirmation
2. Has the central responsibility for meeting the educational needs of adolescents
3. Should shape its programs to provide adolescents with a definable set of learnings
4. Must have the necessary resources and personnel to function effectively

Adolescents:

5. Need direction in the selection of programs and courses
6. Need a healthy, safe environment in which to learn
7. Should actively participate in the community of the school
8. Need to explore and develop themselves in a microcosm of society

Public High Schools:

9. Should provide experiences that will ensure the intellectual development of each student
10. Should structure opportunities for the personal development of their students
11. Should prepare their students to function as members of society

---

commission, in turn, presented its modified report to the State Superintendent later that fall. The state board then acted on many of these recommendations by adopting a new state bylaw on July 29, 1985.

The New Requirements

Maryland's new requirements, effective for the class of 1989 and subsequent classes, stipulated one additional credit in mathematics, as well as one credit in a fine arts course and one credit in a practical arts course. This latter requirement could be fulfilled by earning a credit in either computers, home economics, industrial arts, or vocational arts. Students were also expected to earn four credits during their senior year. The new requirements are compared with the previous ones in Table 1.2.

An additional and unique feature of the requirements was the Certificate of Merit option. This option stipulated additional credits (one credit in a foreign language and a third credit in science), a minimal grade point average of 2.6, and the requirement that 12 of the 20 credits be from advanced-level courses. This option required that all departments—not just the academic ones—select and offer advanced courses that satisfy the Certificate of Merit guidelines. Each local district was free to decide what qualifies as an advanced course.

OUTLINE FOR REMAINDER OF THE BOOK

With this background in place, we are ready to address the five questions outlined earlier. Data addressing each of those five questions form the basis for the presentations in Chapters 3 through 7. These five chapters are first introduced by a review of pertinent literature in Chapter 2 and are summarized by our view of the implications for future action in the final chapter.

Chapter 2 provides a detailed discussion of the issues, including a framework for understanding state-initiated reform and a review of the research on graduation requirements and tracking. The focus on tracking helps provide a balance for the concerns of equity with a policy context that pays primary attention to issues of excellence. We offer a framework of three strategic choices that capture both substantive decision making about reform policies and the processes of local implementation. These strategies include rational planning, market incentive, and political interaction. We suggest that Maryland incorporated all three strategies in their reform.

The review of state efforts to raise standards includes national, single-state, and multiple-state studies. Two patterns emerged from this review. First, schools are offering more academic courses, and more students are enrolling in them, but the shift is toward lower-level remedial or basic courses. Second, the pressure of competency testing is forcing schools to offer more remedial courses so that students can pass these tests.

The tracking literature documents the extent to which schools serve a sorting function by classifying students into groups, labeling those groups, conferring status on them, and certifying those statuses to the larger society. The concern in the literature is that through this process,

Table 1.2.
COMPARISON OF NEW AND OLD MARYLAND HIGH SCHOOL GRADUATION REQUIREMENTS

New	Old	Difference
	Maryland High School Diploma	
Credit Requirements		
English—4 credits	English—4 credits	Same
Science—2 credits	Science—2 credits	Same
Fine arts—1 credit	No credit specified	1 Fine arts credit added
Mathematics—3 credits	Mathematics—2 credits	1 Mathematics credit added
Social studies—3 credits (1 U.S. history and 2 unspecified)	Social studies—3 credits (1 U.S. history; 1 contemporary issues; 1 unspecified)	Only U.S. history specified
Physical education—1 credit	Physical education—1 credit or 2 years of physical activity	Physical activity option eliminated
Computer studies or home economics or industrial arts or technology education or vocational education—1 credit	No credit specified	1 Credit in computer studies or home economics or industrial arts or technology education or vocational education added
Electives—5 credits	Electives—8 credits	3 Required credits added, thus reducing the number of elective credits
Total Required Credits		
20 credits	20 credits	Same total credits but 3 additional specified credits

Senior-Year Credits

4 credits earned after 11th grade

No specified credit requirement after 11th grade

Senior must earn at least 4 credits during senior year

State Competency Tests

Functional reading, functional mathematics, citizenship skills, writing

Functional reading

All 4 tests will be phased in for the class of 1989

Maryland Certificates: Certificate of Merit

In addition to the diploma
Effective: Class of 1989
Certificate for completion of a more challenging education program

No provision

Provision is made for a certificate in addition to the diploma for graduates who meet certificate stipulations in the graduation requirements bylaw

Credit Requirements

English—4 credits

Science—3 credits

Fine arts—1 credit

Mathematics—3 credits

Social studies—3 credits (1 U.S. history)

Physical education—1 credit

Computer studies or home economics or industrial arts or technology education or vocational education—1 credit

Foreign language (level II or above)—1 credit

Electives—3 credits

(cont'd)

Table 1.2. (cont.)

New	Old	Difference
Advanced Courses		
12 credits in advanced courses from the above listing		
Grade Point Average		
At least 2.6 (on a 4.0 scale)		

Maryland Certificates: High School Certificate

New	Old	Difference
In lieu of the diploma	No provision	Provision is made for a certificate in lieu of the diploma for special education students who cannot meet the specified requirements in the IEP and in the graduation requirements bylaw
Effective: Class of 1986		
Certificate of completion of a special education program for students who have been enrolled for at least 4 years beyond 8th grade		

Other Provisions for Earning Credit Toward Graduation

New	Old	Difference
Summer school	Summer school	Same
Evening school	Evening school	Same
Correspondence courses	Correspondence courses	Same
Tutoring	Tutoring	Same
Work study programs	Work study programs	Same
College courses	College courses	Same
	Examination	Credit by examination eliminated

Alternatives to 4-Year Enrollment Requirement in a Public High School

Early college admission program	Same
Early admission to vocational, technical, or other postsecondary school	Same
Accelerated 20-credit program	Graduation in less than 4 years eliminated
Job entry training program	Job entry training eliminated as an alternative to 4-year enrollment
General Educational Development Testing Program	Same
Maryland Adult External High School Diploma Program	No provision	Maryland Adult External High School Diploma Program is referenced as an alternative approach to earning a diploma in the graduation requirement bylaw

certain groups of students may be denied access to educational opportunities. Although the evidence on the deleterious effects of tracking is fairly convincing, there is also recent evidence to suggest that tracks are not nearly as tightly defined as some earlier research suggests.

This complex web of past conceptual work and research helped set the stage for our investigation of the effects of changes in one state's graduation requirements. By documenting effects at the school level over time and by investigating patterns both before and after the policy was in place, the study captured not only the diversity of responses across schools but also the policy's influence on educational opportunities offered to different groups of students. Five key questions mentioned earlier emerged from this review and guide the data presentations in Chapters 3 through 7. To remind the reader, those five questions are:

1. What is the local variation in response to the policy change?
2. How has the policy affected tracks and tracking systems as a form of access to resources?
3. What impact has the policy had on students and teachers at risk?
4. How has the policy altered educators' perceptions of their influence over their work?
5. What was the intent of the policy, and how well has that been met as perceived by those outside the secondary education community?

Chapter 3 addresses local variation in response to the requirements. The documentation on local variation is organized around three themes. The first theme centers on whether students have different experiences as a result of the reform, using evidence from course-taking patterns and interviews. Four key questions are the focus of the transcript analyses in this chapter and the following two chapters. These include: (1) Are students earning more credits? (2) Are students being exposed to a more rigorous curriculum? (3) Are students struggling more with their course work? and (4) Is the balance of credits shifting across content areas? Dramatic differences in course-taking patterns exist across the five schools. To balance this view of course-taking patterns, the second theme addresses students' perspectives on their overall educational opportunities and the effects of the requirements on them. The final theme captures teachers' views of curriculum change as a result of the new graduation policy. The results from all three themes highlight the importance of local context in shaping how school people respond to, modify, adapt, and even ignore state-mandated change.

Chapter 4 looks at how tracking systems work in the five schools and whether, given a policy that emphasizes the academic track, those systems become rigid and less inclusive or whether they become permeable and permit students more upward mobility. This was accomplished through transcript analyses of student course-taking patterns, as well as through interviews with students and teachers. We begin with a detailed description of students' views of their opportunities and the constraints placed on them. Student comments were dramatic in detailing the deleterious effects of tracking. Formal and informal mechanisms in the five high schools constrained the hopes and aspirations of at least some of the students. Next, we look at differential course-taking patterns by track. The strong differences by track were not diminished as a result of the policy change in graduation requirements. Teachers' comments, offered in the final section, document how the Certificate of Merit helped define a new track and how uneven dissemination of information about the Certificate helped maintain track inequity. Taken as a whole, the data in this chapter suggest that the new graduation requirements did not diminish powerful means for sorting students and for sustaining status systems.

Chapter 5 explores how and to what extent various groups of students and teachers have become more vulnerable because of reform in graduation requirements. These issues are studied by analyzing interviews with teachers about at-risk students; by analyzing course-taking patterns according to race, academic performance, and gender; and by analyzing teachers' perceptions of their own jeopardy. The transcript analyses have several gloomy findings and only a handful of bright ones. Among gloomy findings were that minority students and low performers continued to have limited access to and participation in academic resources. On the brighter side, gaps across race, academic performance, and gender in mathematics credits declined. Teachers also reported a sense of vulnerability and voicelessness in the policy implementation process. A number of them questioned whether they would have jobs in the future and how the new requirements would constrain those jobs.

Chapter 6 describes the influence that people who were involved with the graduation requirements felt they had on school actions. Specifically, the chapter discusses the perceptions of people in different role groups about their impact on students' lives and about how the new graduation requirements affected their perceived influence. Four different role groups were studied: state department staff, central office administrators, building administrators, and counselors. State staff felt they had significant potential to influence education in a constructive way. Yet despite all that potential, there appeared to be significant impediments standing in the way. District administrators offered two perspectives on their influence. On one hand, they talked about how local systems often moved beyond what the state required; on the other hand, they expressed concern about limitations of their control once an issue reached their level. Likewise, principals appeared ready to deal with the new requirements but criticized the state or their own system for not taking full advantage of the opportunity the policy change presented them. Counselors' responses were also two-dimensional. On one hand, they talked about the importance of shaping students' course selections and, by implication, their high school careers. However, they also felt themselves to be "constrained decision makers." Students' opinions of counselors' influence were not always flattering but were less constrained than as perceived by counselors themselves. Overall, we found a generalized expression of little control over policy implementation and, hence, students' careers at all levels. We refer to this as a policy vacuum where key actors see other people, events, and local context as powerfully constraining their actions.

Chapter 7 describes the original policy intentions of the graduation requirements and documents their effects on those within the school systems. The chapter concludes by discussing how college admissions officers and local employers perceive the effects of the new policy. The major intent of the reform was to raise standards for students and to provide them with a more well-rounded set of experiences. From students' perspectives, the requirements made high school more challenging, but often those who were more challenged were the ones who were already succeeding. School staff reported that students were getting increased exposure to curriculum areas they may have otherwise bypassed and that their education was more well rounded. However, this positive response was not shared by individuals outside the schools. College admissions staff and local employers, the consumers of the policy product, saw few positive effects as a result of the increased requirements. They reported little knowledge of the specifics of the requirements and made almost no use of the information about the changes in admission or employment decisions.

Chapter 8 puts the implications of the research findings into perspective, grounding them in discussion of a major reform focus of the day: restructuring. Specifically, the issue addressed in this chapter is how to strike a match between 1990s' reform challenges and 1980s' policy initiatives, such as increased graduation requirements. Accepting the premise that for educational improvements to take place, significant restructuring efforts must be initiated, the report concludes with seven challenges for schools and five for state policymakers. The challenges for schools include creating a vision of inclusive, caring schools; reorganizing how students are brought together to learn; building more flexible time schedules; altering the role of counselors; infusing the curriculum with higher-order thinking and problem solving; making data bases more comprehensive and diverse to better inform decision making; and enhancing communication within districts and between schools.

The primary challenge for the state is to devise ways to encourage and support local district restructuring along these seven lines. To accomplish this, the state needs to articulate a broad vision for its educational systems; redistribute state funds so that investment is increasingly in the human capital that serves children directly; devise policy mechanisms that allow schools to try creative and flexible time schedules, learning environments, and teaching strategies; build greater capacity to provide districts with timely and comprehensive information; and build communication structures that ensure the accurate and thorough flow of information between districts and the state. The call is for the state to move away from the mandated changes of the first wave of reform and to embrace a strategy of capacity building and system changing.

*

This research has essentially been a story of the difficulties in initiating and sustaining systemic change. A key reason for those difficulties has been our inability to frame the problem in a comprehensive way. These challenges cannot be addressed piecemeal. We conclude the book with a call to conceptualize systemic change through four frames: the technical, the political, the cultural, and the moral. Only by combining them all can we help meet the challenges that our students will face in the 21st century.

2

THE ROLE OF THE STATES
IN THE REFORM MOVEMENT
OF THE 1980s

Governmental oversight agencies are in place to mold the relationship between policy and practice. In the United States, that oversight has been divided among federal, state, and local agencies. Nowhere is that more true than in education, where the federal government has played a minimal role, where the constitutional authority rests with states, but where most authority has been delegated to local school districts and their governing boards. As D. K. Cohen and Spillane (1992) point out, such weakness at higher levels (when compared internationally) is quite unusual. The American system is best described as having a fragmented governance system, with thousands of local districts having wide influence. Many analysts would argue that such a design was purposeful, reflecting Americans' distrust of central power.

Yet at the same time, there is "an abiding hope for the power of government and a wish to harness it to social problem solving" (D. K. Cohen & Spillane, 1992, p. 7). This hope, coupled with the fact that states have taken increasing responsibility for the financing of education, has produced a growing involvement and influence for states in the policy arena. Despite this growth of state involvement, there is ample evidence of varied responses to state reforms (Corbett & Wilson,

1991) and recognition of the wide gap between state policy and local practice (Firestone, 1989a). A more careful analysis of the relationship between the two, particularly in this time of ferment, is essential if we want to understand what it will take to improve our nation's schools.

The decade of the 1980s was a period of intense state involvement in education. Growing concern over the quality of American education found expression in the National Commission on Excellence in Education's *A Nation at Risk* (1983) which described schools as wallowing in a "rising tide of mediocrity" (p. 5). Spurred by such evocative rhetoric, state policymakers initiated a series of reforms. Prodded by growing awareness that the American economy was no longer preeminent in world markets, early reforms targeted student outcomes, curriculum, testing, and standards for teacher training and certification. Taken together, these were efforts to "forcefully repair the sinking vessel" (Hawley, 1988, p. 418) of American education.

To the surprise of some, the movement has not withered away, as have so many previous reform movements. Instead, responsibility for reform seems to be shifting from the state house with an exclusively regulatory emphasis to a shared responsibility between the state and local districts. The current interest in restructuring is an example of this shift; although some states have enacted legislation that mandates site-based management and portfolio assessment, for example, they have not closely constrained the particulars of those reforms (see Shanker [1990] for a discussion of incentives for restructuring). Similarly, some states (e.g., Massachusetts and Vermont) have recently legislated or funded grants for local school districts to experiment with fully integrating special needs students into the regular curriculum. Again, the specifics of implementation are local decisions. States have several policy instruments available to either mandate or encourage local districts and schools to move in desired directions (McDonnell & Elmore, 1987). Perhaps we are entering an era of complex state strategies that employ a mix of "carrots" and "sticks."

The decade-long reform effort is fascinating to observe and describe; however, the interest here is in its beginning—the "first wave" of the reform movement, when states enacted more rules and regulations affecting education in a 3- to 4-year period than they had, in total, since the early 1960s (Timar & Kirp, 1989). This flurry of legislative activity has been estimated at over 700 new policies between 1983 and 1985 (Darling-Hammond & Berry, 1988). Much of this activity focused on what has come to be called "student standards"— that is, curriculum reform that would establish higher standards for students to achieve in order to graduate from high school. These policies, most often tightening credit requirements for graduation, also addressed competency tests, "pass to play" provisions, and promotional standards.

INCREASED GRADUATION REQUIREMENTS
AS ONE STATE INITIATIVE

One of the most common state-level reform initiatives in the early 1980s was tightening high school graduation requirements. The curriculum was thought to be the culprit in many educational woes, and the most common way to strengthen the curriculum was to regulate course offerings and course-taking patterns (Clune, White, & Patterson, 1989). A review of *Clearinghouse Notes*, produced by the Education Commission of the States (1990), documents the pervasiveness of this state policy initiative (through either the legislature or the state board of education).

In 1980, 37 states had responsibility for defining minimal graduation requirements. The remaining 13 delegated most or all of that responsibility to local school boards. By 1990, 43 states had assumed the responsibility. Thirty-nine states made some changes in the number of Carnegie units required for graduation. Most of that movement occurred in the first half of the decade, with only four states adding credits between 1985 and 1990. In 1980, the average number of credits that states required for high school graduation was 17.40. By 1985 the average had increased to 19.47, a jump of just over 2 credits. By 1990, that number had taken another small jump to 19.76 credits. A separate analysis of just those states that had control over credit requirements during the entire decade reveals a 3.27 average increase in credit requirements.

With the 35 states that controlled requirements during the entire period between 1980 and 1990 as a baseline, the evidence is convincing that states attempted significant changes in the number and kinds of required courses for students. For example, in nearly all cases (32 of the 35 states), course requirements were increased in either math or science. In 25 of these 35 states, both math and science requirements increased. Policymakers did not just pass their reform brushes over traditional academic curricula. Indeed, approximately half of the states instituted new or tightened requirements in either fine arts or practical arts. Only one state besides Maryland required a full credit in both fine arts and practical arts.

What were the driving forces behind some of these state-initiated changes in graduation requirements? In the next section, we review several state initiatives and organize them around three strategic choices outlined by Timar and Kirp (1988).

Specific State Initiatives

In 1983, when Maryland initiated a set of reforms targeting the high school curriculum, graduation requirements, and attendant diplomas (among other initiatives), states all over the nation had begun similar programs of reform. These efforts were shaped in part by the specifics of the National Commission on Excellence in Education's call for high school students to take a minimum of four year-long courses of English, three of mathematics, three of science, three of social studies, and a half year of computer science. In addition, for college-bound students, a foreign language was recommended (National Commission on Excellence in Education, 1983).

Using a typology of state reform strategies developed by Timar and Kirp (1988), we discuss the "bellwether" states (Naisbitt, 1984) of California, Texas, and South Carolina, as well as Maryland, in terms of their overall approaches to the early reform efforts. We include a discussion of each state's specific requirement changes in light of those called for by the commission's attempt at "trickle down reform" (Ginsberg & Wimpelberg, 1987).

Timar and Kirp (1988) characterize state strategies in managing both the substantive decision making about reform policies and the processes to implement those policies at the local level. Using Texas, California, and South Carolina as examples, they present a typology of three strategic types: rational planning, market incentive, and political interaction.

States that have the rational planning strategy approach school improvement as a set of efficiency problems that are amenable to adjustments in some aspect of the technology of education. "Problems" such as underachievement or poor teacher preparation are fixed through proper diagnosis and prescription. Policies and their attendant procedures thus become a set of remedies for educational problems that are assumed to be implemented uniformly across districts. The role of the state is to be the problem definer and diagnostician; the local district's role is to implement the "cure." This strategy assumes rationality in the behavior of organizational members and an efficiency criterion as the single best measure of effectiveness (Wise, 1979). It also assumes a like-mindedness on the part of all parties to assent to the prescribed policy and a skill level sufficient to implement it.

States that adopt the market incentive strategy make a different set of assumptions about educational excellence and the policy process. Although policy development rests squarely within the purview of the state, implementation of specific policies is bargained through market mechanisms (e.g., competitive grants). Local variation and discretion in implementation are assumed, although the state shapes that discretion through the creation of artificial markets. For example, in a competitive grants school improvement initiative, the state creates an artificial market in which school improvement efforts are exchanged for grant money. This strategy assumes an economic model of behavior in which compliance can be induced through incentives.

The third type of strategy discussed by Timar and Kirp (1988) is political interaction. Here, political actors from all levels in the state education enterprise engage in an elaborate policy conversation, constructing parameters of the policy features that are acceptable. The process relies on dialogue and the delegation of decision making. Although the state assumes responsibility for articulating broad policy goals, the specifics of those policies are negotiated among important actors. Political interaction also assumes variability in local implementation, but much effort goes into ensuring that the state's goals are consonant with local conditions. Using these three broadbrush types, we next examine Texas, California, South Carolina, and Maryland because these states are generally recognized as being in the vanguard of this reform and have also been studied.

TEXAS.   Rational planning characterized the Texas approach to educational reform in the early 1980s, where an emphasis on the application of business principles to education took hold early (Timar & Kirp, 1988). Led by H. Ross Perot, the reform movement was structured in a highly centralized, hierarchical model where administrative restructuring proceeded apace with curricular changes, teacher testing, and a host of other mandates. Most notable and visible nationally were the provisions for competency testing of all teachers and a career ladder program. Also receiving national attention was the "no-pass, no-play" standard for participation in high school extracurricular activities. Social promotion was prohibited in the omnibus legislative act (House Bill 72).

The specific stipulations for graduation from high school (effective with the class of 1988) included 4 years of English (increased from 3), 3 years of mathematics (increased from 2), 2 years of science (the same as before), and 3 years of social studies (increased from 2-1/2 years). The core academic requirements increased overall from 9.5 to 12;

other requirements and electives increased from 8.5 to 9, resulting in a total of 21 credits required for graduation compared with the previously required 18 (Clune, White, & Patterson, 1989).

CALIFORNIA.   Prior to the publication of *A Nation at Risk*, California legislators had designed and enacted comprehensive school improvement legislation. Although the legislation provided incentives to implement various changes at the local level, it contained very few specific mandates. Senate Bill 813 called for improvements in grades K to 12, including changes in high school graduation requirements; encouraged teacher merit pay options, mentor programs, and higher salaries; provided incentives to lengthen the school day and year; called for transportation consolidation; provided rewards for increased student achievement; and fostered a mini-grants program for the improvement of classroom teaching (Randall, 1990).

The specific guidelines for local districts to consider for high school graduation included three credits in English, two each in mathematics and science, and three in social studies. A total of 10 core subjects were required and 3 other credits were required, totaling 13 credits (Clune, White, & Patterson, 1989). This seemingly small number is misleading, however, as local requirements far exceeded those suggested by the state. In fact, California districts required an average of 22 credits total for graduation (McDonnell, 1988).

Characterizing California's approach as providing "market incentive[s]" (p. 76), Timar and Kirp (1988) note that the legislation "urges much and commands little" (p. 80) and is quite permissive procedurally. They describe the market approach as one where policy formation is controlled centrally but implementation rests on bargaining between the local district and the state. Corroborating this market incentive notion is a study of California mathematics curriculum reform (Schwille et al., 1988) that describes the state's approach as "prescriptions without challenge to local authority" (p. 37).

Further reform occurred in 1984, when an accountability program was instituted. Focusing on student outcomes, the program called for enrollment increases in certain academic courses, improved scores in tests statewide, reduction in the dropout rate, and increased performance in advanced placement (AP) classes and all college-bound classes. Indicators were established and assessments were made beginning in 1984 by the recently created Policy Analysis for California Education (PACE).

Other policies enacted around the time of high school graduation reform that affected student course work were changes in the University of California and California State University systems' entrance requirements, local district curriculum frameworks, and state and district standardized testing (McDonnell, 1988).

SOUTH CAROLINA. Political processes dominated South Carolina's approach to first-wave policy initiatives (Timar & Kirp, 1988). The state articulated broad policy goals while allowing local districts wide discretion and flexibility in implementation. First articulating a broad reform agenda, the state leaders began a process of building local support for and involvement in the reform efforts. Largely due to its history of segregated schools and low public funding for education, South Carolina proceeded cautiously so as to preserve the "integrity of the process" (Timar & Kirp, 1988, p. 84).

South Carolina's Education Improvement Act contained provisions for 4 years of English; 3 of mathematics, 1 of which may be in computer science (increased from 2); 2 in science (increased from 1); and 2 in social studies (increased from 1). Required core courses thus totaled 12 credits, increased from 10. Other required courses remained the same, at 8.

Schwille et al. (1988) describe South Carolina as "prescriptive of content, cautious about standards" (p. 33) and report that the state had gone further than any others in their study of mathematics curriculum reform in mandating what teachers should teach. At the same time, the state was reluctant to enforce strict standards and used their tests of basic skills diagnostically.

MARYLAND. Maryland's graduation reform initiative was enacted in 1985, effective with the class of 1989. The requirements did not include an increase in the total number of credits (remaining at 20) but did narrow options by reducing elective courses. Students were required to increase their mathematics credits from 2 years to 3 years. In addition, a full credit was required in both the fine arts and practical arts areas. To encourage more academic rigor, a Certificate of Merit was introduced for students who enrolled in more challenging courses.

The approach in Maryland can best be described as a combination of the three approaches offered by Timar and Kirp (1988). On one hand, there were components that reflected a top-down, rational planning approach. All districts were expected to implement the same policy with no regard for local contextual differences. The problem was clearly defined as an imbalance of courses, and the solution was a different balance: more math and diversity with the fine and practical arts. Yet there were also signs of the other two approaches.

The market incentive strategy was also evident: Although rules were in place, implementation became a matter of local discretion. For example, there was wide variation across districts in terms of what courses could be included in the practical arts requirement. Likewise, districts and individual schools varied significantly in the emphasis they placed on the new Certificate of Merit as a meaningful label of advanced achievement.

Finally, from the political interaction model came the process by which the policy was developed (extensive and widespread participation by all the key constituent groups) and the discretion of local districts to define what constituted the Certificate of Merit.

Typologies

Typologies of state policy reform strategies such as those developed by Timar and Kirp (1988) and descriptions of the specific changes initiated in each state provide an important context for what actually takes place. However, those perspectives only provide a partial picture. A more complete picture can be obtained by also reviewing available evidence from research on the effects of those policies. In this next section, we review the recent research in this area.

RESEARCH ON HIGH SCHOOL GRADUATION REQUIREMENTS

Historically, high school graduation requirements have been viewed as a minimal set of standards that students must fulfill to receive a diploma. They are well within a state's legislative purview, although local districts can enact even stricter requirements. In the 1980s, partly as a reaction to the proliferation of courses added to high school curricula in the late 1960s and 1970s, as well as to declining standardized test scores nationally, policymakers implemented stricter requirements with one goal in mind: to raise standards and thereby increase achievement.

Their assumptions were linked to the growing body of research that demonstrates a significant association between increased course work and student achievement as measured on standardized tests (Alexander & Pallas, 1984; Ekstrom, Goertz, & Rock, 1988; Schmidt, 1983; Sebring, 1987). In summarizing this research, Goertz (1989) notes the strong consensus that has emerged among researchers that increased course work is positively associated with increased academic achievement. Thus, the implicit logic in reforming student standards was to boost achievement through stricter and more academically oriented graduation requirements.

Many of these initiatives were announced in 1983 or 1984, with the class of 1987 or 1988 the first full student cohort to pass through high school under a new set of requirements. Beginning in those same years, local districts began to assess existing curricula and make necessary revisions, alter staff assignments or recruit new faculty to accommodate newly required course work, and ensure thorough training for staff who advised students.

Most policy researchers who tracked the effects of high school graduation requirements have focused on curriculum reform and its impact on student course-taking patterns. Clearly, the intent of the student standards legislation was to alter the academic course work available to students and, by implication, the overall intellectual tone of students' high school careers. As discussed earlier, such a policy would then presumably lead to greater achievement.

The bulk of the large data base research has focused on course offerings and course-taking patterns and has linked these to either school or student characteristics. This body of research can be categorized as (1) preform national profiles of course offerings and course-taking patterns, (2) single-state in-depth profiles of both early patterns and assessments of changes, and (3) recent multiple-state assessments of changes. Clearly, each major type of research—national, relying on large data bases, or state, relying on multiple sources of school, district, and state-level data—complements the other, providing a multifaceted portrait of major educational reform in the 1980s. Each type is considered in turn.

Baseline Studies Using National Data Bases

Relying on national, longitudinal data bases such as the High School and Beyond (HS&B) study supported by the National Center for Education Statistics (NCES) and conducted by the Educational Testing Service, policy researchers analyzed course-taking patterns among students across the nation. Most of these studies used data gathered in the HS&B First Follow-Up Survey and transcript data gathered in 1981–1982, before most states initiated curriculum reform. These analyses serve as baseline data for changes that occurred as a result of state-initiated reform.

One topic of high interest in several of the studies was student enrollment in mathematics and science and whether there was systematic variation by track, race, gender, socioeconomic status, or other demographic variables. *An Analysis of Course Offerings and Enrollments as Related to School Characteristics* (West, Miller, & Diodata, 1985a) assessed the availability of and student participation in mathematics and science courses, vocational education, and computer science. The analyses were based on the 1982 HS&B Course Offerings and Course Enrollments Survey, the 1982 HS&B Transcripts Survey, the 1980 HS&B Base Year Survey, and the 1982 HS&B First Follow-Up Survey. The data were gathered from over 1,000 public and private secondary schools across the nation, over 18,000 sophomore transcripts, and approximately 30,000 sophomores in the First Follow-Up Survey. Some interesting findings emerged when researchers analyzed course taking according to school characteristics:

- When minimum competency requirements were present, there were more course offerings in math, science, vocational education, and computer science.
- Advanced mathematics and science offerings decreased when fewer than two thirds of the students were enrolled in college preparatory programs.
- Schools that had up to one quarter (between 1% and 24%) of students classified as disadvantaged offered more mathematics, science, vocational education, and computer courses than schools that had none.
- Vocational course enrollments represented 18% of all enrollments; mathematics, 10%; science, 7%; and computer science, less than 1%.
- Schools with a minimum competency testing requirement had a greater percentage of students enrolled in general mathematics and a lower percentage enrolled in algebra courses and geometry than schools without a minimum competency testing requirement.
- Schools with a higher percentage of students in an academic program or with at least three quarters of the students expecting to attend college had higher overall science and computer science enrollments and higher advanced mathematics and science enrollments and lower vocational enrollments than schools without a high percentage of students in academic programs.
- Vocational enrollments were higher in schools where the dropout rate was over 2%.

Many of these findings are not surprising. What stands out, however, are the low levels of enrollment in mathematics and science courses relative to vocational courses and the suggestion that minimal competency testing pushes students toward basic or remedial courses, at least in mathematics. The patterns also suggest that smaller schools might have more difficulty in responding to state mandates that require them to offer more courses overall and more advanced courses specifically (Firestone, 1989a; Timar, 1989). The presence of students of color, non-native English-speaking students, and students of poverty seems to press the curriculum toward more varied offerings, especially in mathematics and science.

A second study by the same researchers (West, Miller, & Diodata, 1985b) focused on patterns in course offerings and enrollments as a function of student characteristics. This study found four categories of course takers in mathematics/science and four in the vocational area:

Mathematics/Science	*Vocational*
1. Concentrators	1. Concentrators
2. Four-year college bound	2. Limited concentrators
3. General	3. Samplers
4. Nonparticipants or limited participants	4. Nonparticipants

Some of its more important findings include:

- About half of the students took general mathematics or science, while fewer than 10% of the students concentrated in mathematics.
- About half of the students had a strong vocational orientation (concentrators or limited concentrators); however, participation in vocational education was associated with decreased mathematics and science participation.
- Over one third of the students defined their programs as general and earned fewer credits in mathematics, humanities, and science than those in vocational programs.
- High-SES students were more likely to participate more intensively in mathematics, science, and computer science.
- Low-SES students participated more intensively in vocational and general education.
- Race/Ethnicity was unrelated to participation in vocational education, while white students participated more intensively in mathematics, science, and computer science.
- No differences were noted between male and female participation in mathematics and computer science.

- Generally, immediate postgraduation plans were not related to course-taking patterns, although the largest differences found were between plans to attend 4-year college and plans to work full-time.

Single-State In-Depth Profiles

Two research studies of single-state reform initiatives are summarized here. Both California and Florida led the movement to make state policies a more significant force in high school students' course selections.

CALIFORNIA.   The PACE group has initiated periodic assessments of education in California. One early report, *Curricular Change in California Comprehensive High Schools: 1982–83 to 1984–85,* (Grossman, Kirst, Negash, Schmidt-Posner, & Garet, 1985) tracked changes in the course offerings of 20 comprehensive high schools in response to an omnibus educational improvement bill (Senate Bill 813). Prior to this legislation, which encouraged stricter and more uniform graduation requirements, California had vested full control of graduation requirements in local districts. Thus, legislation that targeted the class of 1987 made few intrusions on local autonomy. Guidelines suggested that students take 3 years of English, 2 each of mathematics and science, and 3 of social studies. In addition, students were urged to take courses in fine arts or foreign languages, physical education, and health/driver's education. Locally required academic and nonacademic courses, as well as a minimal number of electives, brought the average number of credits to 22 in most districts (McDonnell, 1988).

Based on analyses of course descriptions and master schedules for the 1982–1983 and 1984–1985 academic years, the study concluded that as a result of tighter curriculum policies: (1) schools offered more courses in academic areas, especially math and science, and (2) by 1984–1985, schools offered fewer courses in industrial arts, home economics, and business education. Within mathematics, the more advanced courses (calculus, analytic geometry, trigonometry, and geometry) showed the biggest growth. In addition to more academic courses, schools in the sample offered more AP courses. AP course offerings grew 34% over the 2-year period. After adjustment for enrollment changes, this grew to 117%.

One explanation for declines in industrial arts and home economics is that students had less time for electives in their programs of study and thus demanded fewer of those courses. These shifts toward more academically oriented curricular offerings and more advanced courses within academic departments pose several policy issues. Although the curriculum is focusing on advanced academic courses for college-bound students, students in general programs have fewer nonacademic electives—courses in home economics, business education, and industrial arts—from which to choose. The PACE study asks important questions: What will the erosion of nonacademic electives mean for non-college-bound students? What are the implications for general students? Are their curricular offerings becoming impoverished? Are students of color or poverty continuing to be excluded from the rich educational resources of upper-level course work?

Moreover, the growing number of mathematics and science courses comes at a time when teacher shortages are severe, especially in those subjects. Are increasing numbers of teachers being assigned to teach out of field? The PACE report notes, "As many of the increases have occurred at more advanced levels, for example, in calculus and advanced placement, it becomes even more important to ensure that teachers teaching these courses have sufficient background in, and knowledge of, their subjects" (Grossman, Kirst, Negash, Schmidt-Posner, & Garet, 1985, p. 4). Although McDonnell (1988) found little evidence of out-of-field assignments, the possibility of underprepared teacher placements should be taken seriously.

FLORIDA.   The PACE study was replicated in Florida, and the results were published in 1989. Sponsored by the Center for Policy Research in Education (CPRE) and based on data available through the Florida Department of Education, *Curricular Change in Dade County, 1982–83 to 1986–87: A Replication of the PACE Study* (Hansen, 1989) compared course offerings and enrollments in Dade County in 1982–1983 and 1986–1987. Although not strictly a replication because its analyses rest on districtwide rather than statewide data, the study is of interest here.

Prior to 1983, Florida had no state-mandated credit requirements for high school graduation; requirements were set locally and varied from 17 to 22 year-long courses. The Raise Academic Achievement in Secondary Education (RAISE) Bill stipulated 24 credits, distributed as follows: four credits in English; three credits in mathematics; three credits in science, two of which must have a laboratory component; one credit each in American and world history; half a credit each in economics, practical arts education, performing arts education, life management skills, and physical education; and nine elective credits, but not more than two of those credits in remedial and compensatory courses. This latter stipulation was revised by 1985 legislation that increased the number of allowable compensatory courses from two to nine. In addition to legislated changes in high school graduation requirements, schools had to respond to changes in entrance requirements made by Florida state universities. Effective in the fall of 1984, students who applied for admission had to have one more English and math course than required by the state for high school graduation, as well as two foreign language courses. Other changes were stipulated for social studies and natural sciences, effective in 1986.

The largest enrollment increases reported over the 4-year span (1982–1983 to 1986–1987) were in science and foreign languages; small enrollment increases took place in computer education. Meanwhile, vocational and physical education enrollments declined, as did language arts enrollments, albeit modestly. Enrollments remained relatively stable in mathematics and social studies.

Some department shifts did take place. In mathematics, general math and geometry enrollments increased substantially while algebra, computer applications, and "other" enrollments declined. This suggests an internal redistribution toward more basic or remedial courses.

A substantial effect of the reform of graduation requirements was the redistribution of course offerings and staffing patterns across departments within schools. The biggest loser was vocational education, with physical education a close second. Science was called the biggest winner, with foreign language a distant second.

A comparison of the California and Florida studies of curricular change (Grossman, Kirst, Negash, Schmidt-Posner, & Garet, 1985; Guthrie et al., 1988) reveals the following similarities and differences.

- Science enrollments increased substantially in both Dade County and California.
- Vocational enrollments declined substantially in both places.
- Math enrollments remained relatively stable but had substantial internal redistribution.
- Foreign language enrollments increased significantly in both places.
- Social studies remained stable in Dade County and declined slightly in California.
- Arts enrollments increased somewhat in Dade County, while declining moderately in California.
- Music enrollments declined substantially in California but remained stable in Dade County.

When examined in light of the specifications of each state's new requirements, reasons for some of the more subtle differences become clear. For example, Florida stipulated course work in fine arts. It seems reasonable, then, that overall enrollments in two arts areas would remain stable (music) or increase a bit (art). California's requirements, in contrast, included course work in fine arts or foreign language, suggesting that enrollments in both art and music might well decline in favor of foreign language course work, which was required for entrance into the California college and university system. Social studies requirements were similar in both states and included American and world history, economics, and civics. California also required course work in geography.

Recent Comparisons Across States

The CPRE conducted several recent cross-state case studies (in addition to the Dade County study discussed earlier) as part of its research on the implementation and effects of state policies. Two studies by McDonnell and Clune are of particular interest here.

McDonnell (1988) interviewed over 600 policymakers and educators in 5 states, 19 districts, and 30 high schools. Her interviews produced the following observations:

- Schools reported a 20% to 30% increase in the number of sections of any given course for each additional year that the state required that subject.
- Most of the new sections were offered in lower-level classes.
- Increases in course offerings in some subjects led to decreases in others.
- Local response was often minimal compliance and some shirking at the school level. At the same time, districts used the new policies as leverage to standardize curricula far beyond state requirements.
- Messages about the effects of the policy on dropouts and on tracking systems were mixed.
- The most important effects of increased course requirements were due to their interaction with other state policies (e.g., competency tests).

McDonnell (1988) concluded the research with a discussion of the different norms that state policymakers and local educators hold for course work. Although principals, counselors, and teachers acknowledge the need for higher standards, she found that their primary concern is to move students through the system, and in so doing, they tailor course work to individual ability levels even if it means "watering down" courses. Policymakers, on the other hand, tend to follow norms concerned with electorate accountability, the public welfare, and balance of competing interests. Practitioners' and policymakers' norms do not always conflict, but when they do, implementation deviates from expected outcomes.

Clune, White, and Patterson (1989) collected interview data on the intent and effects of new graduation requirements in 6 states, 24 districts, and 32 high schools. The sites were chosen to ensure significant policy impact and variations in state and local capacity. Much of the data collected by Clune and McDonnell overlapped. Clune's interviews with over 700 educators led to the following conclusions:

- Typically, the reforms did not affect affluent schools and districts and college preparatory students.
- Four of the 13 intensively studied districts had credit requirements that equaled or exceeded the state requirements, and almost all districts had some preexisting requirements that reduced their burden in meeting the new state requirements.
- Most schools added math and science courses. Just over a quarter of the students took an additional math class, and a third took an additional science class.
- The new courses were overwhelmingly at the basic, general, or remedial level.
- The requirements did not necessarily increase dropout rates, and concerns still exist about the quality of education offered at-risk students to keep them in school.
- Respondents perceived strong but mostly uninformed public support for higher standards.
- Perceived disadvantages (fewer electives and vocational offerings) outweighed the most often cited advantage of the new policy initiative: better college preparation.
- States did not regularly monitor course taking or compliance with the new requirements.

Clune, White, and Patterson (1989) concluded that reform policies that increased graduation requirements both succeeded and failed:

> They succeeded in getting a lot more students into basic academic courses and in satisfying a concerned public; they failed in getting students into the most rigorous possible courses, in producing a reasonably uniform education for all students, and, probably, in conveying the higher-order skills necessary for a competitive economy. (p. 47)

These more aggressive goals require policies that address the content of courses, target courses for certain groups of students, and offer more technical assistance to schools and teachers.

Conclusions from Requirements Studies

Two clear patterns emerge from the national, single-state, and multiple-state studies. One is the shift in emphasis within the high school curriculum: Schools are offering more academic courses, and more students are enrolling in them, but they are taking lower-level, remedial, or basic courses. This pattern appears most often in mathematics but is also true in science. Social studies course offerings, however, are declining, as are some fine arts (art and/or music) courses. Most profound are declines in vocational education courses, specifically home economics and industrial arts. A second pattern emerges from the pressure that competency and basic skills tests appear to be exerting on course offerings: To ensure that all students pass the required tests, schools offer more remedial courses. Again, this is most striking in mathematics.

The research discussed thus far has documented course-taking patterns among high school students before state reform and comparisons of course-taking patterns before and after reform within a state or across a few states. The most recent studies gathered multifaceted data from schools, districts, and states to assess implementation issues and ongoing patterns of response to state policy changes. One consistent theme in these studies is access to educational resources. Whether assessing participation of students of color and poverty in the academic curriculum or evaluating the shift from a general and vocationally oriented curriculum to an academic one, the issues of excellence versus equity have been a topmost concern.

RESEARCH ON TRACKING

Equity has been a major focus of researchers who have investigated the internal organizational processes of schools. Our goal in calling attention to this body of literature is to bring to the forefront the issue of equity in the investigation of first-wave reform initiatives such as increased graduation requirements. What is the distribution of student course taking when analyzed by race, ethnicity, language-minority status, poverty level, or gender? Are students of color, poverty, young women, or non-native English-speaking students disproportionately in lower-status courses or lower-status tracks? Have the new reforms increased these students' access to valued resources?

There is ample evidence that historically harmful patterns persist. Intradepartmental shifts (i.e., those resulting in more remedial or basic level courses) represent a kind of internal resegregation within the academic track. If disproportionate numbers of students of color and poverty, Spanish-speaking youths, and young women continue to be found in these lower-level but nonetheless "academic" courses, schools have done little to address equity. Requiring all students to take more academic courses and attempting to reduce intertrack differences may have created patterns of intratrack inequities.

Because graduation requirements reform directly shapes the curriculum, how students are sorted into various tracks or programs must be included in a complete analysis of this reform. Supported by recent research on the effects of tracking, the following discussion seeks to uncover the frequently tacit processes by which students are sorted, learn to lower their expectations, and thus are persistently excluded from the full range of educational choices.

Curriculum grouping, or tracking, is one organizational system for sorting and classifying students. As Oakes notes in her recent work (1992), "tracking practices are diverse, complex, and dynamic. . . . All these practices organize schools so that students who seem similar can be taught together, separately from other students" (p. 12). Clearly, various high school tracks have a profound influence on the types, variety, and quality of students' educational experiences, easing access to intellectual challenge and appropriate course work for college for some while limiting information and reducing mobility for others.

Grouping systems most often sort students into the academic or college-bound track, the general track, and the vocational track. By sorting students into groups, labeling those groups, conferring on them certain statuses, and certifying those statuses to the larger society, schools are powerful mechanisms for influencing students' life chances. Understanding selection systems within schools is critical for understanding the educational and occupational attainment process (Rosenbaum, 1978) and how educational resources are allocated. Despite progress in understanding the link between the sorting of students and their future occupational choices, researchers know "very little about the structure of opportunity within schools and its influence on youths' opportunities in society" (Rosenbaum, 1978, p. 236).

In a case study of one high school, Rosenbaum (1978) found administrators and teachers articulating one set of norms, suggesting an open system where all students had equal access to educational opportunities. In examining school records, however, he found a stable tracking system structured so that students in the highest track stayed in that track and noncollege track students stayed in their tracks. Although lower-track college-bound students moved into noncollege tracks, the reverse rarely happened. Rosenbaum concluded that the differences between the "apparent" opportunity structure and the "actual" one were real and persistent: Although the former appeared to be open and grounded in norms of fairness, the latter belied those assumptions and revealed patterns of constrained opportunities and misinformed choices for lower-track students.

Rosenbaum (1978, 1980) presents an important concept—the structure of opportunity—for studying how access to educational resources within schools is patterned into an elaborate, stable tracking system. Oakes (1985, 1990) has extended this concept, helping to build a growing literature that documents the perverse effects of tracks and ability grouping for certain categories of students, notably children of color and lower socioeconomic levels. As she notes (1992), "track-related differences demonstrate that tracking—however well intentioned and seemingly objectively implemented—leads to an unequal distribution of school resources, with academically and socially disadvantaged students receiving less" (p. 16). Also contributing to this literature is the work of Gamoran and Berends (1987), who review current research on tracking and make a useful distinction between large-scale surveys and ethnographic studies to achieve a more complete understanding of stratification. The following discussion relies largely on their work.

Research on Tracking: The Surveys

The impetus for much of the survey research was a need to further explore within-school variations in achievement found in previous research, notably the Coleman report of the mid-1960s (Coleman et al., 1966). Several studies have found that participation in the academic or college-bound track is associated with higher achievement levels (Alexander & Pallas, 1984; Gamoran, 1987; Kerckhoff, 1986). In addition, HS&B and College Entrance Examination Board (CEEB) data (Sebring, 1987) support the notion that academic track placement shapes higher achievement levels, even when controlling for aptitude. Although some researchers have found smaller effects when ability (Jencks & Brown, 1975) and pre–high school achievement (Alexander & Cook, 1982) are controlled, there seems at least some consensus that achievement is shaped in part by track placement. At least in mathematics and science, much of this achievement is explained by course-taking patterns (Gamoran, 1987).

Post–high school plans are more consistently associated with track (Alexander, Cook, & McDill, 1978; Rosenbaum, 1980). This is not surprising because the labels given tracks—academic or college preparatory, vocational, and general—are predictive of those plans. Students in the academic or college preparatory track are more likely to attend college than their general or vocational peers (Alexander & Eckland, 1975; Jencks & Brown, 1975; Rosenbaum, 1980) and to have higher overall educational attainment (Wolfle, 1985).

In analyses of the National Science Foundation's 1985–1986 National Survey of Science and Mathematics Education (NSSME), Oakes (1990) examined the distribution of opportunities of various groups of students to participate in science and mathematics. Relying on teacher reports of the ability levels of students in randomly sampled science or mathematics classes, Oakes found that access to "rich and meaningful topics and skills" (p. 7) was disproportionately allocated to students judged to be of high ability. Those in lower-track classes were, in contrast, taught curricula "dominated by exercises, workbooks, and commercially produced basic skills kits" (p. 7). Thus, determinations of students' ability profoundly shape their opportunities to participate in rich, variegated, and complex learning situations, at least in mathematics and science.

The stability and persistence of track assignments, as well as their exhaustiveness as constructs that describe a student's educational experiences, have been thorny empirical problems that have recently come under challenge (Garet & DeLany, 1988; Oakes, 1985). This critique centers on the robustness of the track variable. Although two studies reviewed by Gamoran and Berends (1987) used more refined and empirically based measures of track (Hotchkiss & Dorsten, 1987; Kerckhoff, 1986; Westat, Inc., 1988), the bulk of large-scale surveys relied on student self-reports or on the reports of others in the school. Because of concerns about validity when students are asked about their course taking, Goertz (1989) compared the HS&B 1982 student transcript data with student self-reports. Her analyses "found that the quality of student reports on amount of course work . . . differed by subject area" (pp. 18–19) with correlation coefficients ranging from 0.87 to 0.40.

Related concerns about track assignments arise from close scrutiny of the 1990 work of Oakes. In determining the track or ability level of students, Oakes relied on the NSSME survey item in which teachers assessed the ability level of an entire class of students: In that data base, "teachers detailed the race, gender, . . . and *ability levels* of students in their classes" (p. 9, emphasis added). If, as she asserts, those "designations of 'ability' are suspect" (p. 7) for sorting students into tracks, they may well be suspect for empirical analyses. Clearly, more fine-grained and judgment-free assessments of ability and track are needed. We return to this discussion in Chapter 4. Now, however, we examine the evidence from ethnographic studies, as reviewed by Gamoran and Berends (1987).

Research on Tracking: The Ethnographies

Noting that surveys do little to unpack the complex tracking processes within a school, Gamoran and Berends (1987) turn to ethnographies to provide rich descriptive detail about the "subjective meanings of the events and patterns of life in schools" (p. 420). One finding of interest comes from Oakes' (1985) work in 25 middle and high schools. Although high school track placement overlaps substantially with the distribution of ability—more-able students tend to be found in academic tracks and less-able students in general or vocational tracks—those descriptors do not capture the complexity and subtlety of the stratification. Oakes (1985) and Goodlad (1984) found that "nearly all the schools grouped students by ability for several subjects, but few had curricular programs as clearly defined as in the school studied by Rosenbaum (1976)" (Gamoran & Berends, 1987, p. 421).

Ethnographic research has also documented well the instructional differences between tracks. Some tracks tend to simplify and fragment instructional tasks for some groups (Finley, 1984; Hargreaves, 1967; Metz, 1978; Oakes, 1985), resulting in what Page (1984) describes as a "skeletonized" and "univocal" curriculum for lower-track students. Moreover, the assignment of students to teachers is not random in schools: Ethnographic work suggests that "the more experienced teachers and those regarded as more successful are disproportionately assigned to the higher tracks" (Gamoran & Berends, 1987, p. 423). And teachers in higher-track classes seem to devote more time to instruction, teach with more energy and enthusiasm, and vary their instructional approaches more than teachers in the lower tracks do (Oakes, 1985). The ethnographic research, then, provides a pattern of findings that strongly suggests that there are dramatic differences in the educational resources available to students in lower-track classrooms and upper-track classrooms.

Ethnographic research also focuses on the social context of tracking, showing how differential status accorded track labels shapes attitudes toward school. Students placed in lower-ability and lower-status tracks tend to develop antischool attitudes; those accorded the higher status of academic tracks are more likely to bond to school and schooling and are therefore less likely to disengage from the schooling process (Finn, 1989). Teachers contribute to this dichotomizing process as well (Finley, 1984; Hargreaves, 1967; Rosenbaum, 1978), as do other students (Oakes, 1985; Rosenbaum, 1976; Willis, 1981). But when placed in mixed-ability groups, low-ability students showed dramatic increases in confidence, work habits, and dependability (Veldman & Sanford, 1984), suggesting a greater sensitivity to class placement than high-ability students (Dawson, 1987).

In summarizing the ethnographies, Gamoran and Berends (1987) note that this "literature brings a consistent message about the effects of tracking—here, that it creates differences in students' attitudes and behavior that may be further linked to achievement and post–high school aspirations" (p. 428).

A Questioning of the Track Concept

As noted earlier, some recent research calls into question the notion of rigid tracks in American high schools. Garet and his colleagues take a more micro perspective on student course-taking patterns and challenge much of the conventional thinking. They conducted case studies of six high schools to capture science course taking among students who entered the schools as freshmen in 1979. Relying on student transcripts and interview data, Garet and DeLany (1984) attempted to redress the lack of attention in tracking research on "the fine-grained structure of the curriculum in individual high schools" (p. 3) and found great variation in the initial science courses that 10th graders took when each school was studied in depth. Although socioeconomic status contributed to much of the difference, the 11th- and 12th-grade course-taking patterns of those students who took biology in 10th grade varied substantially, suggesting that "for many students, the curriculum sequences observed resemble a somewhat random-appearing collection of courses, not easily classifiable according to track" (p. 11). This challenges the whole concept of track, with its coherent set of courses, rigidity, impermeability, and exclusivity.

One explanation for these seemingly random patterns is that the shifts might well represent informed, reflective choices made by students as they grew in intellectual self-knowledge. Another is that the curriculum wobbled from year to year because of the idiosyncratic nature of teacher choice, staff turnover, and the like. Furthermore, irregular course-taking patterns (and hence idiosyncratic or "incoherent" student choice) might well be the result of scheduling conflicts. Garet and DeLany (1984) conclude that course-taking irregularities might not be intentional but instead the result of the "operation of multiple, loosely connected standard operating procedures at the schools. . . . [the result of] constraints and organizational choices" (p. 12).

Building on data they gathered on students entering high school in 1979, the researchers conducted a second study (Garet, Agnew, & DeLany, 1987) focusing on the four California high schools and found that the actual or enacted curriculum was the result of linked decisions about course offerings and student distribution across the available courses. A set of loosely related decision waves had occurred: (1) The course offerings ("menu") was constructed, (2) information was disseminated to parents and students, (3) formal information was collected and consolidated, (4) negotiations took place, (5) the master schedule was built, and (6) the master schedule was altered to incorporate not only student requests but also the needs of the school and district (DeLany, 1991). This process was characterized by uncertainty and constraints and was made all the more fluid and unpredictable by changes in the student population, student programs of study, and the course menu. Thus, the decision process was one of not only uncertainty and constraints but also of adjustment and adaptation.

The literature discussed earlier suggests that although perhaps not as rigid or impermeable as early research found, tracks and tracking systems persist in the American high school today and have especially negative consequences for students at risk of school failure because of minority status, poverty, or lack of previous educational achievement. One could argue that first-wave reform efforts such as stricter high school graduation requirements would have little overall effect on these groups without simultaneously confronting tracking systems.

Current calls for reform fortunately focus specifically on ability grouping and tracks. For example, at the national level, the National Governors' Association (1990) has called for the elimination of tracking, as has the Carnegie Council on Adolescent Development (1989). Moreover, the National Council of Teachers of Mathematics (1989) has recently proposed a common core of mathematics learning for all students—one that avoids the premature tracking of students into "either college-preparatory sequences or 'general mathematics' sequences on the basis of narrow perceptions of performance or curricular goals" (West, 1992, p. 8). At a regional level, the New England League of Middle Schools (n.d.) has taken the position that tracking is inconsistent with sound middle school philosophy. As a further example, state departments of education have adapted policies intended to promote experimentation with alternative grouping arrangements (see, for example, Massachusetts Board of Education, n.d.).

These recent efforts can be seen as attempts to reinfuse equity into the reform discourse, thereby providing what Dawson (1987) calls a "tremendous opportunity to teach a lesson of lifelong significance: the value of diversity" (p. 367).

CONCLUSION

The first wave of reform in the 1980s has been criticized as being excessively regulatory and limiting the discretion of teachers and administrators (Conley, 1988; McNeil, 1988; Wise, 1988). Teachers found they had little authority to determine what they taught, not only in classrooms but also with regard to the total school curriculum. Myriad regulations emanating from the state capital buffeted administrators (Rossman, Corbett, & Firestone, 1988). And although students' voices are not often heard in policy studies despite their centrality to reform, students found they had fewer choices in high school than did their older brothers and sisters, who attended "shopping mall high schools" (Powell, Farrar, & Cohen, 1985).

In addition, critics of this first wave of reform charge that from an organizational perspective, the reform policies do not sufficiently take into account the idiosyncratic nature of schools and variations in local responses to state mandates (Corbett & Rossman, 1989; Corbett, Rossman, & Dawson, 1984; Metz, 1988; Timar, 1989). Sensitivity to local variability, however, is a relatively recent issue for the research community. In fact, what has been called the "first generation" of policy implementation research (McDonnell & Elmore, 1987) took a decidedly state-level perspective, assessing the success or failure of policies using as a criterion fidelity to original intent. Fidelity-to-intent research documented local variation but construed that variation as "noise" in an as-yet imperfect policy system: Rationality had not yet uncovered the best mix of variables to ensure smooth implementation. These studies helped shape conventional wisdom that implementation of state mandates was limited and walled off from the technical core of schools and that mandates were adapted to local conditions in ways that altered their original intent (Berman & McLaughlin, 1975), if not ceremonialized (Meyer & Rowan, 1977).

As early as 1980, Murphy urged a shift away from traditional studies of policymakers' intentions to studies of local variation. Thus, during the last decade, the study of policy implementation developed from a first-generation assessment of policymakers' intent to variability in local response (McDonnell & Elmore, 1987). Exemplifying second-generation research, Timar and Kirp (1989) recently described success-ful implementation as resting on "organizational features of individual schools." They note that "schools shape policies as much as policies shape schools" (p. 506). McDonnell's (1988) work is also representa-tive of this growing perspective. McDonnell found evidence of shirking and minimal compliance in local responses to state policy initiatives. She explained this phenomenon in contextual terms—for example, the scope of Florida's mandates encouraged minimal compliance. In Pennsylvania, conflicts between course work requirements and voca-tional education precluded anything other than a pro forma attention to mandates. As a further example, McLaughlin (1987) describes how "policy effects are complex, sometimes hidden or invisible, often unan-ticipated or nominalistic . . . even when they are apparent, they may be transitory" (p. 175).

Supporting the notion that the proof of the policy is in its imple-mentation, Elmore (1980) developed the strategy of "backward map-ping," where research begins at the level of implementors and works up through the local district to the state system in search of explana-tions for the reform as it was eventually implemented in the school. This call to focus on local variation and to concentrate resources on the targets of policy reform was influential in defining both the design and the key questions of our research.

Another influence was the first wave's emphasis on excellence and achievement, often at the expense of the concerns about equity and social justice that were prominent in federal policies of the 1960s and 1970s (Apple, 1988; Hawley, 1988). Although some commentators gloss over larger social justice questions in the first wave of reform (Finn, 1988; Murphy, 1989), growing evidence from urban and rural centers suggests that educational standards grounded in meritocratic principles may create patterns of injustice by systematically excluding certain students from educational opportunities. Thus, it is essential that research on policy reform explore the extent to which all students are afforded enhanced learning opportunities.

This complex web of research sets the stage for our investigation of the effects that changes in Maryland's graduation requirements had on education in that state. By documenting the effects at the school level over time (from just after the bylaw was enacted to 4 years later) and by investigating course-taking patterns before and after the policy was enacted, we can capture not only the diversity of responses across schools but also the policy's influence on opportunities for different groups of students.

Building on concerns from second-generation policy research (McDonnell & Elmore, 1987), we are curious about how state-initiated reform differentially affects schools. Moving away from the homogeneous assumptions of early 1980s' research, we focus on the local school and its context to better understand local implementation and effects and ask: *(1) What is the local variation in response to the policy change?*

Next, our focus turns to the issues of tracks and tracking systems and how these powerful structures are or are not shaped by curricular reform. Exploring areas uncharted in previous research on student standards reform, we probe the effects of policy reforms on tracks and resulting students' course-taking experiences, asking: *(2) How has the policy affected tracks and tracking systems as a form of access to resources?*

Third, and related to the second set of concerns, are questions that probe the experiences of students and teachers identified as at risk, either because of the policy reform or because of entrenched patterns of lack of access to educational resources. For students, we focus on race, gender, and achievement as important lenses to understand the impact of the reform. For teachers, we assess departmental shifts and how perceptions of risk vary with a more objective assessment of risk. This leads us to the large question: *(3) What impact has the policy had on students and teachers at risk?*

Fourth is a focus on how various actors in the policy arena perceive their influence on that policy system. Trying to understand where important policymakers and policy implementors feel they can lay claim to affecting students' experiences in high school, we ask: *(4) How has the policy change shaped various actors' perceptions about their influence in the implementation of educational reform?*

Finally, we take a broad perspective on high school graduation requirements reform and focus on the policymakers' intent in framing the policy changes and how well that intent has been achieved: *(5) What was the intent of the policy, and how well has that been received by the key consumers of high school graduates, institutions of higher education, and the business community?*

These five broad questions provide the framework for the presentation of our research findings. The following five chapters are devoted to an exploration of these questions.

3

WHERE'S THE ACTION? STUDENTS, TEACHERS, AND THE CURRICULUM

Early research on planned change in schools began with the assumption that innovations should be implemented in a form as true as possible to what their designers intended. Fidelity to original design was the hallmark of successful implementation. As researchers analyzed planned change efforts, however, it soon became patently clear that such a perspective was inappropriate for understanding the complexities of school change. Work by Berman and McLaughlin (1977) identified *mutual adaptation* as an often-found outcome of planned change and innovation. This finding turned around theoretical thinking, resulting in increasing sensitivity to the power of the local context to shape innovations and the implementation process.

This chapter begins the exploration of data from our 4-year study of high school graduation reform, building on the notion that local schools and districts vary enormously in their responses to state-mandated policy. A complex mix of historical factors, local economic conditions, characteristics of the population being served, and school-specific conditions such as culture, internal resource allocations, and posture toward the state accounts for this variation. Yet policy mandates rarely take this mix into consideration: They assume similar capacity in individuals or agencies to respond to the required change (McDonnell & Elmore, 1987). Policymakers also assume that schools and districts will assent to the intended meanings and presumed value of the mandate. Thus, the policy mandated for Fast Track is the same policy installed at Urban and Rural. Because the local capacity to respond varies considerably, however, differences in implementation emerge across sites. This chapter looks at curriculum changes and course-taking patterns across the five schools and offers convincing documentation of varied responses to the centralized policy initiative of increased graduation requirements.

This theme—local variation—is woven throughout our discussion of the findings but is addressed more explicitly in this chapter. We detail schools' differences here to foreshadow much of the discussion that follows in Chapters 4 through 7. We begin by posing four key questions designed to address whether the policy is affecting the depth and breadth of student exposure to high school curricula:

1. Are students earning more credits?
2. Are students being exposed to a more rigorous curriculum?
3. Are students struggling more with their course work?
4. Is the balance of credits shifting across different content areas?

These four questions guide the presentation of much of the data for the next three chapters. In this chapter, we will explore the variation across schools in answering these questions. After each specific question is addressed, we look at students' views of the overall influence of the new graduation requirements policy. And we conclude this chapter by portraying how teachers' perspectives varied across the five schools. In subsequent chapters, we investigate the role that track, gender, race, and academic performance also played in understanding students' schooling experiences.

The data used to assess local variation include a mix of qualitative and quantitative results. The quantitative portion involves analysis of a sample of student transcript records from the class of 1986, the last to graduate before any of the new requirements took effect, and the classes of 1989 and 1990, the first two cohorts expected to meet all the requirements. Complete transcript records were analyzed for just under 2,000 students across the three cohorts. The qualitative data derive from interviews conducted with students, teachers, counselors, and administrators from all five schools. Three separate visits were made to each of the schools for the purpose of interviewing more than

800 staff and students. Appendix A documents the methodology in more detail. Samples of interview and transcript data protocols can be found in the technical report (Wilson, Rossman, & Adduci, 1991).

ARE STUDENTS EARNING MORE CREDITS?

The policy initiative did not require an increase in the total number of credits earned. However, with the reduction in elective credits resulting from the specification of certain courses (e.g., a third year of math, a fine arts credit, and a foreign language as part of the Certificate of Merit) and the national attention on high school standards, students' opportunities to take more courses, as well as the absolute number of courses they did take, may have been altered. Another reason for considering the number of credits is that it is an easily understood variable when making comparisons across schools, track, gender, race, and academic performance.

Most analyses of transcript records either focus in detail on one subject area or are a global representation of curriculum exposure. Our data base is unique because of its detail and comprehensiveness. Each course across all 4 years of a student's high school experience was included in the analysis. More specifically, for each course, four separate features were analyzed: the subject (e.g., science or math), the grouping (e.g., vocational, general, academic, or honors), the grade (A through F), and the number of credits earned (anywhere from 0.25 to 2.00). Thus, one student exposed to a semester grading system with eight separate subjects would have a total of 128 variables (8 subjects x 4 codes x 4 years) in the transcript analysis.

To address this first question regarding the number of credits earned, an individual student's total was computed by scanning across all 4 years of courses taken; those individual results were then combined to create an overall school score. To compute the number of credits earned, the computer checked each course that a student took to ensure that the student had received a passing grade; when that condition was met, the number of credits was added to the total. These results are displayed in Figure 3.1, with separate averages presented for each school across three cohorts: the class of 1986 (before the new graduation requirements policy) and the classes of 1989 and 1990 (the first 2 years after complete implementation of the policy). Two years of postpolicy effects are presented throughout the transcript analyses to allay claims of unique first-year changes or of missing longitudinal effects. Bar graphs summarize many of the findings in this book because they offer a clear visual comparison for the nontechnical reader. Analyses of variance are also reported below each bar graph to summarize the statistical relationships.

The prepolicy data (class of 1986) in Figure 3.1 show that the average number of credits earned ranged from a low of 22.3 to a high of 25.4. That variation represents a significant difference; graduates at Rural in 1986 earned over three more credits during their high school careers than did students at Urban. This situation reflects a structural variation in which some schools had only six-period days while others had seven-period days. As a result, some students could choose from among 24 different full-year courses over 4 years while other students could choose from 28. Those with the greater number of courses available had more flexibility and opportunity to tailor schooling to meet their special needs. The two schools with the lowest averages (Urban and Middle Class) both had six-period days.

In Figure 3.1, we also see that in four of the five schools the number of credits that students earned went up after the policy went into effect. Only Rural experienced no change in the number of credits earned. The increase in credits earned ranged from a low of less than

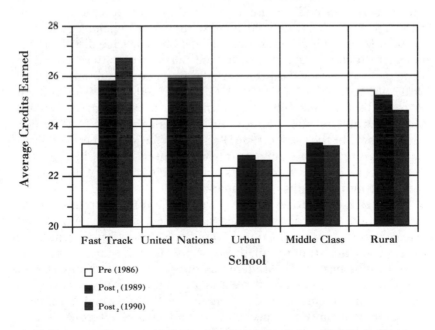

FIGURE 3.1. Credits earned by school, pre- and postpolicy. Statistical effect by school: $F = 206.0, p \leq .001$.

half a credit increase at Urban (22.3 to 22.6) to a high of 3.5 credits (23.2 to 26.7) at Fast Track. In the latter school, much of the increase might have been due not only to the new course requirements but also to the school's increase in the number of its periods from six to seven in 1986–1987, thus allowing students to take more courses. A similar structural change at United Nations—the creation of an eight-period day for the magnet school students—had more to do with the increase in credits earned than with simply the new policy. It is difficult to untangle the two, however. Many people we interviewed argued that the new policy was one of the major forces behind the move to have more periods in the school day. Thus, although the number of periods has a big impact on the number of credits that students earned, the new requirements were probably an added incentive for schools to increase the number of periods each day.

ARE STUDENTS TAKING MORE ACADEMICALLY RIGOROUS COURSES?

To answer this question, we investigated the ratio of advanced credits that students earned to the total credits that students earned. Advanced courses were defined as those that were eligible for the Certificate of Merit. This criterion was selected because each district determines which courses are eligible for the Certificate of Merit, and thus the analysis allows for local contextual differences. Although the Certificate of Merit did not exist for the class of 1986, there was enough comparability in course offerings from 1986 to 1989 that any course that was eligible for the Certificate of Merit for the class of 1989 was coded as such for the class of 1986. Ratio was considered a more appropriate measure than a simple count of advanced credits, because the five schools have different numbers of periods in the day, which makes a straight count of credits not comparable.

Figure 3.2 summarizes the proportion of advanced credits earned at each school. Students in the class of 1986 in one school, Urban, earned a very low proportion of credits (10%) that qualified as advanced, while students in three of the four remaining schools showed ratios near 25%. Students in the other four schools earned between two and a half and three and a half times as many advanced credits as did students at Urban. Students at Rural earned the largest proportion of advanced credits before the policy took effect (36%).

Four of the five schools showed large increases in the proportion of advanced credits their students earned after the implementation of the

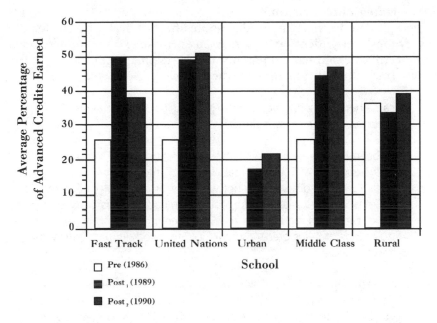

FIGURE 3.2. Percentage of advanced credits earned by school. Statistical effect by school: $F = 107.5$, $p \leq .001$.

new policy. Rural was the only school that did not show an increase; it remained about the same with just over one third of students' course offerings classified as advanced. At Fast Track and United Nations, the proportion of advanced credits earned nearly doubled, going from approximately one quarter to just under one half for the first postpolicy cohort. That increase remained stable at United Nations but dropped at Fast Track. The increases at Urban more than doubled by the second year of implementation, but the proportion was still lower than that of any of the other four schools prior to the policy change.

An assumption that is often made by policymakers during policy reform is that everyone will be reasonably knowledgeable about the changes. We tested that assumption by interviewing students. We found that students' knowledge of the Certificate of Merit varied widely across the five high schools. At Fast Track, the Certificate of Merit was a centerpiece for curriculum and guidance. In 1986, we interviewed several students who described how they had been counseled into Certificate of Merit courses only to be failing several of them. When we returned in 1988 and 1990, we heard students tell about being in Certificate of Merit classes early on, failing, and having to "straighten out" their course work. In addition, Fast Track students were unique in their knowledge about the certificate, except for the very top-level students, who surpassed even the extra requirements of the certificate and had no real need to be familiar with them. Typical Fast Track student responses are the following:

> I came here my sophomore year. The principal told me about it—the certificate—when I was making my course selections.

> I've been told by my counselor that the Certificate of Merit helps you in college courses. At Towson State University, they say it makes no difference. They can't differentiate between Certificate of Merit and regular. In a lot of courses, teachers don't make any distinctions between Certificate of Merit and regular. But they say even if it doesn't help you get into college, it helps prepare you for college work. I guess with some classes it does.

> My freshman year I didn't learn much about it in Baltimore County. When I came here, I learned about it. Messed me up because I didn't take Certificate of Merit my freshman year—I'll be short two classes. I added them up already.

> The guidance counselor has been telling us since eighth grade, and we've signed up for courses. Every year, the guidance counselor tells us the same thing. From what I've been told, Maryland is the only state that has it and if I go to other states and try to show that as an accomplishment, they'll be like, "What's that?" Classes are not that much different. Some teachers may take it seriously, but for the most part they teach it as a normal class.

In contrast were students at Middle Class and Urban, many of whom had little knowledge of the certificate and yet told us that they were interested in earning it. Sadly, at both schools, students repeatedly told us that they knew vaguely about the Certificate of Merit and would have wanted to earn it but that it was too late for them now. And when we asked students to tell us which students they thought were earning the Certificate of Merit, fully half of the students interviewed at Urban said, "above average students." This stood in marked contrast to Middle Class, where over half of the students said the Certificate of Merit was designed for "top honors students." Thus, Urban students had a more democratic concept of the certificate—one could be above average and earn it—while those at Middle Class seemed to have a more elitist concept—only the best and brightest could qualify. The clear message throughout our student interviews was the different ways in which schools responded to the press for more rigorous courses, as well as schools' individual interpretations of that press.

ARE STUDENTS STRUGGLING MORE WITH THEIR COURSE WORK?

One of the arguments against increasing course requirements is that the extra pressure will make it more difficult for students to complete their work. This would particularly affect students on the borderline—that is, students who were just barely able to get by. To examine this question quantitatively, we looked at whether students were failing more courses after the policy change. To do this, we made the assumption that grading policies were relatively stable over time. This assumption derived from the facts that the teacher populations in the five schools were stable and that no other major reform influenced grading practices.

Figure 3.3 compares failure rates in the five schools before and after the new requirements took effect. These figures represent the proportion of all courses in which students received failing grades, either for low performance or poor attendance. Across all five schools, the failure rate was less than 10%. However, there was marked variation across the five schools, with the highest failure rate (at Urban) being three times the lowest failure rate (Fast Track) before the new graduation requirements policy took effect. Balancing these two extremes were more middle-of-the-road rates at the other three high schools. When we compare students who were enrolled before and after the requirements took effect, it is very clear that the increased requirements did not have a detrimental effect on the course failure rate. Indeed, in three schools (Urban, Middle Class, and United Nations), there was a substantial drop in failures. At Urban, where the biggest drop occurred, the failure rate declined by 64%. The other two schools showed only small declines. The small change at Fast Track reflects a bottoming out, with proportions about as low as they could go. On the other hand, the lack of change at Rural is indicative of that small school's response to policy reform. Because of its size, the school has very little flexibility and consequently made few changes in the way it went about its work.

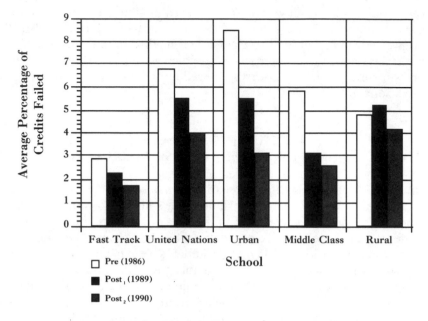

FIGURE 3.3. Percentage of credits failed by school. Statistical effect by school: $F = 19.0, p \leq .001$.

HAS THE BALANCE OF CREDITS
IN DIFFERENT SUBJECT AREAS CHANGED?

In this section, we focus on specific subject areas in which the require-ments may have had an effect. We review credit distributions in four different subject areas: math, fine arts, practical arts, and academic sub-jects. The new policy changed courses in the first three subjects: It increased the math requirement from two to three credits and added a fine arts and practical arts credit. With the added emphasis on rigor introduced by the Certificate of Merit, we hypothesized that increased attention might be paid to academic subjects.

Math

Figure 3.4 displays data on the average number of math credits earned in each of the five schools before and after implementation of the new policy. As was the case with almost all the data, there were some important differences across the five schools prior to implementation of

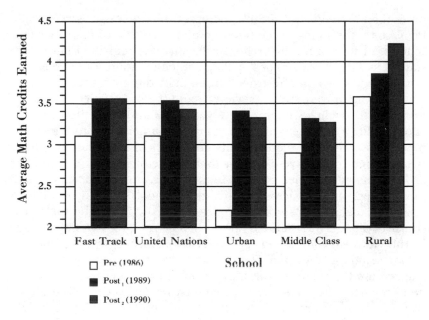

FIGURE 3.4. Math credits earned by school. Statistical effect by school: $F = 29.2$, $p \leq .001$.

the policy. In four of the five schools, the average number of math credits earned was near the three credits required by the new policy. That is, on average, students were taking three or more math courses even before the requirements took effect. A separate analysis revealed that in those four schools, approximately 68% of the students had enrolled in three math credits. At Urban, this figure was a low 43%. It is interesting that the school in which students earned the most math credits was Rural, which had a strong commitment to at least 3 years of mathematics even prior to the requirement. The most obvious disparity is between Urban and the other four schools for the class of 1986. Students in the other schools far exceeded the required two credits, but Urban students on average just met the two-credit requirement.

A comparison of the three cohorts suggests that although most of the schools were already encouraging students to take three credits of math, the formal requirement still had a positive effect on math credits earned. There was a significant increase in math credits across all five schools in the first year after the policy was implemented. In four of the five schools, the average increase was in the range of a half credit. The most dramatic increase occurred at Urban, where a leap of more than a credit (i.e., a 50% increase) took place. This reflects an increase that is almost three times greater than that of the other four schools. In four of the five schools, the increase remained fairly constant across the 2 years of post–policy implementation. The one exception was Rural, where the growth in math credits continued.

How varied were students' views about the importance of an additional math credit? Students were generally muted in their feelings about taking a third year of math. As noted earlier, prior to the implementation of the new requirements, fully 60% of all of the students in the five high schools were already taking at least 3 years of math. We probed students on their reasons for selecting a particular course and found some variation across the five high schools. At four of the high schools, a majority of students reported that they took the third-year course because it was required rather than because they wanted to take it. This view was widespread at United Nations, where just over half the students said that they had taken the third-year math course because it was required of them. In the fifth school, Rural, over half of the students reported that they had selected a particular course because they wanted to; one third of students said they took a particular course because it was required. This is consistent with transcript data that show Rural students with the highest average number of math credits.

A third interesting pattern appeared at Urban, where a small proportion of students—under 15%—told us that they had selected the third-year course because it was required. Students justified their math course selections at Urban in much the same way they justified their other courses: by saying their counselors told them which courses to take. When asked why they had selected particular math courses, students responded:

Business math: They gave it to me.

General math: The guidance counselor gave it to me.

Algebra 1A and 1B: Since I'm in a business course, the guidance counselor said I had to take it.

Algebra I, geometry, algebra II, and advanced math: Because the counselor put me in that stuff. Math was stopping me from being in work study, which is what I really need to do.

Applied math I, applied math II, and algebra I: The counselor gave me these courses.

These students' comments suggest that they felt they had little influence in shaping their course selections and, hence, their high school careers. There are, however, alternative ways to interpret these data. For example, counselors might have been constrained by the school's course offerings, which in turn were constrained by central curriculum decisions and by teacher shortages. Thus, the options available to any one student for his or her roster might well be quite small. We did not find the same pattern of responses at Rural, however, which had the least flexible scheduling and curriculum offerings of the five high schools. Urban students might well have been voicing a generalized ennui with their high school careers.

Fine Arts

Fine arts was a new course requirement added by the policy change. Students usually met it by enrolling in a music, art, dance, or drama class. A review of student transcripts prior to the policy's implementation found, somewhat surprisingly, that on average, students were already enrolling in at least one fine arts class. However, averages can sometimes be misleading. A separate analysis found that the percentage of students in the class of 1986 who earned at least one fine arts credit ranged from a low of 50% at Urban to a high of 71% at United Nations. Two schools (Fast Track and United Nations) averaged almost two fine arts credits per student, while Rural averaged one and a half credits. The remaining two schools averaged closer to one credit.

In all five schools, the requirement had a significant effect on fine arts enrollment (see Figure 3.5). The average number of credits earned went up in all of the schools, but the increase varied significantly from a low of just over a quarter of a credit increase at United Nations to a high of almost one and a half credits at Rural during the first year of full implementation. In four of the five schools, small declines marked the trend between the first year and the second year after the policy was in effect. The biggest jump occurred at Rural, where the number of fine arts credits almost doubled. This is somewhat surprising given the scheduling and staff constraints at the small school and is largely attributable to its seven-period day, which gave students more opportunity to take additional course work than at either Middle Class or Urban.

Practical Arts

The policy initiative also added a practical arts requirement. Intense lobbying by various content area specialists during policy formulation

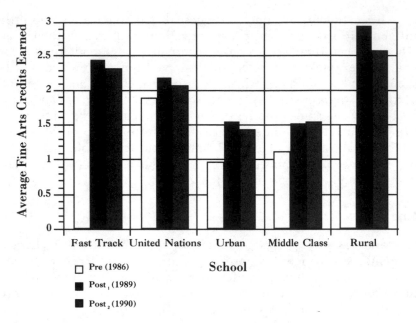

FIGURE 3.5. Fine arts credits earned by school. Statistical effect by school: $F = 34.5$, $p \leq .001$.

led to a very broad compromise definition of what was acceptable under the general rubric of practical arts. The acronym for this requirement, CHIVE, represents four different disciplines: computers, home economics, industrial, and vocational education. In addition, most business courses were considered acceptable under this requirement. With such a broad range of acceptable courses, it would not be surprising for students to accumulate a number of credits under this general rubric. Upon inspection of the quantitative data, that is exactly what happened. Prior to implementation of the practical arts requirement, students had enrolled in a wide range of these courses.

The results in Figure 3.6 illustrate this last point. The average number of credits earned in these combined disciplines was substantially more than what the policy required. Indeed, almost all students in all five schools (94%) had taken at least one practical arts course in their high school careers even before the requirement was put into place.

There were variations in the numbers across the five schools, however. For instance, Urban students enrolled in almost twice as many practical arts classes as Fast Track students did prior to the policy

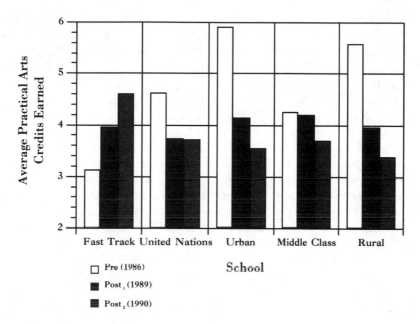

FIGURE 3.6. Practical arts credits earned by school. Statistical effect by school: $F = 5.0, p \leq .001$.

change. This is not at all unexpected given the different missions of the two schools. The vast majority of Fast Track students go on to postsecondary education, while the majority of Urban graduates move into the work force.

The most surprising finding was in the number of practical arts credits that students took after the new policy was implemented. In four of the five schools, the average number of practical arts credits went down. The schools with the biggest drop, Urban and Rural, were schools that had the largest average practical arts enrollments prior to the policy change. Those declines were substantial; at Urban, practical arts credits were down by more than two and a third credits, and at Rural, they were down by just less that two and a quarter credits. The obvious anomaly in this trend is Fast Track. Prior to the policy change, Fast Track students enrolled in the fewest practical arts courses by far, on average one credit less than the closest other school. After 2 years of implementation of this requirement, Fast Track students had the highest average: a full credit more than any other school.

These declines reflect what is often the zero-sum nature of curriculum offerings. Even though the practical arts requirement was a key component of the new policy, there are only so many periods in a school day; if additional requirements are added, something must be eliminated. As these schools had already clearly exceeded the minimal practical arts requirement spelled out in the new policy, these courses were the first to be reduced.

Fine and Practical Arts: Students' Views

We asked students to explain their views about the fine arts and practical arts requirements. When we compare the five high schools, students' responses varied. At Rural, most students (close to three fourths) reported that they selected fine arts and practical arts courses because they wanted to. The same was true of students at Fast Track. However, more students at Urban than at any other school explained that they took the courses they did in fine arts and practical arts to fulfill the requirements because their counselors told them to. In fact, this justification was rarely mentioned at the other four high schools.

Many students at Urban explained that they were infrequently consulted on course selections and had only minimal involvement in their own program planning. Students were simply assigned to courses. For example, here's what Urban students said:

> The drawing/painting class? They gave it to me.

> Auto mechanics? I was put there. I failed a business class, so the counselor put me in auto mechanics the following year.

> They never told me about the requirements. They just said, "Here are your classes."

> There's not too much you can take here. You just take what they give you to get your diploma.

> Art/Designs? The counselor gave it to me. They gave me home economics because I finished PE [physical education] credits and it was the only class open.

> I wanted to take home ec, but I couldn't take it because they didn't have another half-credit class to continue the year. So, they took me out of home ec and put me in sociology.

> Because I was in Pregnant School last year, this year I was given a schedule. I had no choice in the courses I took.

Students at Urban responded this way often enough to indicate that such course assignments were not an uncommon phenomenon. In fact, over one quarter of the students interviewed justified their course selections by saying they were told to take a particular course by their counselors.

THE REQUIREMENTS' OVERALL INFLUENCE

We asked the students to assess their overall education and to make a judgment about the influence of the new requirements on the quality of that education. More students at United Nations (over half) than at the other schools reported no influence by the requirements; the greatest proportion of students who said the requirements influenced them were at Urban (over three fourths) and Fast Track (just under three fourths).

One explanation for students at United Nations reporting few overall effects of the graduation requirements could be the influence of the local magnet program. All students, even those not in the magnet program, considered the magnet requirements more salient and more strict than any put forward by the state. As one student stated, "There's not much influence. All the magnet requirements really affect me, not the graduation requirements." Another said, "It's hard to evaluate because the requirements before were 20. The magnet requirements exceeded those requirements anyway, so it didn't really change anything anyway."

United Nations students also reported that they would have taken the required courses anyway and thus that the requirements were not much of a motivator:

I went beyond the requirements anyway.

I never had problems with passing classes; I would have gotten those credits anyway.

I didn't think about the requirements at all. I knew I was going to take history and math all the way through.

I would have done it anyway. For some of my friends it [the requirements] did help, but not me.

At Urban and Fast Track, students described how the requirements shaped their high school educations. The requirements, they said, broadened their exposure to new areas by demanding a level of effort that they might not otherwise have put forward and also prepared them well for college. Some college preparatory students stated that they would have taken the same courses anyway because they needed them for college admissions but that the requirements were probably important motivators to others. In describing the broader exposure they got to new areas as a result of the requirements, students said:

> They forced me to take classes I needed. I learned that science is fun.

> Yes, because you're a little bit educated in every little thing when you leave here.

> The requirements made me take classes I didn't want to take but knew it would be best for me. If I didn't, I would have all electives.

> Yes. They encouraged me to become more well rounded because I have had to take a variety of courses. I couldn't narrow my options. It opened my mind to a lot of opportunities.

These students also talked about how the requirements demanded more of them and of others:

> They move you in the right direction; from there, I went on.

> It forced some to take more challenging courses. It helps prepare you for the real world.

> It made sure I took all the classes I need, and I got to learn more. It helped set the goals and criteria I needed to meet.

Students spoke, at times eloquently, about their desires and aspirations, about why they took particular courses, and about how they viewed their worlds. It was clear from both the transcript and the interview data that local variation was expressed in the students' perspectives. In this last section, we look at how teachers' views varied across the five schools.

CURRICULUM CHANGE: TEACHERS' VIEWS

As discussed earlier, one persistent goal of the research was to discover, document, and describe local variations in perceptions of the policy change. We were particularly interested in teachers' perceptions of the curriculum changes, because teachers were significantly affected by the changes. We were also interested in how teachers' views might or might not have changed over time, particularly as structures and processes to support the new requirements became institutionalized in the fabric of the schools. It is also interesting to note how teachers' perspectives on the policy changes varied across the five schools, as well as across time. It is our intention that such analyses should inform future policy deliberations, promoting policy development that is more sensitive to local context.

We structured interviews with teachers to capture their perceptions of the policy and its effects on the curriculum in fairly open-ended ways, probing for more detail and clarification when appropriate. Three sets of interviews were conducted in each school. The first took place in 1986, just after the policy had been mandated but before there was much local response. The latter two rounds of data collection yielded richer information about local response to the policy, and it is these interviews—74 conducted in 1988 and 174 in 1990—that form the nucleus of this analysis.

Some differences were uncovered when teacher interviews from the five schools were analyzed separately. First, in both 1988 and 1990, Urban and Middle Class had the highest proportion of teachers who reported substantial curriculum changes due to the requirements. These schools, however, also had considerable proportions of teachers who reported no changes at all. In 1988, about two thirds of the teachers interviewed at Urban (64%) and Middle Class (63%) described curriculum changes caused by the new requirements. The changes most frequently mentioned at Urban were enrollment shifts and the addition of new courses; Middle Class teachers also described enrollment shifts, but they added initiatives to rewrite the curriculum as a result of the new requirements.

By 1990, once again, there were some modest shifts. Urban and Middle Class teachers continued to identify substantial curriculum changes in response to the new requirements, but the proportions had fallen from 64% to 48% at Urban and from 63% to 36% at Middle Class. In these two schools, then, as changes and adjustments in the curriculum became institutionalized, teachers' reports of change declined. What is most puzzling about Urban were the low levels of information regarding the new requirements in 1986. How can we account for such high levels of reported effects in 1988 and 1990? Also, are there commonalities in the responses of individual teachers at Middle Class and of those at Urban?

Middle Class and Urban stand in contrast to United Nations and Rural, where substantial proportions of teachers reported that their schools had made no curriculum changes at all in response to the new requirements. In 1988 at both schools, nearly half of all teachers interviewed reported no effects. By 1990 at Rural, the proportion rose from 45% to 67%. Even more telling is that by 1990, only a handful of teachers at Rural (less than 9%, a decrease from 27%) talked about any curriculum effects at all. Meanwhile at United Nations, the proportion who reported curriculum changes had increased to nearly one half. Thus, Rural teachers reported decreased curriculum changes, and United Nations teachers reported increased curriculum changes. Two interesting questions emerge: (1) Given the vast contextual differences in the schools, how can we explain the mid-implementation (1988) similarities in teachers' responses? and (2) What do responses about curriculum effects suggest about the two schools?

Fast Track teachers, in yet a final local variant, described ongoing curriculum changes but consistently attributed them to other causes. In 1988, nearly half of the teachers interviewed told of curriculum revisions and adjustments but said the changes were precipitated by events other than the new requirements. By 1990, the proportion had dropped a bit (to 40%). And although some teachers described curriculum changes carried out in response to the requirements, their proportion dropped from over one third (33%) in 1988 to under one tenth (9%) in 1990. The major question we need to ask about Fast Track is why the teachers' reports are substantially different from those of the other four high schools.

The contextual differences among the schools provide some possible explanations for these differences. Both Urban and Middle Class teachers discussed curriculum changes due to the requirements, more so than teachers in the other three high schools. Middle Class was operating on a six-period day. Teachers went into some detail about how this put enormous pressure on students to pass every class, to take few electives, and to be sure that they met the requirements as promptly as possible. With so little room in the schedule for new courses, it seems likely that teachers would consider the stricter requirements to be squeezing an already tightly structured curriculum. Middle Class also experienced substantial declines in student enrollment over the 5 years of the study: Enrollment dropped from 1,417 students in 1985–1986 to 1,152 students in 1989–1990. It is possible that teachers perceived changes caused by that decline to be the result of the new requirements.

Urban is a more difficult school to explain. In the first round of data collection (1986), we were struck by the lack of knowledge that teachers, administrators, counselors, and students had about the requirements. The lack of teachers' knowledge was especially noticeable. By 1988, however, a large number of teachers attributed changes in the curriculum directly to the new requirements. By 1990, although still high, the proportion had declined somewhat. Our judgment is that Urban teachers interpreted any changes as curricular in nature; thus, staffing declines or shifts between departments were reported as curriculum changes. The interview data support this interpretation. For example, when asked about changes in the curriculum as a result of the new requirements, a business education teacher responded, "We lost students and teachers; there was a shift from business to general." It is also likely that the changes reported were not the sort intended by the new requirements. For example, when asked about curriculum changes, a math teacher said:

> Basically, they offer the same thing they always offer. What they've done is water down the curriculum. For example, they used to have algebra II and trigonometry in the 11th grade. Now, they have algebra II in the 11th grade and trigonometry and analytic geometry in 12th grade. They don't go into more depth either, because of the caliber of the students and [because] the seniors get out in May. The teacher is not going to be able to cover the entire curriculum this year.

Rural and United Nations, although very different schools, seemed to foster similar responses to the new requirements. Rural was unable to make substantial adjustments to accommodate the stricter requirements because of its size. That is, there was little room to design new courses, install them in the curriculum, or respond overall to a set of requirements that focused on academics. In fact, teachers described how advanced placement students were forced to double up with students in non–advanced placement courses because of their small number. United Nations, as a magnet school, already had in place a diversified curriculum designed to meet the multiple needs of students drawn from across the county, of local students needing college preparatory and advanced courses, of general students, and of vocationally oriented students. In developing the magnet curriculum, teachers had anticipated many of the demands of the Certificate of Merit and already had appropriate courses in place.

Finally, Fast Track is located in what Firestone (1989b) calls an "active user" district. Aggressively academic parents push the school to provide a substantial, college-bound program of study. Continuous renewal of the curriculum, attention to the admissions requirements of state colleges and universities as well as of highly selective institutions, and strong pressure on students to take advanced courses all lead to Fast Track being at least one step ahead of the state in its graduation requirements. Thus, it is hardly surprising that teachers would describe changes in the curriculum but not attribute them to the new requirements. The school could relatively smoothly incorporate any new state requirements into its own requirements. Teachers noted "tinkering" with courses, especially Certificate of Merit courses, in response to some of the requirements.

CONCLUSION

The views of teachers, when combined with the thoughts and performance of students, give us more complete, textured descriptions of the five high schools.

Rural's smallness gave it both more and less flexibility to accommodate major policy changes: more, through the teachers' and students' knowledge of one another and willingness to adjust and modify, to experiment and learn, to best meet students' and teachers' needs and policy demands; less, because scarce resources constrained multiple and varied curriculum choices.

Middle Class's rigid schedule and tracking system created sequenced pathways for students that left little room for experimentation or failure. We characterize this school's response to the new requirements as mechanistic.

Urban's challenge to meet minimal student needs with its few and shrinking resources was almost overwhelming. In retrospect, we aren't surprised at a muted response. Given low student (and many teacher) aspirations, a limited district-mandated curriculum, and pressing social and family problems, to respond more fully would have taken critical attention away from more pressing survival needs.

In stark contrast was *Fast Track*, with its aggressive community, teachers, and students. Achievement—academic only—was the standard at Fast Track, so much so that some students were miscounseled into Certificate of Merit courses and failed them. But Fast Track's response to the new policy was full, complete, and well orchestrated. Fast Track may well be a school well ahead of the state in policy considerations.

Finally, *United Nations* offered a wide range of course offerings to its diverse student population. With district requirements stricter than

those of the state and with special magnet, vocational, and ESOL programs already in place, a wide range of options made the new state
requirements seem like a nonevent.

These portraits help contextualize the findings in the four chapters
that follow. We next discuss tracks and access to resources (Chapter 4)
and students who are consistently excluded from those educational
resources (Chapter 5). We then take a larger view of the policy process
and discuss overall influences in that process (Chapter 6) and overall
effects of the policy reform (Chapter 7). Before those larger views,
however, we turn to a discussion about how opportunity is structured
and how scarce educational resources are allocated.

4

WHO'S WINNING?
TRACKS, TRACKING SYSTEMS,
AND ACCESS TO RESOURCES

The importance of local variation in response to the state's new policy on high school graduation continues to be a central theme in the discussion of all our findings. In this chapter, we turn toward a more sociological interest: stratification systems in high schools and how these promote and constrain students' access to educational opportunities. As discussed in Chapter 2, stratification systems, or tracking and ability grouping, powerfully shape students' experiences in school. As Oakes (1990) notes:

> Although the decisions are usually well-intentioned, considerable evidence suggests that tracking, especially as secondary schools, fails to increase learning generally and has the unfortunate consequence of widening the achievement gaps between students judged to be more and less able. (p. xi)

The net result is that students placed in lower-track classes (i.e., judged less able) may well have reduced access to educational resources.

Our tasks in this chapter are to describe the stratification systems in place in the five high schools prior to the policy reform and then to assess any changes in those systems that might be attributable to a policy that promotes increased course work for all students. We specifically examine how the tracking systems shaped students' overall participation in course work, their course failure rates by track, and whether they earned more credits in specific subject areas (mathematics, practical arts, and fine arts) after the new policy was implemented. We also discuss how the tracking systems allocated the scarce resources devoted to merit courses and what changes in those allocations occurred over time.

In exploring some of these issues, we relied on transcript data from the classes of 1986, 1989, and 1990 and on interviews with students and teachers. We begin with a detailed description of students' views of their opportunities and the constraints placed on them—that is, their definition of the mechanisms and role groups that they saw as holding the keys to more advanced courses and of the support that students received in their academic endeavors. Then we turn to the quantitative data—students' course records—to help describe the tracks and their permeability and how students' course experiences varied by tracks. This is complemented by a third section that details teachers' views of how the new policy affected student tracking.

This chapter demonstrates that tracking systems are much more fuzzy and ambiguous (at least for the large middle groups in the five high schools) than conventional wisdom would have us believe and that access to college preparatory courses was often blocked (perhaps unwittingly). One major finding is that although the new graduation policy was designed to encourage more students to take more advanced and challenging courses, full implementation of the policy was stymied at the school level because some students thought they would be discouraged in those pursuits and because teachers and counselors acted as substantial gatekeepers.

OPPORTUNITIES AND CONSTRAINTS: STUDENTS' VOICES

As noted in the literature review, two strands of research characterize research on high school tracking systems: surveys and ethnographies. We make use of both methods to gain a more complete picture of what resulted from an important policy change. We begin by using the students' words to capture how they viewed the opportunity structure in their schools. Students' perspectives are crucial to understanding how school structures and norms coalesce into various formal and informal sorting mechanisms and opportunities or lack thereof. These mechanisms shaped student course taking and, subsequently, their high school careers.

The majority of students interviewed stated that if they wanted to take advanced courses (i.e., move across tracks), they could. Their responses fell into two categories. The more optimistic response was to embrace that freedom and take advantage of it: "Any class I've wanted to take, any option I've wanted has been available to me. No one has ever held me back from doing whatever I wanted." Another student commented: "It's up to me. If I want to, I can." The other category of response acknowledged the lack of barriers but also admitted to little individual effort to capitalize on those opportunities. One student stated, "I'm free to enroll in advanced-level courses, but I haven't been motivated," and another said, "I'm free to, but I chose to drop out—it was too much pressure."

Although in the minority, some students claimed that barriers did exist that prevented them from taking full advantage of all of the opportunities that were theoretically open to them. Students talked about both formal and informal mechanisms restricting their opportunities. Neither of these mechanisms altered in any significant way as a consequence of the change in graduation requirements.

Formal Mechanisms

Students suggested three categories of formal barriers: The first barrier was made up of adult gatekeepers—teachers and counselors who controlled access to certain classes. The second barrier was tests that had the potential to block enrollment in courses. And the third barrier consisted of restrictions placed on enrollment in certain courses.

Teachers or counselors were the most frequently mentioned barrier to course enrollment. Student comments indicated that these groups were seen as gatekeepers who controlled access to courses:

> It's mostly the teachers who hold students back from higher classes. If they think you won't do well, they won't offer it to you.

> Teachers don't like you to take advanced courses if you aren't able to do the work. Teachers decide who should be in or out.

> Sometimes teachers will discourage students who maybe can't do it.

> The teacher picks students. Even though I did well on the test, the teacher didn't pick me.

> It's your counselor who decides. . . . It is a major struggle to get into advanced classes if you are not in the program.

It was also common for students to talk about test results as a barrier to taking some courses. Tests were considered a control mechanism at both ends of the continuum of course difficulty. That is, students stated that if they didn't do well, they couldn't gain access to advanced courses, and that if they passed minimal competency tests, they would be denied access to some introductory courses:

> You can't be involved in AP [advanced placement] classes unless you take the tests. Kids are handpicked for the tests.

> When I first came to the school [transfer from Catholic school], I was placed in a Certificate of Merit class. I was tested and scored lower than the other students so was removed from that class.

> I'm taking geometry for the second year, and I am in danger of failing it again. I wanted applied math, but I couldn't take it because I had passed the Maryland Functional Math Test and applied math is only for people who didn't pass.

> Last year I wanted to take English 3 honors. I didn't pass the reading test, so I couldn't stay there.

The final barrier, although not mentioned as frequently as the first two, had to do with the phenomenon of labeling. We found direct evidence of this only at Middle Class. Students talked about being identified as a particular kind of student and, once that label was applied, it was difficult to shed. Several students stated that the labels were pinned on them even before they entered high school:

> Once you come over from the middle school, they phase you. Then you go in sequence.

> At the eighth-grade orientation, they gave us help [about what track they would be in]. So, my path was pretty well laid out for me.

One student even commented that students in advanced-level courses received preferential treatment: "I feel the advanced program gets a lot more attention. If we had as much as they do—if teachers put as much time into the regular courses—it would bring us up. If the teachers were more enthusiastic, students would be more enthusiastic also."

These three mechanisms—teachers, tests, and track labels—created procedures that (at least for some students) dampened aspirations. Perhaps even more powerful, although we have no measure of this, were the informal mechanisms—attitudes of others encoded in norms—that constrained and shaped student aspirations in subtle yet pervasive ways.

Informal Mechanisms: The Attitude of Others

When interviewing students about their high school experiences, we also asked them how others would react if they were to enroll in more challenging courses. Specifically, we sought students' views of four "significant others": teachers, counselors, peers, and parents. Students saw parents as being the most supportive and encouraging. Counselors and teachers were also generally supportive, although less so than parents. Typical positive responses included:

> Some teachers would be happy for me; they'd say I have potential. And some could care less.

> My counselor would encourage me to get into a better course.

> My counselor would jump up and down; it would be cool.

> My parents would throw me a party; they'd be thrilled.

> My parents would push me.

However, students also mentioned four "significant other" reactions that discouraged them from seeking more challenging course opportunities. Of these four, other students' reactions were easily the most indifferent or discouraging. Analysis of their perceptions of other students, as well as those of teachers, parents, and counselors, revealed four categories of informal barriers. The first two came from students' thoughts about how others assessed their ability and the amount of work if they were to attempt more challenging courses. The latter two barriers focused on peers and included a fear of losing social cohesiveness and social acceptability. Each of these is discussed in the following.

ABILITY.   Students expressed concern about the confidence that adults would have in them if they were to take advanced courses. Some judgment of capability was often the focus; that is, students wondered how parents, teachers, and counselors would evaluate them. Counselors and teachers, in particular, were often seen as assessors of ability. Students suggested that these significant others determined whether they "could handle" advanced courses. As one student stated about his teacher, "She knows me as a student so could estimate how well I could do." Other comments about how teachers and counselors reacted to students' ability were:

> They discourage you if they don't think you're capable.

> They'd be worried—not sure I could do it.

> The counselor would say I don't think you would be good at it. We'll give you help, but I'm not hopeful.

> The teacher would say you know you can't do it, why bother?

> If they thought I was smart enough to pass it, they'd encourage me to. But in my case, they wouldn't encourage me.

Peers were also identified as assessors of ability, as people who: "if they thought advanced courses were too hard for me, they would tell me." Students regularly expressed this in a common language: "Friends would probably say it was too hard for me," "They would tell me it's hard and try to talk me out of it," and "They would tell me not to take it; they'd think it would be too hard for me."

Grades, as a concrete reflection of ability, were often mentioned as barriers to students' taking on increasingly challenging opportunities:

> My parents might have concerns if my GPA [grade point average] goes down.

> A few teachers would think I wouldn't be able to do it because I've had some problems with grades.

> My counselor wouldn't allow me to take advanced courses because of previous grades.

> It would depend on the kind of grades you were getting. You should probably be allowed to move up if you're getting really good grades.

> My counselor would probably look and see how I did in those classes in the past and tell me if I'm capable of making it.

First thing the teachers would do is look at my grades and tell me it's nice, but your grades aren't as good as they should be to take this course.

The tone of these comments is clear. If there was any doubt about a student's ability, then the safest course of action was not to be challenged. The most obvious conclusion that students drew from that message was: Don't go beyond the minimum; just do enough to get by.

AMOUNT OF WORK.   Students anticipated having parents, teachers, counselors, and sometimes friends caution them if they were taking on courses that were more challenging than they could handle. Typical concerns were about increased pressure, amount of homework, and performance:

My friends would have thought I was crazy, because it takes a lot to study for advanced and business courses.

My parents would say take the challenge as long as I don't have to struggle too much and get in over my head.

My counselor is afraid the work overload would be too much. He wants to make sure we do well.

My teacher would ask why would I want to take more classes and increase the pressure on myself.

SOCIAL COHESIVENESS.   As emerged in interviews, one factor in students deciding which courses to take was their friendships; they often took classes to maintain contact with their friends. Taking the same classes as their friends also gave students a certain comfort level in a school. The importance placed on students being in the same classes with their friends was illustrated by the following comments:

My friends would be upset if you were leaving their classes. They would be happy if you were joining them.

My friends would think I'm crazy for taking hard classes. Many feel we should be in easy classes together; we shouldn't be separated.

My friends would think I was trying to get away from them.

SOCIAL ACCEPTABILITY.   How students are viewed by their peers was very important because they are at an age when development of their social self is at its peak. For example, students repeatedly used the term "nerd" when projecting peer reactions to their taking more challenging courses. It became clear that the reaction of their peers was a very strong element in decisions to reach for higher levels of attainment. Students expressed this concern as follows:

> Some people tell that to others, like magnet students. They are nerds, don't have any friends, their friends are their books.

> Some friends would think I was a nerd-bucket.

> They would call me a nerd because I'm doing more than the minimum.

Some criticism was also directed to seniors who worked too hard. The acceptable norm was to take a light load during the senior year as these two comments suggest: "Are you nuts? It's your last year." "You're crazy—lots of kids slack off senior year."

Building a sense of identity and belonging is an important part of the socialization process in high school. Much of that identity comes from friendships. Until a new culture pervades high schools so that learning and achievement define student belonging, factors such as social cohesiveness and acceptability will continue to influence students' course choices. It is quite clear that the graduation requirements policy did little to shift some of these widely entrenched norms.

Taken together, formal and informal mechanisms at the five high schools constrained to varying extents the hopes and aspirations of at least some students. These students were given a signal that they might best stay right where they were rather than aspire to a more rigorous curriculum or set of challenging courses.

Teachers were also queried about whether tracks existed and to what extent the new graduation policy exacerbated tracking patterns. Although at first reticent to discuss a practice that has come under so much criticism, the vast majority of teachers acknowledged their existence. It is interesting that the teachers were quick to put the blame elsewhere. Students and parents were the ones whom teachers held responsible for the increased track pressures:

> There is definitely more tracking—in the sense that kids track themselves. There is more of an opportunity for self-tracking, which could be positive or negative.

It's gotten worse but not because of Certificate of Merit or graduation requirements. It's all voluntary; kids choose their own track.

We don't track in this school, but it is happening; it's parent- or self-imposed.

It is parent sponsored to give high achievers another recognition.

Parents demand student recognition. Kids didn't care about the Certificate of Merit until their parents found out about it. Parents love the little stars denoting Certificate of Merit recipients on the graduation program because [they] differentiate their children from the pack. You better not be the secretary who leaves the stars off!

I hear about parents who are pushing for their kids to be in higher-track courses.

Perhaps much of the blame for this may be a by-product of the new Certificate of Merit and the process by which this certificate led to a new track in several schools. As parents and students pushed to earn this certificate, a new student classification emerged. Teachers talked extensively about the Certificate of Merit as replacing the college-bound track.

How did all this actually play out in the kinds of courses that students selected to shape their high school experiences? In the next section, we explore some of those relationships.

TRACKS AS CHARACTERIZED BY COURSE-TAKING PATTERNS

Because tracking is such a powerful force in the literature on high schools, we also wanted to capture its complexity through transcript analyses. Transcript records from the classes of 1986, 1989, and 1990 allowed a very fine-grained analysis of course-taking patterns. Recording each course separately according to four variables (subject, track, credit, and grade) permitted our analysis to be much more detailed than any previous research. This section describes our exploration of student movement across tracks, builds a more empirically grounded definition of tracks, and then uses that empirical definition to assess whether different tracks of students experienced the new requirements policy in similar or dissimilar ways.

Almost all of the quantitative research on tracking systems has used a very simplistic measure of tracks. Researchers have relied on either the counselor's identification of a particular track placement, a student's self-report, or a review of the level of difficulty of one subject area (typically mathematics) during one school year. Although we were convinced by the interview data that tracks were an important part of the ethos of these five high schools, we were skeptical of adopting such past measures of review. A few examples from our data reinforced the difficulty of replicating a simple measure.

Movement Across Tracks

We began by exploring the movement of students across a single subject area: mathematics. We chose mathematics because it is the one area where fairly clear distinctions can be made about the difficulty of courses and where there is general agreement on the sequence of courses that students pursue. Each course a student took was coded by difficulty level. Four major categories were created: honors/advanced placement, college preparatory, general, and vocational/business. By analyzing the level of difficulty across all 4 years of high school enrollment, we were able to chart each student's path through high school mathematics. They could take four logical paths. First, they could work their way *up* from a general course (e.g., math 9) to a college preparatory course (e.g., algebra I). Second, they could take all their mathematics courses at the *same* level (e.g., general or college preparatory level). Third, they could move *down*, as signified by enrollment in algebra I in the ninth grade (college preparatory) and perhaps in an applied math class in the 10th grade (general). A final path is for students to move both *up and down* at different points during their high school years.

An analysis of math course–taking patterns allowed us to assign each student into one of those four paths. Much of the literature on tracking maintains that students are pretty well locked into one track and, once in place, remain there for their entire high school career. Our coding of the transcript data allowed a much finer-grained analysis of course-taking patterns than is common in many other analyses and let us look closely at movement across a student's 4-year experience. Figure 4.1 depicts students' math course–taking patterns both before (class of 1986) and after (classes of 1989 and 1990) the new policy was in place.

The data provide a rather striking finding: Fewer than half of the students maintained the same level of difficulty in their mathematics courses. That trend was consistent whether comparing students' course selection prior to or after implementation of the new graduation requirements. The least likely movement was downward (approximately 10%), and an equal proportion (nearly a quarter in each case)

	Class of 1986 (Pre)	Class of 1989 (Post₁)	Class of 1990 (Post₂)
Up	27%	26	19
Same	46	34	44
Down	10	13	9
Up/Down	17	27	28

FIGURE 4.1. Student movement across tracks in mathematics courses. (*Note:* Each column totals 100% of students.)

opted for increasingly challenging courses or bounced back and forth. If there is so much movement in one subject, were we likely to encounter the same trend in others?

We decided to explore that issue using science as a second subject for analysis. Science was chosen over other academic subject areas because, like mathematics, prerequisites often preclude students from enrolling in more advanced courses. There is, moreover, a general perception that students take a progressively more difficult sequence like biology, chemistry, and physics. To explore the degree to which science course–taking patterns were similar to mathematics course–taking patterns, we cross-tabulated science movement with mathematics movement for all 3 years of data. That is, we constructed a four-by-four cell with the four categories of movement (down, same, up, up/down) for each of the two subject areas. Figure 4.2 displays that four-by-four cell.

The number in each cell represents the number of students whose course taking in math or science corresponded to the labeled movement. For example, there were 173 students (13% of the entire sample) in the upper-left-hand corner who moved "up" (i.e., took more academically rigorous courses as they progressed in their high school careers) in both math and science. In review of the row and column

SCIENCE

		Up	Same	Down	Up/Down
M A T H	**Up**	12.9%	7.0	0.7	5.2
	Same	12.3	16.5	2.8	8.5
	Down	5.1	3.7	0.9	2.0
	Up/Down	8.6	7.4	1.5	4.8

35%

FIGURE 4.2. Track movement by subject area. (*Note:* The entire matrix totals 100%.)

totals, a fairly similar pattern appears. In both math and science, fewer than half of the students stayed in the same track for all their courses. Indeed, in math, only two in every five students stayed in the same track, while in science, it was more like one in three. In both subjects, the least likely pattern of movement was downward (i.e., taking less academically rigorous courses), with only 1 in 8 students moving downward in mathematics and 1 in 16 in science. Two surprising findings were the percentage of students moving up (39% in science and 26% in mathematics) and the large number who moved both up and down (just over one in every five students).

Even more surprising than any of the findings within a given subject area is comparison across the two subjects. If the pattern of movement across mathematics and science were consistent (i.e., if one moved up in math, one would also be likely to move up in science), then the vast majority of students would fall in the four shaded cells along the diagonal. Yet the numbers reveal that only one in three students (35%) moved the same way in both subjects. That is, track movement in science was not highly correlated with track movement in mathematics.[1]

All of this fine-grained analysis leads to one of two conclusions: Either the portrait of rigid tracks is a myth or this analysis contains so much noise that overall patterns are obscured. We lean toward the latter conclusion. The qualitative data from students and teachers in the previous section convince us that movement across tracks does exist.

Redefining Tracks

Rather than look at individual subject areas and trends from 1 year to the next, we developed a more global indicator that incorporates all of a students' course-taking experiences. As each course was categorized as college preparatory (Certificate of Merit eligible or above), general, or vocational, we could compute three simple ratios: (1) college preparatory courses to the total number of courses, (2) the general to the total, and (3) the vocational to the total. A simultaneous review of those three ratios revealed wide variation across all three, with some interesting combinations. It was clear that in addition to the "pure types" (i.e., students enrolling only in college prep, or in general, or in vocational courses), there were also many "mixed types." That is, students took courses in more than one category and did not fall into tidy, generic track categories.

After careful review, we developed a decision rule. A pure type was defined as a student who took two and a half times as many credits in one category as in either of the other categories. A mixed type took less than a two-and-a-half times difference between the two highest categories and more than two-and-a-half times between the lowest. Finally, a mixed-type student with courses from all three categories was a combination for whom no category was separated from another category by more than two and a half times. These definitions led to the following distribution of students across all three student cohorts (classes of 1986, 1989, and 1990):

Pure: college preparatory	16%
Mixed: college preparatory/general	28%
Mixed: college preparatory/general/vocational	12%
Mixed: general/vocational	6%
Pure: general	39%

It is interesting to note that there were no pure vocational students and also no mixed-type college prep/vocational students.

Once these categories were established, we analyzed the relationship of these track assignments to student course-taking patterns.

These analyses addressed the same general questions that were outlined in the previous chapter. What is of interest here is whether a differential effect is related to a student's particular curriculum track. A complete breakdown of the sample sizes by track is presented in Table B.1 in Appendix B.

Are Students Earning More Credits?

Table 4.1 summarizes the mean number of credits that students earned by school, by year, and by track (the number of cases associated with each cell for the next five tables is presented in Appendix B). From earlier analyses, we knew that there were significant differences by school and by year. The question was whether there were differences by track as well. There were no differences across the tracks for the students unaffected by the new state requirements (class of 1986). After the new requirements took effect, some differences by track emerged. The typical pattern was for students in the general track to earn fewer credits than those in other tracks. At United Nations, there was more than a four-credit difference between students in the general track (23.2 credits) and students who took college prep courses (27.9). This reflects the fact that many college prep students at United Nations were in the school's magnet program and enrolled in eight courses rather than the usual seven each term. There was almost a two-credit difference at Fast Track and a one-credit difference at Urban. There was less of a difference across tracks at Middle Class and Rural. It appears that students in the general and general/vocational tracks took the bare minimum of credits, doing only what was required and little more.

Are Students Taking More Rigorous Courses?

As there is considerable overlap in the definition of track and rigorous courses (e.g., college prep track students enrolling in more advanced courses), the relationship is tautological and thus not appropriate for data analysis.

Are Students Struggling More?

Although the findings in Chapter 3 showed that students were not struggling more as a result of the new requirements, the evidence was quite convincing that there were differential effects by track (see Table 4.2). Very consistent results across all five schools show that students in the college prep classes failed the lowest proportion of courses and

TABLE 4.1.
CREDITS EARNED—BY SCHOOL AND TRACK

	CP	CP/Gen	CP/Gen/Voc	Gen/Voc	Gen
Fast Track					
1986 (Pre)	—	23.8	23.9	—	23.0
1989 (Post$_1$)	26.6	26.1	26.0	—	23.9
1990 (Post$_2$)	27.5	27.2	26.7	—	25.8
United Nations					
1986 (Pre)	25.5	25.1	25.3	24.9	23.3
1989 (Post$_1$)	28.1	25.0	25.6	—	23.6
1990 (Post$_2$)	27.9	25.5	25.8	—	23.2
Urban					
1986 (Pre)	—	22.8	22.2	22.8	22.1
1989 (Post$_1$)	—	23.5	23.6	23.9	22.4
1990 (Post$_2$)	—	23.0	23.2	23.7	22.1
Middle Class					
1986 (Pre)	—	22.9	23.4	22.3	22.0
1989 (Post$_1$)	23.4	23.2	23.3	—	23.3
1990 (Post$_2$)	23.5	23.2	23.6	—	22.8
Rural					
1986 (Pre)	26.1	25.5	25.3	24.8	25.0
1989 (Post$_1$)	—	25.1	—	26.2	24.8
1990 (Post$_2$)	—	25.6	23.3	24.8	—

CP, college preparatory; Gen, general; Voc, vocational.
Statistical effect by track: $F = 73.6$, $p \leq .001$.
Note: Number of cases for each cell are presented in Appendix B, Table B.1.

that those in the general track failed the most. The most obvious example of this occurred at Fast Track, where students in the general track were six times more likely to fail courses than their counterparts who took a combination of general and college prep courses. Even in the

TABLE 4.2.
PERCENTAGE OF CREDITS FAILED—BY SCHOOL AND TRACK

	CP	CP/Gen	CP/Gen/ Voc	Gen/ Voc	Gen
Fast Track					
1986 (Pre)	—	2.8	1.9	—	3.1
1989 (Post$_1$)	0.0	1.3	1.0	—	8.4
1990 (Post$_2$)	0.0	0.7	1.3	—	4.5
United Nations					
1986 (Pre)	2.0	3.0	5.9	3.2	10.3
1989 (Post$_1$)	1.0	6.4	5.0	—	12.5
1990 (Post$_2$)	0.8	3.7	3.4	—	10.5
Urban					
1986 (Pre)	—	6.1	6.3	6.3	9.9
1989 (Post$_1$)	—	2.7	2.6	1.2	7.1
1990 (Post$_2$)	—	2.2	1.3	1.1	4.0
Middle Class					
1986 (Pre)	—	3.0	1.8	5.8	8.6
1989 (Post$_1$)	0.8	2.7	4.0	—	5.6
1990 (Post$_2$)	1.1	2.2	2.1	—	5.2
Rural					
1986 (Pre)	2.9	3.6	5.0	5.6	6.8
1989 (Post$_1$)	—	3.9	—	4.4	8.4
1990 (Post$_2$)	—	0.5	6.4	5.6	—

CP, college preparatory; Gen, general; Voc, vocational.
Statistical effect by track: $F = 86.4$, $p \leq .001$.

least powerful case (Urban), general track students failed courses at twice the rate of those who enrolled in college prep classes. The findings clearly point out that different experiences existed in these schools depending on a student's track.

Are Students Earning Different Credits Across Subject Areas?

This section focuses on specific subject areas in which the new policy might have had a direct effect because of explicit changes in mathematics, fine arts, and practical arts requirements.

MATHEMATICS. Table 4.3 breaks down mathematics course taking across the five tracks. Students in the college prep track took the most math courses, followed by those in a mixed track with some college prep. There was another drop in mathematics course taking for students in the general track and for students in the combined vocational/general track. This latter group took the fewest math courses. The most probable explanation for this last finding is that students who were enrolled in a vocational course of study had to take vocational courses while also meeting the requirements for a general diploma. That is, they had to enroll in four English, three math, three social studies, and two science courses in addition to courses in their vocational program. This left them almost no flexibility for another math class. Consequently, they enrolled in the barest minimum to get by.

The trend across years was for differences by track to diminish. That relationship was true across all schools. For example, at Rural, students in the general/vocational track enrolled in half as many math credits as did the college prep/general students prior to the shift in policy. By the time the policy had been in place for 2 years (class of 1990), the gap between these same two groups was less than one credit.

FINE ARTS. The data in Table 4.4 summarize the number of fine arts credits earned by students in the different tracks. Only one consistent difference was evident by track. Students who enrolled in vocational courses took fewer fine arts courses than did other students. As noted with the math credits, this was undoubtedly a function of the fact that these students were sacrificing their elective options to complete their vocational requirements. The most obvious example of this was at Urban, where vocationally oriented students enrolled in almost no fine arts credits before the requirements and took only the bare minimum after the requirement was in place.

PRACTICAL ARTS. At first glance, one might contend that the argument for this data presentation is tautological. That is, as vocational courses are a major part of practical arts requirements, vocational students would by definition enroll in more of them. However, two factors counter this. First, the practical arts requirement included more than

TABLE 4.3.
MATH CREDITS EARNED—BY SCHOOL AND TRACK

	CP	CP/Gen	CP/Gen/ Voc	Gen/ Voc	Gen
Fast Track					
1986 (Pre)	—	3.54	3.00	—	2.94
1989 (Post$_1$)	4.29	3.54	3.50	—	3.34
1990 (Post$_2$)	3.60	3.63	3.41	—	3.59
United Nations					
1986 (Pre)	3.88	3.65	3.07	2.33	2.75
1989 (Post$_1$)	3.82	3.45	3.08	—	3.10
1990 (Post$_2$)	3.72	3.45	3.08	—	3.10
Urban					
1986 (Pre)	—	3.61	1.55	1.07	2.64
1989 (Post$_1$)	—	4.09	3.29	3.17	3.40
1990 (Post$_2$)	—	3.34	3.17	3.14	3.41
Middle Class					
1986 (Pre)	—	3.44	3.00	2.08	2.57
1989 (Post$_1$)	3.53	3.19	3.08		3.22
1990 (Post$_2$)	3.36	3.40	3.36	—	2.98
Rural					
1986 (Pre)	4.79	4.42	3.22	2.13	2.88
1989 (Post$_1$)	—	4.06	—	3.20	3.91
1990 (Post$_2$)	—	4.62	4.31	3.75	—

CP, college preparatory; Gen, general; Voc, vocational.
Statistical effect by track: $F = 46.3$, $p \leq .001$.

just vocational courses; it also included computer science, business, and home economics. But more important, we created separate variables for the subject and track. Thus, it was possible for a student to enroll in practical arts courses with a college prep track affiliation (e.g., an advanced computer design course). In other words, the subject and

TABLE 4.4.
FINE ARTS CREDITS EARNED—BY SCHOOL AND TRACK

	CP	CP/Gen	CP/Gen/ Voc	Gen/ Voc	Gen
Fast Track					
1986 (Pre)	—	2.47	1.00	—	1.96
1989 (Post₁)	1.57	2.75	1.72	—	1.94
1990 (Post₂)	3.10	3.16	1.30	—	2.18
United Nations					
1986 (Pre)	1.38	2.55	0.95	0.42	1.92
1989 (Post₁)	2.12	2.72	1.54	—	1.85
1990 (Post₂)	1.79	2.79	1.78	—	1.95
Urban					
1986 (Pre)	—	0.78	0.40	0.35	1.31
1989 (Post₁)	—	1.24	1.14	1.17	1.72
1990 (Post₂)	—	1.59	1.11	1.18	1.50
Middle Class					
1986 (Pre)	—	1.20	0.70	0.25	1.26
1989 (Post₁)	1.49	1.63	1.75	—	1.40
1990 (Post₂)	1.51	1.68	1.14	—	1.60
Rural					
1986 (Pre)	1.50	2.63	1.33	0.13	1.44
1989 (Post₁)	—	3.03	—	2.60	3.00
1990 (Post₂)	—	3.53	1.56	1.69	—

CP, college preparatory; Gen, general; Voc, vocational.
Statistical effect by track: $F = 35.4$, $p \leq .001$.

the track assignment for that subject were independent in at least some subject areas.

As expected, students in the vocational track took more practical arts courses, but students in the general track took a large number of practical arts courses as well (see Table 4.5). College prep students took the fewest practical arts courses. The starkest contrast was at Urban,

TABLE 4.5.
PRACTICAL ARTS CREDITS EARNED—BY SCHOOL AND TRACK

	CP	CP/Gen	CP/Gen/ Voc	Gen/ Voc	Gen
Fast Track					
1986 (Pre)	—	1.79	5.75	—	3.27
1989 (Post1)	4.00	3.39	5.50	—	5.50
1990 (Post$_1$)	3.70	2.42	6.63	—	5.29
United Nations					
1986 (Pre)	1.96	2.30	7.69	10.08	5.13
1989 (Post$_1$)	2.60	3.05	6.35	—	5.23
1990 (Post$_2$)	2.13	3.41	6.85	—	5.07
Urban					
1986 (Pre)	—	1.56	7.23	9.01	4.87
1989 (Post$_1$)	—	1.06	5.18	7.70	3.98
1990 (Post$_2$)	—	1.06	6.03	7.45	3.53
Middle Class					
1986 (Pre)	—	1.87	6.40	9.08	4.94
1989 (Post$_1$)	2.50	3.05	7.83	—	6.35
1990 (Post$_2$)	2.78	2.79	6.57	—	4.94
Rural					
1986 (Pre)	2.21	2.58	6.33	10.50	7.76
1989 (Post$_1$)	—	1.38	—	8.80	5.36
1990 (Post$_2$)	—	1.62	3.75	6.63	—

CP, college preparatory; Gen, general; Voc, vocational.
Statistical effect by track: $F = 361.1$, $p \le .001$.

where college prep/general students earned just above the minimal number of practical arts credits and general/vocational track students earned four times that many.

These analyses provide a portrait of students' pathways through high school. They yielded some surprises and confirmed some things we would expect. One surprise was the amount of movement across tracks: Students seem to have taken courses at various levels of difficulty depending on their need, inclination, and course availability. Another surprise was the apparent independence of tracking in science and mathematics. These two findings challenge our traditional conceptions of lock-step tracks.

In response to other questions about numbers of credits, academic credits, and so on, the data confirmed what we would expect: that students in college preparatory and college preparatory/mixed tracks used the educational resources (i.e., courses) of the school in more depth and variety than did students in the general and general mixed tracks. Thus, students with access to rigorous educational opportunities that would prepare them for college took advantage of those opportunities disproportionately.

Highlighting the students' views on tracking focuses on only one side of the coin. The other side is formed by the adults who had a great deal to do with shaping students' high school experiences. How these adults viewed the complex dynamic of developing students' educational experiences went a long way toward shaping those experiences.

EFFECTS ON THE TRACKING SYSTEM: TEACHERS' VIEWS

An equal number of teachers felt that tracking had and had not been affected by the new requirements. The percentage of teachers who believed that tracking systems had been affected in 1990, however, almost tripled since the question was first asked in 1988. This suggests that tracking had indeed changed, although exactly how was still unclear.

When addressing the issue of tracking and the new requirements, most teachers talked about the Certificate of Merit, the certificate given to students who had enrolled in a more academically rigorous curriculum (12 of 20 credits in advanced courses, 3 science credits instead of 2, and 1 foreign language credit beyond the first year) and who had been more successful (minimum GPA = 2.6). Teachers' comments clustered around the role of the Certificate of Merit in defining a new track and around uneven dissemination of the Certificate of Merit as a means of maintaining track inequities.

Certificate of Merit as the College-Bound Track

Again and again, teachers discussed the Certificate of Merit as if students who took those courses were enrolled in a track in and of itself.

Certificate of Merit was referred to as another delineation in the per-
petual hierarchy of students. Several teachers faced the issue head on
by stating: "[The Certificate of Merit] is just a new label on the same
old thing. We've always tracked kids who are college bound" and "The
Certificate of Merit is a new name for the old academic track. It's
exactly the same thing. What goes around comes around."

This was most apparent at Fast Track High School, where teachers
and other school officials viewed the Certificate of Merit as "giving
legitimacy to the academic track," "enhancing the academic track of
students when applying to college or a job," and "forcing kids to see
differences between academic prep for college versus nonacademic
prep for industry." Students who are pursuing the Certificate of Merit
at Fast Track can, according to one teacher, be identified early on in the
high school years: "It's not unusual by 10th grade to know which kids
are going to get the Certificate of Merit."

For many teachers, the positive effects of recognition and reward
attached to the Certificate of Merit were far outweighed by its negative
effect of isolating some students, as evidenced by these three comments:

> Instead of democratizing education, we're elitizing it. Kids are not being
> exposed to the same things, and there are very few places for them to
> all come together.

> The Certificate of Merit is an attempt to give credit to students who
> have excelled. I'm not sure I agree with that. When you start doing
> those kinds of things, you tend to track students more.

> There is a tendency to pay attention more to the student who does well
> rather than the ones who don't.

There were also concerns from an entirely different perspective.
Unlike Fast Track teachers, who worried about the potential of two
tracks (Certificate of Merit and non–Certificate of Merit) developing
Urban High School teachers were concerned that given the limitations
of an urban school facing enrollment and staffing declines, they simply
could not remain competitive without offering a viable Certificate of
Merit program. According to one counselor, "Last year we had three
students [who received a Certificate of Merit], and this year I think
only one. We can't afford to give students some advanced classes if we
don't have enough students to fill them." Their program simply could
not accommodate an additional track.

Dissemination of Information About the Certificate of Merit

If the Certificate of Merit has the potential for redefining tracks in schools, it is important to know more about the extent of teachers' knowledge and how they communicate it to students. In many cases, teachers are the primary disseminators of information within a school, serving as the link between policy, administration, and students. If teachers don't know about the Certificate of Merit, they can't tell students about it or encourage them to obtain it.

In many cases, students reported hearing about the Certificate of Merit first and then asking their teachers about it. As one teacher who was not new to her school stated, "I had to ask what the Certificate of Merit was when a student asked me. Nothing was said about it," and another said, "Some kids asked me in homeroom, and I told them they would have to see their counselors."

Although many teachers believed they had a clear understanding of the Certificate of Merit, their responses indicated otherwise. For instance, one teacher said it "allows those going to college to waive certain courses," apparently confusing it with advanced placement courses. Another stated, "It is for students who can't meet the academic requirements; they are given a certificate instead of a diploma," confusing it with a certificate of attendance awarded to special education students.

Teachers who had the most knowledge and the most accurate information about the Certificate of Merit were those who taught advanced courses and who worked with college-bound students. This unevenness in knowledge helped perpetuate inequities in access to academic opportunities for students.

This may help explain why certain students were much more knowledgeable about the Certificate of Merit than others. College-bound students were more likely than others to find out about the Certificate of Merit through teacher encouragement. About one half of the teachers we interviewed reported encouraging the Certificate of Merit; teachers who did so said they tended to encourage students "who could handle it." However, in most cases, those students included mostly college-bound or honors students, according to teachers. As one teacher stated, "If I taught ninth graders, I would go after the ones that seem to be in the college-bound track." Other teachers' encouragement of certain students was also apparent:

> I encourage the ones who can do the work easily and who don't feel like it's an extra burden.

I don't encourage lower-level students.

In these comments, it is apparent that some teachers believe either that tracks are not a significant feature of their schools or that they are not responsible for the perpetuation of tracking systems. On the other hand, their reports of their own actions (for example, disseminating information about the Certificate of Merit), corroborated by students' reports of teachers' actions, suggest persistent patterns in which some students are denied access.

CONCLUSION

This chapter has addressed the crucial question of who has access to scarce educational resources under a policy intended to encourage more students to partake of more rigorous resources. We paraphrase this question as "Who's winning?" seeking to capture a sociological concern with stratification systems that sort students into winners and losers. This chapter has looked at who seems to have continued access to resources (suggesting that many are denied that access) through the tracking system.

Our conclusions are threefold. First, tracks are both less easily defined and more permeable than previous research suggests. We like to call this "fuzziness." Nevertheless, there are clearly identifiable clusters of course taking, with college preparatory and college preparatory mixed students retaining all the rights and privileges to which they have become accustomed.

Second, formal and informal local mechanisms constrain access to scarce resources, whether more classes or more rigorous classes. Teachers are especially viewed as powerful shapers of students' pathways; peers are also quite important in encouraging or dampening higher aspirations.

Our third conclusion is that the Certificate of Merit might well serve as an incentive if knowledge were widespread and access universally encouraged.

Taken as a whole, this discussion suggests that sorting students and sustaining status systems are not lessened by the reform of graduation requirements. That is, those who won in the past are the same ones who are winning today.

5

WHO'S LOSING?
STUDENTS AND TEACHERS
AT RISK

C ritics of American education (Banks, 1987; Grant & Sleeter, 1988; Perrone, 1987) voice concerns about persistent patterns of inequity in schools. Focusing most frequently on race, gender, and social class, these analysts demonstrate how students of color and poverty and often girls participate less frequently than their more privileged peers in high-status classes and the educational resources of schools. In Chapter 4, we documented how students judged to be of lower ability and thus counseled into lower tracks have unequal access to the knowledge resources of schools. In this chapter, we examine how race, gender, and academic achievement shape that access. We were particularly interested in achievement because it is often confounded with ability to make judgments about appropriate pathways through high school. That is, students are often judged to be of lower ability based on past records of achievement rather than on more complex assessments. As Oakes (1990) describes it, "Designations of 'ability' are suspect . . . even though they may relate to students' prior school performance; and 'ability-based' inferences about students' curricular and instructional needs are often wrong" (p. 7). Thus, minority students, girls, and low performers may well be at risk of full participation in the educational resources of a school. We also wanted to assess the effects of social class but had difficulty creating a useful indicator of it.[1]

Teachers, in turn, may perceive themselves at some risk as a result of the shifting curricular demands of a policy that stipulates course work in some areas and not in others. The research reviewed in Chapter 2 showed how some departments suffered losses in student enrollments while others showed substantial gains. No longer assured of sufficient enrollments to justify a particular number of students, some departments might well have felt themselves at risk of losses, too. This chapter describes the perceptions and experiences of student groups historically at risk and those of teachers who saw shifts in the curriculum as a result of policy reform. We pose the question: In what ways do these groups benefit or lose from the policy reform of graduation requirements?

We begin this exploration by examining teachers' views of students who have historically been excluded from educational benefits and are considered most at risk: dropouts. Next, we explore patterns of student participation in various educational resources. We reasoned that participation in high-status course work gave students access to future educational benefits—that is, college admission. We assessed those participation rates by race, academic performance, and gender to see if there were significant differences. We conclude this chapter by looking at adults potentially at risk: teachers in vulnerable departments. Although teachers did not have to fear losing their jobs, they did feel squeezed by reduced flexibility.

Taken together, these analyses of students' experiences and teachers' views of both students at risk and their own work suggest two conclusions: (1) patterns of exclusion and oppression by race continue to plague high schools and (2) accommodation to policy changes proceeds slowly because perceptions often lag behind a more "objective" set of circumstances.

DROPOUTS

The most obvious losers in education are the ones who never graduate—school dropouts. One of the strongest arguments against tightening standards has been that it would only increase these numbers. We probed teachers' perceptions of this possibility as they gained increasing experience with the new policy. In addition to summarizing the overall view across the five schools, we also offer a more detailed analysis of Urban, where the dropout problem was most acute.

Teachers' views of the effects of the policy reform on students' dropping out shifted as the research progressed. In 1986, many teachers with whom we spoke indicated that students would be "pushed out" of school because of the new, stricter requirements. In fact, opinion was about evenly split, with half of the teachers expressing strong concern about students dropping out and the other half saying that the new requirements might encourage students to do more and try harder. These teachers were interviewed early in the implementation of the new policy, when courses and procedures were not all in place or running smoothly. At that time, a full cohort of students had not completed high school or come near completion under the new requirements. Lots of questions and worries were apparent. By 1988 and 1990, opinions had shifted somewhat, with the most dramatic shift occurring from 1986 to 1988.

By 1988, almost two thirds of the teachers told us that the new requirements were not increasing the school dropout rate. This proportion had risen to nearly three fourths by 1990. Clearly, the schools adjusted as time passed: Courses were tried and modified, fine arts and practical arts requirements were met, and the third-year math requirement was being implemented. Teachers anticipated graduating students with a somewhat new set of credit requirements, but in general, their fears about increasing numbers of dropouts were unfounded. Typical comments were:

> I really don't see any changes in the dropout rate because of the new credits.

> With a seven-period day, students have more room. For example, if they failed English 11, they have space to take English 11 in 12th grade. They don't have the same sense of hopelessness.

> My initial impression is to say yes, but I don't think it has that big an impact. I believe that they drop out in seventh grade. I don't think the requirements influence them.

> It just seems to me kids aren't dropping out like they used to. Kids stay—kids come back next year even though they have failed. I'm not sure why that is.

When talking about students dropping out, teachers said the school had little effect in general. One noted, "Sometimes I think whether they succeed or fail—we don't influence it. If it's harder, they come up to it;

if we make it easier, they still fail." In contrast, a few teachers from Fast Track told of how the school provided special support for students at risk, thereby decreasing their chances of dropping out: "We have programs designed to help students that have difficulty meeting the requirements" and "We have courses for them, general-type courses. It shouldn't be a problem here. They've always taken those courses."

Across all five schools, however, teachers described other circumstances that caused students to disengage from or never fully connect with school, including home circumstances, student characteristics, and life choices. For example, teachers spoke of home situations: "Domestic problems cause kids to drop out" and "Dropping out has more to do with SES, child abuse, and drug addiction. These have a bigger impact on dropping out." However, home was also frequently mentioned as an important source of support: "I feel they'll stay in if they have encouragement from home. They may say they're dropping out because of the requirements, but that's just an excuse."

Some teachers spoke of student characteristics that caused students to drop out. One academic subject teacher said, "Dropouts are students with a lack of interest. Even if the requirements were 15, you would still have the same number of dropouts"; another stated that "kids dropping out turned off long before." Others noted age as a factor: "Kids who drop out are so far from meeting any of the requirements. Age plays a role: When they are 14 years old and have 4 more years left, they want to get a job and drop." Yet others talked about how teenagers live: "Dropping out has to do with the life-style students have (pregnancy, drugs, alcohol) and it has nothing to do with the graduation requirements."

Teachers also gave the desire to earn money as a reason for students' dropping out: "Kids drop out for money, cars." And another teacher said, "Kids have no real reason for staying in this school. They need the money more than the credit, they think. So they often quit to work and help support their families." Another told us, "We're in a blue-collar area, and their priority is to get a job. We have a small number who are interested in higher education, but most of those kinds of students go to the citywide schools." Dropping out to work was discussed often at Rural, where the local water-related industry was a viable alternative for teenagers. Teachers described how "watermen" families often "let kids work as soon as they are big enough. By 15, many have their own boats. We lost them before graduation." At times, students of color were seen as being most at risk: "Hispanic males are number one to drop out; next, black males. They have the poorest attendance records."

Teachers in all five schools thought that the new requirements were causing more students to leave high school early, but these teachers were in the minority. They said that the increased pressures of the new requirements would put students already at risk in greater jeopardy. Their general logic was that the requirements and less flexibility would compound difficulties for students struggling with high school anyway. A teacher told us, "I would think for students who have become less successful with fewer requirements, with more it would be even harder." Another teacher echoed this, saying, "[Now there was] more potential for them dropping out. Twenty-two credits for some—it would be an eternity for them to get it. I know some students who are in ninth grade for the third time."

Some teachers identified students whom they thought would be affected because of their lower ability. They spoke of how these students have become "overwhelmed" and of how they "do not have study skills" and were "not part of the planning in 9th and 10th grades." Others noted how the requirements "have made life tougher for lower achievers" and how "borderline kids are having more trouble." This teacher went on to describe how "previously we were going down. It should be our charge to kick enough butt to get them through." This perspective is best summarized as one teacher put it:

> Graduation requirements are so restrictive that students who are at risk—with handicaps other than mental capacity—their frustration level is so quick. They make it through 2 years, even 3 years, then they hit a wall. They don't have the flexibility in the requirements for them to attain a diploma.

Dropping Out at Urban

Although teachers at Urban thought that the new graduation requirements wouldn't particularly affect the dropout rate, they did tell us that dropouts were a major problem at the school. Many thought the causes to be a need for money either to assist the family or to support oneself, a community that was unsure about the value of higher education, or disaffection with school. We include their accounts of what it was like to have a substantial number of transient students—students dropping in and dropping out of their classrooms—because their voices were so eloquent.

In describing the community and its influence on students dropping out or not, one teacher offered the following:

It's a unique community: blue collar, first high school graduate in the family. There's a work ethic, not an academic one. There's a heavy immigrant population—the widest ethnic diversity in the city. This all impacts dropouts.

From this teacher's perspective, the community ethos and population weaken the ties to high school.

Several teachers mentioned ninth grade as a critical year, one in which the highest number of students left school. Many gave explanations for this:

It's always a greater number of ninth graders who drop out. The reason I say ninth graders is that when they get to ninth grade, it hits them that they have to pass the tests. In middle school and elementary school, they pass along and don't have to do well. It happens back in 9th/10th grades. There's a steadily decreasing rate up to 12th grade. Seems to me that it's a combination of things. They get two or three failing grades and give up or want money. A few don't give a damn. I see the influence of the home weakened, but the system is trying to get to these kids before they drop out.

Falling out occurs in 9th/10th grade. It's not tougher requirements; it's other factors, more community based. I don't teach ninth grade, but by the time they get to the senior year, they've made a commitment to stay. We're trying something next year to use block scheduling—hopefully, it can identify problems early and work with them. Middle schools do a lot of social promotion.

Others described how their class size shrank from first to second semester, sometimes quite dramatically:

The dropout rate is terrible. I begin with 32 9th graders in homeroom and end with 16 in 10th. They've either dropped out or failed. I don't know if it's a direct result of the new requirements; I couldn't say.

We're losing more ninth graders—I could prove it with the roll book. At one point in my ninth-grade class, I had 48 to 49 students. There are 30 on the roll now. In eighth period, I had 38 to 40; I now have 25. I'm still carrying the names but don't have the bodies. With seniors, I have not seen such a drastic drop; they stick with it.

Despite these grim pictures of young adolescents leaving school, several teachers mentioned how the city had a dropout prevention initiative and how the school was addressing the problem. Some seemed hopeful:

> Ninth grade is a real problem. There are smaller classes the second half of the year. . . . I see a large dropout rate. We had a faculty meeting to get a handle on ninth grade—they drop by the wayside, and they're too young. If we could keep closer to them, we have to give them more support. For example, I have a girl in ninth grade for the fourth time. I think the city is working on this as a whole.

Views on the dropout rate were generally uniform, with teachers identifying other factors—largely ones outside the school—as the prime causes. Experiences at Urban were particularly poignant. Teachers' perceptions of racial/ethnic- and language-minority students varied, depending on their experience with those students. Fast Track and Middle Class teachers had the least diverse student population; United Nations had the most. Finally, perceptions of how students with special needs and students who wanted vocational programs were faring under the new requirements were generally tame. Most teachers felt that accommodations were being made at the school level and that even though juggling and planning were necessary, students were able to meet the requirements.

STUDENTS AT RISK: TRANSCRIPT PROFILES

In this section, we explore the possibility that certain groups of students were affected differently by the new requirements. In particular, we analyzed three criteria to assess students' opportunities to learn. Our purpose was to see if students experienced different effects. The three categories were race, academic performance, and gender.

The findings presented in this chapter suggest that minority students continued to have less access to and participation in various educational resources. Evidence of this came from patterns of earning fewer overall credits, enrolling in fewer advanced courses, failing more courses, and earning more practical arts credits. With some few positive exceptions, this pattern was consistent across schools and years. The same pattern appeared for achievement levels. That is, students with higher overall grades tended to take more courses overall, more advanced credits, and fewer practical arts credits than did students who received lower grades. Gender patterns were less clear, with girls failing fewer courses and more equality noted in math credits.

Effects by Race

The data presentation follows the pattern set out in Chapters 3 and 4. Of primary interest are the same questions outlined earlier:

1. Are students earning more credits?
2. Are students taking more challenging courses?
3. Are students struggling more with their course work?
4. Are students altering course-taking patterns in specific subject areas?

The ideal research method with which to address these questions would have been to sample schools with balanced enrollments across racial groups. Unfortunately, the demographics of American high schools in general, as well as of the five high schools under study, simply don't fit the demands of traditional experimental designs. One high school (Fast Track) had so few nonwhite students that their data were eliminated from the analyses by race. Two other schools (Middle Class and Rural) had only small numbers of African-American students. Consequently, comparisons in these schools must be made cautiously. (The statistical results [ANOVAS] reported in the tables compare white and African-American student experiences across the four schools.) The student populations at the final two schools, Urban and United Nations, were much more racially diverse. Urban was almost equally balanced between whites and African-Americans.[2] The enrollment at United Nations was a rich mix of whites, African-Americans, Asians, and Hispanics. Our sampling strategy was to oversample some racial groups to ensure an ample sample in each category for comparison purposes. This was achieved in only the latter two schools. A breakdown of the sample sizes by race is presented in Table B.2 in Appendix B.

DIFFERENCES IN CREDITS EARNED. Table 5.1 presents the average number of credits earned by race, broken down by school and by year. The comparisons are between white and African-American students because these were the primary racial groups in the high schools studied.

The biggest difference in credits earned was noticed at the most racially diverse high school in the sample, United Nations. Prior to the policy change, Asian students earned the most credits and Hispanics the least credits. After the second year of implementation, all but African-American students showed significant increases in credits earned (gains from 1.5 to 2.0). African-Americans made no gains. Although Hispanic students made progress, they were still disadvan-

TABLE 5.1.
CREDITS EARNED—BY RACE AND SCHOOL

	Asian	White	Black	Hispanic
United Nations				
1986 (Pre)	25.3	24.4	24.3	23.0
1989 (Post₁)	26.6	26.5	24.9	24.7
1990 (Post₂)	27.3	26.4	24.4	24.5
Urban				
1986 (Pre)	—	22.6	22.1	—
1989 (Post₁)	—	23.0	22.3	—
1990 (Post₂)	—	22.8	22.0	—
Middle Class				
1986 (Pre)	—	22.5	22.3	—
1989 (Post₁)	—	23.3	23.5	—
1990 (Post₂)	—	23.2	23.4	—
Rural				
1986 (Pre)	—	25.3	25.7	—
1989 (Post₁)	—	25.2	25.1	—
1990 (Post₂)	—	24.6	24.4	—

Statistical effect by race: $F = 48.6$, $p \leq .001$.
Note: Number of cases for each cell are presented in Appendix B, Table B.2.

taged in comparison with their white and Asian counterparts. That is, the gap between those groups had not decreased. The other three schools with racially diverse student bodies displayed few differences.

DIFFERENCES IN ADVANCED CREDITS EARNED.   Significant differences existed among racial groups when enrollment in advanced-level courses was considered. Table 5.2 presents these findings. White students consistently enrolled in higher proportions of advanced courses, between one and a half and two times as many advanced courses as African-Americans. In the one school with more than two racial groups (United Nations), white and Asian students enrolled in substantially more advanced courses than both African-American and His-

TABLE 5.2.
PERCENTAGE OF ADVANCED CREDITS—BY RACE AND SCHOOL

	Asian	White	Black	Hispanic
United Nations				
1986 (Pre)	29.4	40.9	17.7	16.0
1989 (Post$_1$)	53.8	62.6	37.5	32.2
1990 (Post$_2$)	68.2	58.8	32.2	35.2
Urban				
1986 (Pre)	—	12.5	10.3	—
1989 (Post$_1$)	—	18.0	15.4	—
1990 (Post$_2$)	—	23.6	17.5	—
Middle Class				
1986 (Pre)	—	27.4	13.4	—
1989 (Post$_1$)	—	45.0	28.3	—
1990 (Post$_2$)	—	48.4	38.8	—
Rural				
1986 (Pre)	—	38.3	23.6	—
1989 (Post$_1$)	—	37.2	19.1	—
1990 (Post$_2$)	—	40.0	24.2	—

Statistical effect by race: $F = 169.0$, $p \leq .001$.

panic students. These findings were consistent across time. Students in all racial groups increased their proportion of advanced credits after the policy was implemented, except students at Rural. With the exception of consistent improvement for African-Americans at Middle Class, however, the gap between minority students and their white peers did not diminish. In other words, the change in requirements seemed to have neither exacerbated nor alleviated racial differences in student enrollments in advanced courses.

DIFFERENCES IN FAILURE RATES. Strong effects in failure rates were associated with race, as evidenced by the data in Table 5.3. In all schools but Middle Class, the pattern across time was for African-American

TABLE 5.3.
PERCENTAGE OF CREDITS FAILED—BY RACE AND SCHOOL

	Asian	White	Black	Hispanic
United Nations				
1986 (Pre)	4.6	4.2	8.2	12.7
1989 (Post1)	4.0	3.7	8.6	8.7
1990 (Post2)	1.1	3.0	6.6	8.4
Urban				
1986 (Pre)	—	6.7	10.2	—
1989 (Post$_1$)	—	4.8	7.4	—
1990 (Post$_2$)	—	2.6	4.3	—
Middle Class				
1986 (Pre)	—	5.5	9.5	—
1989 (Post$_1$)	—	3.2	2.1	—
1990 (Post$_2$)	—	2.6	2.5	—
Rural				
1986 (Pre)	—	4.8	4.9	—
1989 (Post$_1$)	—	4.6	7.7	—
1990 (Post$_2$)	—	3.3	7.1	—

Statistical effect by race: $F = 70.4, p \leq .001$.

students to fail more courses than white students did. At United Nations, African-Americans failed twice the number of courses as did whites. That gap continued after the policy was implemented. Blacks at Urban failed one and a half times the number of courses as their white counterparts. Although there was a general decline in failure rates at Urban over time, the ratio between the two racial groups remained constant. Middle Class made the most progress in this area, with failures declining in both groups and with the proportions equal by the second year of complete policy implementation. Just the reverse trend was noted in Rural, with African-Americans failing twice the number of courses as whites by 1990, when the two groups had started out almost on equal footing.

TABLE 5.4.
MATH CREDITS EARNED—BY RACE AND SCHOOL

	Asian	White	Black	Hispanic
United Nations				
1986 (Pre)	3.8	3.3	2.9	2.3
1989 (Post1)	3.6	3.6	3.5	3.4
1990 (Post2)	3.6	3.4	3.4	3.0
Urban				
1986 (Pre)	—	2.3	2.1	—
1989 (Post$_1$)	—	3.5	3.3	—
1990 (Post$_2$)	—	3.3	3.3	—
Middle Class				
1986 (Pre)	—	2.6	2.6	—
1989 (Post$_1$)	—	3.3	3.1	—
1990 (Post$_2$)	—	3.3	3.4	—
Rural				
1986 (Pre)	—	3.6	3.4	—
1989 (Post$_1$)	—	4.0	3.4	—
1990 (Post$_2$)	—	4.3	3.9	—

Statistical effect by race: $F = 10.7$, $p \leq .001$.

DIFFERENCES IN MATHEMATICS CREDITS.   Data on the number of math credits earned by race offer a ray of hope (see Table 5.4). In the two schools with the most racially diverse populations, early disparities in math credits were virtually eliminated. That is, African-American students, who before the policy took effect were earning fewer math credits than white students were, were earning an equal number by the time the policy was in place. The African-American students at Middle Class saw their situation reverse: White students enrolled in more math classes after the policy took effect, whereas black enrollment remained constant. At Rural, both groups increased their math credits, but the gap between them did not change.

TABLE 5.5.
FINE ARTS CREDITS EARNED BY RACE AND SCHOOL

	Asian	White	Black	Hispanic
United Nations				
1986 (Pre)	1.6	2.1	1.8	1.7
1989 (Post$_1$)	1.8	2.4	2.0	1.9
1990 ((Post$_2$)	1.5	2.3	2.2	1.9
Urban				
1986 (Pre)	—	0.9	1.0	—
1989 (Post$_1$)	—	1.6	1.4	—
1990 (Post$_2$)	—	1.4	1.3	—
Middle Class				
1986 (Pre)	—	1.2	0.7	—
1989 (Post$_1$)	—	1.5	1.4	—
1990 (Post$_2$)	—	1.6	1.0	—
Rural				
1986 (Pre)	—	1.4	1.9	—
1989 (Post$_1$)	—	3.0	2.9	—
1990 (Post$_2$)	—	2.7	2.3	—

Statistical effect by race: $F = 3.9$, $p \leq .05$.

DIFFERENCES IN FINE ARTS CREDITS.   Of all of the comparisons by race, the differences in fine arts credits were the smallest ($F = 3.9$) (see Table 5.5). Although statistical analysis suggests that differences existed, those differences were not nearly as pronounced as any of the other differences. In the two schools with the largest minority enrollments, the comparison between African-American and white students' credits produced a discrepancy of only 0.1 credits in 1990. The biggest difference was between Asian and white students at United Nations (0.8) and between blacks and whites at Middle Class (0.9). When differences did exist, white students were earning more fine arts credits than minority students were. Overall, the gap between different groups has not shifted significantly as a result of implementation of the policy.

TABLE 5.6.
PRACTICAL ARTS CREDITS EARNED—BY RACE AND SCHOOL

	Asian	White	Black	Hispanic
United Nations				
1986 (Pre)	4.8	3.4	5.4	5.4
1989 (Post$_1$)	4.3	3.0	4.5	4.3
1990 (Post$_2$)	3.4	3.1	4.7	5.0
Urban				
1986 (Pre)	—	6.2	5.7	—
1989 (Post$_1$)	—	4.2	3.9	—
1990 (Post$_2$)	—	3.6	3.3	—
Middle Class				
1986 (Pre)	—	4.2	5.0	—
1989 (Post$_1$)	—	4.0	6.2	—
1990 (Post$_2$)	—	3.5	5.4	—
Rural				
1986 (Pre)	—	5.4	6.9	—
1989 (Post$_1$)	—	3.4	6.2	—
1990 (Post$_2$)	—	3.1	4.3	—

Statistical effect by race: $F = 33.2, p \leq .001$.

DIFFERENCES IN PRACTICAL ARTS CREDITS. In this final display by race, comparisons are made for practical arts credits (see Table 5.6). In three of the four schools, the balance was for African-American students to earn more credits than whites (approximately one and a half times as many). Urban was the one exception, where on average white students earned more practical arts credits than African-American students did. The policy did little to change these balances. Consequently, minority students were neither advantaged nor disadvantaged by the shift in policy.

Teachers also addressed their concerns about the impact of the policy on minority students. Differences in the student populations at each school and teachers' daily experiences with them greatly influenced their perceptions, as evidenced by the following discussion.

Teachers' Accounts of Differences by Race

A teacher's capacity to respond to whether racial-minority or language-minority students would be differently affected by the policy change depended directly on the specific student population in the school where the teacher was located. Teachers from Middle Class and Rural had little or no experience with language-minority students and thus could not realistically discuss the requirements' effect on them. Teachers from Middle Class also had few minority students, thus limiting their basis for discussion about students from historically oppressed groups. Teachers at United Nations and Urban had both racial and language mixes in their schools, with United Nations the most diverse. Not surprisingly, teachers at United Nations expressed the most concern about racial-minority and language-minority students. Teachers at Urban spoke eloquently about the enormous problems facing their students, about half of whom were black. Some details from each school follow.

At Middle Class, concerns about racial and ethnic minorities were minimal because of their low number of minority and almost nonexistent limited English–speaking student enrollments. Teachers noted: "Our minorities are so small. I don't see any significant impacts. Blacks we do pull come from lower socioeconomic groups. But whites from low SES also fail"; "I haven't gotten any negative feedback, but it may be the kids I see. Most are middle income or upper income. I have more white students from low-income families with lots of problems"; "The ones I have are great students. I've never had any problem at all with that."

There were no language-minority students at Rural, although one teacher expressed concern for African-American students, whom he linked to waterman students, describing both as being at greater risk: "Both blacks and watermen have trouble because there's no family encouragement and they're not motivated."

Serving the most diverse student population in terms of race and primary language, teachers at United Nations revealed much more complex assessments of their students' responses to new, more strict requirements. Many of the teachers with whom we spoke described the complex interactions of socioeconomic status, racial or linguistic minority status, track placement, and "at riskness." Thus, they told us how educational background made so much difference and how for students from impoverished backgrounds, the requirements could be difficult: "For some, yes; and for some, no. Those with a good educational background, no. Those ill prepared are then pressured to catch up. The requirements may negatively influence them." Another described how the school was better serving low-income minority students than before but that the "new credits are hurting those students because they are at risk anyway." Curricular track placement was a primary concern: "Hispanics and blacks are hurt because more are in low tracks."

At United Nations, language-minority students were found in all tracks. This seemed to foster more broad-based concerns about those students. Many teachers worried about how well these students were faring:

> Language problems create the biggest barriers. The problem is that we aren't told what the student backgrounds are. I find out after the first writing assignment.

> They need extra classes just to learn English, so the extra courses are needed just to catch up. These requirements would take up courses that ESOL students need in basics.

> They don't have the background knowledge in general. They have a difficult time to some degree. They don't have the same reference point—culture. For example, I may refer to Goldilocks, and they have no idea who she is. They may not have language or exposure in their background to handle the work.

> It has had an effect. Even though ESOL students are supposed to be able to understand English when it comes to word problems [and] verbal and written instructions, there is a problem with ESOL students.

At Urban, teachers spoke little about differential effects on minority students. When they did, they seemed to have few concerns. And in contrast to United Nations, the language-minority students at Urban were primarily Hispanic or Greek. In general, teachers felt that these students did quite well, telling us: "Foreign born are the best students. Greek girls were very good; Greek boys were not as good because they are allowed to run wild"; "My Asian kids are fantastic. Some come with no English and get 95s in foreign language—they're learning both languages at the same time. And Hispanics have at least one class in Spanish"; and "With math, foreign-born kids are usually ahead of us anyway. Maybe in English it would be a problem, but not in math and science." A very small number of teachers expressed concern about how well these students were being served: "That is a problem. We have a lot coming here—a lot don't speak English. They'll pair them with another kid—for example, a Greek who translates. We need an ESL class here because it must be hard for them when they don't speak English."

Effects by Academic Performance

A second important category in which clear losers are often identified is academic performance. Students who are poor achievers do not share in the opportunity structure on an equal footing. In this section, we look at whether differential effects of the policy are evident based on student performance. Student performance was operationalized as student grades in their course work. A cumulative grade point average was calculated for each cohort, and three approximately equal-sized groups of students were created: The bottom proportion of the students were defined as low performers, the middle third as average performers, and the top third as high performers. A breakdown of sample sizes by academic performance is presented in Table B.3 of Appendix B.

DIFFERENCES IN CREDITS EARNED.   Table 5.7 presents the average number of credits earned by school, by year, and by the three categories of academic performance. The differences are consistent and dramatic. Across all five schools, students with better academic records earned more credits than those with poorer records. Students at Middle Class showed the least discrepancy between high performers and low performers, with a difference of only l.2 credits by 1990. Students at United Nations showed the greatest discrepancy, with a five-credit difference. The gap between the low performers and high performers increased significantly at United Nations after the policy took effect, while remaining fairly constant at Fast Track and Rural. The gap between the high performers and low performers dropped by about one credit at both Urban and Middle Class. The growth in the gap at United Nations is partly a function of many high achievers being in the magnet program, in which students were enrolled in eight credits per semester rather than the usual seven. The magnet program was not available to the class of 1986. Overall, it does not appear that great strides were made toward increasing the equity in credit distribution after implementation of the new requirements.

DIFFERENCES IN ADVANCED CREDITS EARNED.   Differences by academic performance were very powerful and consistent (see Table 5.8). Students who did well in class (i.e., had higher GPAs) were much more likely to

TABLE 5.7.
CREDITS EARNED—BY ACADEMIC PERFORMANCE AND SCHOOL

	Low Performers	Average Performers	High Performers
Fast Track			
1986 (Pre)	21.3	23.0	23.8
1989 (Post$_1$)	24.4	26.0	26.6
1990 (Post$_2$)	25.4	26.9	27.5
United Nations			
1986 (Pre)	22.2	24.3	25.5
1989 (Post$_1$)	22.8	25.7	27.8
1990 (Post$_2$)	22.8	25.4	27.7
Urban			
1986 (Pre)	21.9	23.6	24.3
1989 (Post$_1$)	22.3	24.0	24.4
1990 (Post$_2$)	22.1	23.4	23.6
Middle Class			
1986 (Pre)	21.2	22.2	23.5
1989 (Post$_1$)	22.5	23.4	23.7
1990 (Post$_2$)	22.5	23.1	23.7
Rural			
1986 (Pre)	22.1	25.1	26.4
1989 (Post$_1$)	22.9	25.3	26.0
1990 (Post$_2$)	23.0	24.8	25.3

Statistical effect by academic performance: $F = 473.8$, $p \leq .001$.
Note: Number of cases for each cell are presented in Appendix B, Table B.3.

take advanced courses than those who didn't do as well. This occurred in spite of the fact that the language of the policy was very clear about making advanced courses available to a wider range of students. In the most dramatic cases (United Nations and Rural), high achievers were nearly three times as likely to enroll in advanced courses as low achiev-

TABLE 5.8.
PERCENTAGE OF ADVANCED CREDITS EARNED—BY ACADEMIC PERFORMANCE AND SCHOOL

	Low Performers	Average Performers	High Performers
Fast Track			
1986 (Pre)	14	20	34
1989 (Post$_1$)	27	52	63
1990 (Post$_2$)	21	38	52
United Nations			
1986 (Pre)	9	19	42
1989 (Post$_1$)	23	41	71
1990 (Post$_2$)	26	39	71
Urban			
1986 (Pre)	9	14	23
1989 (Post$_1$)	15	25	24
1990 (Post$_2$)	20	29	32
Middle Class			
1986 (Pre)	12	23	38
1989 (Post$_1$)	23	41	60
1990 (Post$_2$)	30	42	61
Rural			
1986 (Pre)	16	36	42
1989 (Post$_1$)	24	26	43
1990 (Post$_2$)	22	24	58

Statistical effect by academic performance: $F = 504.8$, $p \leq .001$.

ers. In two of the schools (Fast Track and Rural), the difference between the low performers and high performers remained fairly constant over time, suggesting that the policy had little effect in moving one group more than another to seek more advanced courses. In contrast, in the other three schools (United Nations, Urban, and Middle

Class), there was some moderate movement toward more equity. That is, low performers were adding advanced credits at a faster pace than the high performers. Yet the discrepancy between the two remained quite large, with high performers earning about twice as many advanced credits as low performers.

DIFFERENCES IN FAILURE RATES. No data are presented for this category because the argument is tautological—that is, low performers are defined partially by the number of courses they fail.

DIFFERENCES IN MATHEMATICS CREDITS. The pattern of math credits earned was very consistent when broken down by student performance. Students who did well in course work earned more math credits than did students who did poorly (see Table 5.9). That was true across all five schools and all 3 years. With the exception of Rural (where the small sample size may have had an effect), all the schools showed a lessening of the gap between low achievers and high achievers after the policy was initiated. That is, math credits were more equitably distributed across academic performance categories once the change in requirements took effect. At Rural, the gap remained unchanged when students were compared before and after the policy took effect. Thus, the policy had the positive effect of moving many low performers closer over time to high performers in terms of the number of math credits earned.

DIFFERENCES IN FINE ARTS CREDITS. As with the comparisons by race in the previous section, differences in fine arts credits by academic performance were considerably smaller than any of the other differences (see Table 5.10). In all of the schools but Rural, by the second year of the policy implementation, there was near equity between low performers and high performers. The greatest improvement was at Urban, where, prior to the policy, low performers earned 1.2 fewer fine arts credits than high performers did; by the second year, they were equal. Although fine arts staff noted that the requirements had increased enrollments among 9th- and 10th-grade students, these increases were offset by declining enrollments among upper-level students. The argument was that as students moved through high school, their schedules would allow less room for electives and they would no longer choose an advanced painting course, advanced electronics, or advanced tailoring. This was best captured in words by a choir director, who claimed that the fine arts requirements was robbing her of her experienced and talented singers:

TABLE 5.9.
MATH CREDITS EARNED—BY ACADEMIC PERFORMANCE AND SCHOOL

	Low Performers	Average Performers	High Performers
Fast Track			
1986 (Pre)	2.6	3.0	3.4
1989 (Post$_1$)	3.3	3.4	3.8
1990 (Post$_2$)	3.6	3.4	3.7
United Nations			
1986 (Pre)	2.6	2.9	3.6
1989 (Post$_1$)	3.0	3.4	3.9
1990 (Post$_2$)	3.0	3.3	3.7
Urban			
1986 (Pre)	2.1	2.3	3.6
1989 (Post$_1$)	3.3	3.4	4.0
1990 (Post$_2$)	3.3	3.5	3.5
Middle Class			
1986 (Pre)	2.2	2.7	3.5
1989 (Post$_1$)	3.0	3.4	3.4
1990 (Post$_2$)	3.3	3.0	3.6
Rural			
1986 (Pre)	3.0	3.4	3.9
1989 (Post$_1$)	3.1	4.0	4.1
1990 (Post$_2$)	3.6	4.0	4.7

Statistical effect by academic performance: $F = 78.8$, $p \leq .001$.

The fine arts requirement? What a disaster. It sounded so wonderful, but it isn't working. We're performers, and we're taking a licking. I go out to performances with kids who can't sing. It's a fine thing to have kids in class who can't sing, but the children I trained this year can't come back because the computer says they've already taken a fine arts class!

TABLE 5.10.
FINE ARTS CREDITS EARNED—BY ACADEMIC PERFORMANCE AND SCHOOL

	Low Performers	Average Performers	High Performers
Fast Track			
1986 (Pre)	2.3	1.7	2.2
1989 (Post$_1$)	2.3	2.4	2.6
1990 (Post$_2$)	2.3	2.1	2.6
United Nations			
1986 (Pre)	1.7	1.6	2.3
1989 (Post$_1$)	1.9	2.4	2.1
1990 (Post$_2$)	2.0	2.1	2.1
Urban			
1986 (Pre)	0.9	1.1	2.3
1989 (Post$_1$)	1.6	1.3	1.5
1990 (Post$_2$)	1.4	1.5	1.4
Middle Class			
1986 (Pre)	1.2	1.2	1.0
1989 (Post$_1$)	1.5	1.6	1.4
1990 (Post$_2$)	1.6	1.6	1.5
Rural			
1986 (Pre)	0.7	1.2	1.9
1989 (Post$_1$)	2.8	2.8	3.1
1990 (Post$_2$)	1.6	2.1	3.4

Statistical effect by academic performance: $F = 3.3$, $p \le .05$.
Note: Number of cases for each cell are presented in Appendix B, Table B.4.

The experience at Rural was less clear. Near equity was reached after 1 year of implementation, but a big gap reappeared by 1990, with high performers earning significantly more fine arts credits. On balance, however, the evidence suggests equitable distribution across performance categories for student enrollment in fine arts courses.

TABLE 5.11.
PRACTICAL ARTS CREDITS EARNED—BY ACADEMIC PERFORMANCE AND SCHOOL

	Low Performers	Average Performers	High Performers
Fast Track			
1986 (Pre)	2.78	3.67	2.70
1989 (Post$_1$)	4.94	4.02	3.26
1990 (Post$_2$)	4.96	4.91	3.85
United Nations			
1986 (Pre)	4.90	5.56	3.56
1989 (Post$_1$)	4.20	4.28	2.99
1990 (Post$_2$)	4.59	4.52	2.78
Urban			
1986 (Pre)	5.71	6.68	5.00
1989 (Post$_1$)	3.79	5.18	5.23
1990 (Post$_2$)	3.62	3.39	3.64
Middle Class			
1986 (Pre)	4.81	4.54	3.61
1989 (Post$_1$)	5.16	4.15	3.76
1990 (Post$_2$)	4.12	4.14	3.04
Rural			
1986 (Pre)	5.94	5.45	5.56
1989 (Post$_1$)	4.21	4.70	3.44
1990 (Post$_2$)	4.38	5.00	1.66

Statistical effect by academic performance: $F = 45.4$, $p \leq .001$.

However, that equity was accomplished at the expense of high performers' exposure to fine arts. Prior to the policy, these students had the flexibility to be exposed to several fine arts classes (2.3 credits on average), whereas after the policy was in place, they were forced to reduce this exposure.

DIFFERENCES IN PRACTICAL ARTS CREDITS.   Large differences existed between the practical arts credits earned by low achievers and high achievers, as documented in Table 5.11. The obvious trend was for low performers to earn more practical arts credits than high performers did. The one exception was Urban, where the distribution was quite balanced. The most dramatic example was Rural, where low performers were two and a half times more likely than high performers to earn practical arts credits after the policy was implemented. This trend of low performers' earning an increasing proportion of practical arts credits compared with high performers was also noted in two other schools: Fast Track and United Nations, the two schools with the strongest academic traditions. This suggests that the inequities regarding practical arts enrollments were exacerbated by the policy. Low performers were increasingly encouraged to earn practical arts credits. Although some would applaud this trend, asserting that these students were finally being steered to more appropriate content, the intent of the policy and recent projections suggest that independent thinking and creative problem-solving skills are essential for the work force of the 21st century.

Effects by Gender

The last category that shapes students' exposure to differential learning opportunities is gender. In this section, we address whether the persistent pattern of boys receiving preference over girls was borne out by our transcript analyses and whether those patterns were strengthened or weakened by the new policy. Unlike the other two categories (race and academic performance), where significant differences were detected across all six outcomes, analyses conducted with gender as the independent variable produced statistically significant differences in only three of the six outcomes. The following discussion focuses only on those analyses: differences in failure rates, math credits earned, and practical arts credits earned. An accounting of sample sizes by gender is displayed in Table B.4 in Appendix B.

DIFFERENCES IN FAILURE RATES.   Table 5.12 compares course failure rates of male and female students by school and by year. The general trend (with the exception of Fast Track, which had the lowest ratios of the five schools) was for boys to fail more courses than girls, with boys failing between one and a half and twice as many courses as girls. When the ratios prior to the new policy (class of 1986) are compared with the most recent data (class of 1990), the differences increased across three schools (United Nations, Urban, and Rural), remained constant at Mid-

TABLE 5.12.
PERCENTAGE OF CREDITS FAILED—BY GENDER AND SCHOOL

	Male	Female
Fast Track		
1986 (Pre)	3.6	2.5
1989 (Post$_1$)	2.1	2.6
1990 (Post$_2$)	1.4	1.9
United Nations		
1986 (Pre)	7.5	6.1
1989 (Post$_1$)	5.0	6.0
1990 (Post$_2$)	5.5	2.5
Urban		
1986 (Pre)	9.8	7.4
1989 (Post$_1$)	7.0	4.8
1990 (Post$_2$)	4.1	2.5
Middle Class		
1986 (Pre)	7.0	4.0
1989 (Post$_1$)	3.9	2.2
1990 (Post$_2$)	3.3	1.9
Rural		
1986 (Pre)	6.2	3.8
1989 (Post$_1$)	5.3	5.1
1990 (Post$_2$)	6.2	2.6

Statistical effect by gender: $F = 23.2$, $p \leq .001$.

dle Class, and reversed order at Fast Track. Consequently, the new requirements did little to alter gender differences.

DIFFERENCES IN MATHEMATICS CREDITS.   Research usually documents that girls earn fewer math credits than boys do. Prior to the new requirements, this was the case in four of the five schools (see Table 5.13).

TABLE 5.13.
MATH CREDITS EARNED—BY GENDER AND SCHOOL

	Male	Female
Fast Track		
1986 (Pre)	3.26	3.02
1989 (Post$_1$)	3.65	3.47
1990 (Post$_2$))	3.62	3.48
United Nations		
1986 (Pre)	3.30	2.93
1989 (Post$_1$)	3.60	3.46
1990 (Post$_2$)	3.46	3.40
Urban		
1986 (Pre)	2.71	1.77
1989 (Post$_1$)	3.51	3.32
1990 (Post$_2$)	3.44	3.25
Middle Class		
1986 (Pre)	2.85	2.96
1989 (Post$_1$)	3.32	3.27
1990 (Post$_2$)	3.25	3.30
Rural		
1986 (Pre)	3.88	3.37
1989 (Post$_1$)	4.11	3.56
1990 (Post$_2$)	3.69	4.65

Statistical effect by gender: $F = 20.3$, $p \le .001$.

Middle Class was the exception, with boys and girls earning an almost equal share of math credits. That equality was constant over time at Middle Class, while in the other four schools, the trend was toward increasing equality in the number of math credits earned. The most striking example was Urban, where in 1986, boys on average earned one more math credit than girls did. By 1990, the girls had almost caught up with the boys. The data from this table present one of the few positive impacts of the policy: The third math credit has encouraged girls to earn as many math credits as boys do.

DIFFERENCES IN PRACTICAL ARTS CREDITS. Gender differences were very inconsistent when practical arts credits earned were compared (see Table 5.14). In 8 of 15 comparisons, girls earned more than boys. The most dramatic case was Rural in 1986. At that time, the school had a beautician program that was not available in later years. Three schools offered evidence of increasing gender balance in practical arts exposure when the cohort of students prior to the policy shift (class of 1986) was compared with the 1990 cohort. These three schools were Fast Track, United Nations, and Middle Class. At Urban, the imbalance remained over time, with girls earning more practical arts credits than boys. At Rural, a complete reversal took place, with girls taking significantly more practical arts classes prior to the shift in policy and with boys taking more after implementation. On balance, however, the effect of the policy was to move toward more gender equity in practical arts enrollments.

Summary

These analyses of student transcript data present few findings with which to celebrate the effects of the policy on at-risk populations. Minority students continued to have limited access to and participation in academic resources. They also received failing grades more often than their white peers. Low-performing students' experiences revealed cycles of disaffection, with low performance associated with fewer credits earned, fewer advanced credits, and more emphasis in practical arts courses. As students began to sense that they were failures or at the margins, they participated less intensely in school. Less-intense participation might well have fostered poorer performance, and so the cycle continued.

The only shining light was with mathematics. Across race, academic performance, and gender, the differences were disappearing. That is, minority students, poor performers, and girls were more likely to achieve equity in terms of math credits earned after the third credit requirement was imposed. This finding should be interpreted cautiously, however. As demonstrated in Chapter 4 (see Table 4.1), students showed considerable movement between tracks in mathematics. Thus, many filled the third-year math requirement with remedial or lower-level courses. In fact, at Urban, we discovered an informal policy

TABLE 5.14.

PRACTICAL ARTS CREDITS EARNED—BY GENDER AND SCHOOL

	Male	Female
Fast Track		
1986 (Pre)	3.33	3.01
1989 (Post$_1$)	4.53	3.39
1990 (Post$_2$)	4.80	4.42
United Nations		
1986 (Pre)	4.15	5.08
1989 (Post$_1$)	3.69	3.80
1990 (Post$_2$)	3.67	3.75
Urban		
1986 (Pre)	5.01	6.72
1989 (Post$_1$)	2.96	4.90
1990 (Post$_2$)	2.85	3.95
Middle Class		
1986 (Pre)	4.68	3.60
1989 (Post$_1$)	4.73	3.54
1990 (Post$_2$)	3.72	3.67
Rural		
1986 (Pre)	3.62	6.99
1989 (Post$_1$)	3.89	4.03
1990 (Post$_2$)	4.09	2.80

Statistical effect by gender: $F = 7.52$, $p \le .01$.

that permitted students to satisfy the math requirement with business and vocational math courses, including accounting. These courses had not been previously counted as math credits. Implemented as an emergency measure for the first graduating class (1989), this practice continued for at least another year.

In summary, the question posed at the beginning of this chapter, "Who loses?" seems to demand the answer, "It depends." And what it depends on are the characteristics of the student and the school he or she attends more than any other characteristic. However, potential losers need to be defined more broadly than as just students. As we learned from talking with teachers, teachers were also concerned about their future. They talked about changes to their departments, possible job losses, and diminished flexibility. The final section presents these concerns.

TEACHERS AND DEPARTMENTS AT RISK

Change is always difficult for any organization. Yet despite the many reforms that have passed over the educational horizon, our schools of today look very much like the ones of the past (Cuban, 1990). To what extent did the policy reform of graduation requirements affect the working lives of teachers? The concerns of the professionals who worked directly with students were ones of job tenure, departmental adjustments, and diminished flexibility. We explore these issues by first analyzing quantitative data about the allocation of staff in the schools and then reporting what teachers had to say. We found that at least by objective measures, department staffing patterns were relatively unaffected by the new policy. This is especially interesting in light of the interview data, which suggest that certain departments felt quite threatened. We explain this discrepancy with the notion that deeply held beliefs about vulnerability persisted in the face of evidence to the contrary.

Staffing Changes: Master Schedules

School master schedules were the source of our quantitative analysis. These data allowed us to look at changes in course offerings between the 1984–1985 school year (prior to the policy initiative) and the 1989–1990 school year (after the policy initiative was in place). These documents reported what each teacher was doing during each period of the school day. Complete data were available for only three of the five schools. Although all schools had current master schedules available, two did not keep archival copies, so we were unable to document changes over time.

The results are presented in terms of full time equivalent (FTE) teaching staff. Table 5.15 summarizes FTEs by subject area for each of the three schools, comparing pre- and postreform.[3] The changes were mostly in the positive direction. That is, more teachers were in these departments in 1989–1990 than in 1984–1985. Some of the increases were quite substantial, particularly when compared with the increases in credits earned by students (see Table 3.1). One explanation for the anomaly may be shifting class sizes, something we were unable to control in the analysis. Another explanation is that the student data base covered student enrollments from 1981–1982 through 1988–1989 while the master schedule data were from 1984–1985 to 1989–1990.

The numbers in the columns represent the percentage FTE change between the 1984–1985 data and 1989–1990 data. Adjustments were made in the analyses to control for changes in student enrollment.[4] The first subjects summarized are those that were directly affected by the requirements (math, fine arts, and practical arts). Next are areas that the literature claims usually suffer when requirements change: physical education and foreign language. Those presented last are the academic areas left untouched by the requirements (with the exception of the influence of the Certificate of Merit).

TABLE 5.15.
FTE TEACHER ASSIGNMENTS—BY SCHOOL AND SUBJECT:
ADJUSTED PERCENTAGE CHANGE

Subject	SCHOOL		
	Fast Track	Middle Class	Rural
Math	+12	+14	+56
Music	+46	–01	+75
Art	+56	+68	+25
Industrial Art	+46	–10	+292
Business	+10	–25	–06
Home Ec	+46	+51	+25
PE	+06	+06	+10
Foreign Language	+53	+30	+92
Science	+06	+01	+16
English	+12	+11	+25
Social Studies	+06	+10	+25

Note: The adjusted change column controls for the change in total school enrollment over time. This adjusted figure is: [(Post – Pre)/Pre] – Enrollment Change. The enrollment change between the 1984–1985 and 1989 (Post$_1$) – 1990 school years was as follows: Fast Track, +14%; Middle Class, -18%; and Rural, -25%.

The most striking finding was that in two of the three schools, no single department suffered losses in the number of sections it offered. At Fast Track, the one school with losses, all losses were concentrated in business and vocational subjects. What appeared to be happening was that schools managed to absorb changes in course requirements without reducing staff in other areas.

Some subjects experienced tremendous growth. The most obvious candidate for growth would have been math, with the change from two to three required credits. This was simply not the case. Math teacher allocations grew modestly in all three schools, but nothing on the order of the 50% growth that might be expected with a 50% increase in course requirements. One explanation may be that many students were already taking three credits of math, so only minor adjustments were necessary. As was reported earlier, students took on average 2.86 math credits before the new requirements and 3.55 credits after the requirements, a 24% increase.

Fine arts subjects (music and art departments) were clearly growth areas, albeit inconsistently. At Fast Track, both music and art FTEs grew by approximately one half. But at Middle Class, only the art department saw significant gains, while at Rural, it was the music department that expanded.

In the practical arts areas, there were also important differences across the three schools. Significant growth occurred in industrial arts in two of the three schools (the massive jump at Rural was directly related to the closing of the countywide vocational center and the absorption of many of those staff into the local schools). Home economics saw growth across all three schools. One explanation for the across-the-board increase in all practical arts subjects at Fast Track is that the large college-bound population probably had not enrolled in many of these courses until the requirements forced them to do so. Moreover, this was the same high school that went from a six- to a seven-period day, thus giving students more flexibility in taking these kinds of courses.

Physical education, a department often cited as absorbing big losses because of changes in requirements, managed to hold its own in all three schools. Foreign language was a surprise winner in all three schools. One explanation for the gain in foreign language may be that for students to earn a Certificate of Merit, they had to take at least a second year of one foreign language. The three academic subject areas left pretty much untouched by the requirements (except for the third credit of science required to earn the Certificate of Merit) included English, science, and social studies. These three subjects displayed modest growth across all three schools.

Teachers' Views: Interviews

From a numbers count, there do not appear to be any significant losers. However, teachers made important qualitative distinctions that pointed to the possibility of some losers in the implementation of this reform. Their voices help explain some of the perceived losses.

Early predictions from our first round of interviews in 1986 suggested that wholesale changes could take place at the departmental level, with significant shifts in staff as schools accommodated the new requirements. Later interviews and analysis of master schedules did not bear this out. Although there were some isolated cases of significant departmental reductions, on the whole, departments came through the reform with only minimal change.

Such a summary, however, does not do justice to the concerns of some staff about the negative effects of the policy. Rather than addressing specific departments, most of the concern was with how the requirements restricted the school's options as a whole. Although not saying so explicitly, staff were conveying the message that their flexibility in providing for individual student needs was being rapidly eroded. This was particularly true in the one small, rural high school and in the two high schools that operated on a six-period day. Staff in the remaining two schools, both of which had seven-period days, expressed fewer concerns about constrained flexibility.

In one school, teachers fretted that their efforts to recruit students in the spring for fall courses were wiped out over the summer by district computers that altered students' course selections to accommodate the tightly scheduled six-period day:

> We can only attract kids for one credit. We recruit them every year in May for a second course in that subject area, but we lose them by September. The computer says they have already had a practical arts class, so they aren't allowed to take another.

> All the special areas are hurting the most [e.g., business, home economics, and industrial arts] because these are electives. . . . I'm looking forward to a seven-period day when students will be able to take electives more freely.

In these tightly constrained systems where degrees of flexibility were minimal, adding new requirements tended to put more pressure on everyone. One teacher summarized the problem succinctly by talking about time, the most limited resource: "If you want more programs, you have to give us more time. If you want better teaching, you have to give people more time."

Even teachers not directly affected by the requirements felt the pinch of a tightly constrained six-period school day. One English teacher commented:

> When I came here, there was only one course in world literature/mythology. I built it up to a full-time job. Students really benefited from that, but when we have to fit it into all the other requirements, there is no room [for this course]. I think on the college level they have to be noticing the lack of education in world literature.

Teachers in the practical and fine arts areas were ambivalent about the new requirements and their effect on student enrollments. Although they generally embraced the notion that the requirement exposed many students to content that they would not otherwise have taken, the tightly packed school day inhibited students from exploring these new-found interests beyond the basic introductory level:

> Kids can't continue in advanced music because there is no room in the six-period class day.

> Kids can't fit in advanced courses because of their packed schedules.

> As students have to meet the fine arts and practical arts requirements, they are having to drop languages to fulfill the requirements. We are losing juniors and seniors in the third and fourth years of foreign language.

Another foreign language teacher commented that local certificates required more foreign language than the state's Certificate of Merit. Yet when the state certificate replaced the county certificate, upper-level students (third and fourth years) would be lost to the language program "unless a seven-period day was instituted."

If there were very limited periods in the day, it was also true that teachers would be spread thinly. At small Rural High School, which had tried to increase the number of honors options, one teacher commented: "If there are going to be more honors courses, then drama [fine arts course] and journalism [practical arts course] must be eliminated. There just aren't enough bodies [teachers] to fit it all in."

Teachers also voiced concern about changes in course loads that forced them to take assignments in other academic departments: "We have a couple of people teaching math who aren't in the math department." The concern was that some teachers were teaching in areas where they weren't necessarily skilled or qualified:

> Some people are teaching courses they are not certified/prepared to teach because of the seniority system.

> Some teachers are teaching out of discipline. For example, we have a home economics teacher teaching U.S. history.

Another important concern raised by a number of teachers was that class size might be altered as a result of some of the new requirements.

> Last year, we actually cut half of a person and had to drop two courses and we increased the class size in all the others.

> I'm the only person teaching biology. If you add one course to my schedule, you have to delete something somewhere else. Adding AP [advanced placement] biology caused us to increase class sizes in other classes. In our general science class, we went from 15 to the low 20s when there is only room for 20.

> In the past [before the new requirements], we used to have 300 ninth-grade students enroll in art. Now we have 600. We have added no new teacher, and there are the same number of sections. There are 42 to 46 students in each class on the roll. . . . I see a profound difference when I have a class small enough to work with kids who are frustrated. In larger classes, the frustrated ones give up and I don't have time to help them. The real issue is how to reduce class size.

One of the effects of the new requirements was renewed competition for students among subject-area departments. Some viewed this competition as healthy. One principal commented, "The competition between departments is good. Anyone that sits back and tries to recruit students under the old curriculum will lose students. Each department has to make courses attractive for students." The majority of teachers, however, were concerned about the competition they were drawn into:

> It has taken away some of our students [from the business department]. Students aren't taking our courses; more have enrolled in fine arts classes. . . . We now have borderline enrollments. Shorthand has 16

students and needs 15. If two kids change their mind this summer, we
lose our course.

Computer science is cutting the throat of the other practical arts
subjects.

We lost a teacher in business because of lower enrollments due to students enrolling in fine arts classes.

Teachers in nonrequired subject areas had long voiced concerns
about their second-class status. Interestingly, several teachers said their
status had not changed even when their courses became required:

I have this big conflict. I think the new requirements are hurting business education even though business courses count as part of the practical arts requirement. We are still stigmatized, and there's no need for
that. The conception of what we teach—that it is vocational—we still
have to deal with that, being second class.

We in home economics are always overloaded in the second semester.
Our courses are dumping grounds for failures from academic courses in
the first semester. We used to have a maximum of 24 students for
safety reasons, but now we are up to 32. It's like a zoo; I need a whistle
to control them.

And yet another teacher in a subject area that was required (science)
commented on how that subject area suffered from neglect and from not
being part of the increased requirements. The focus on one area (e.g.,
mathematics) took focus away from other areas (e.g., science):

It is difficult for scientists and science teachers to understand how little
emphasis is placed on science education in this state. Science and technology impact on everyone every day. I think this lack of emphasis is
going to tell in the future.

We need to increase science credits and not just math.

Administrators do not take into consideration the kind of courses taught
when making staffing decisions. They just use gross formulas—x students, y teachers—without considering that lab classes take longer to
prepare for and there should be more student contact.

None of these comments make the most obvious loss voiced by teachers—that of their jobs—any easier. Although not as problematic as was initially hypothesized, job loss was nevertheless on teachers' minds:

> In theory, there should be an increase in staff in the vocational department because of practical arts, but it's not happening. We have lost a wood-shop and print-shop teacher. A retiring teacher may not be replaced. Most of the reduction is in the vocational areas.
>
> We may lose teachers to make room for teachers in required areas. For example, we will lose business teachers and the business courses they teach as they hire new foreign language teachers.
>
> One social studies teacher is retiring in June. There is concern about him not being replaced.
>
> I have lost, lost, lost in business education. Six years ago, I had 13 teachers. We are now down to 7. In the 1970s, we had 18 or 19.
>
> Teachers are getting surplused and moved to another school. In the future, we might lose our jobs.

These concerns cannot be ignored, despite the master schedule analyses that show few, if any, negative effects of the requirements on departmental size. Teachers quite clearly felt vulnerable and voiceless in the policy implementation and in discussions about whether they would have jobs and how these jobs would be constrained by the new requirements.

CONCLUSION

Through the use of quantitative (transcript and master schedule) and qualitative (interview) data, this chapter has detailed perceptions about students and teachers most at risk as this new policy was implemented. Two general conclusions are noteworthy here: First, patterns of exclusion by race, gender, and academic performance persist despite the new policy's intent to encourage all students to take more academic courses. Second, teachers felt diminished flexibility and feared further squeezes on their time and professional prestige because of the policy.

6

WHO'S IN CONTROL?
KEY ACTORS AND THEIR
INFLUENCE ON POLICY
IMPLEMENTATION

O nce policies have been formulated and encoded as law or regulation, they must be implemented. From Elmore's perspective (1980; see Chapter 2 for a discussion), those charged with enacting the policy demands on a daily basis have the most direct influence on the scope and fidelity of implementation. These "street-level bureaucrats" (Lipsky, 1983) shape, modify, repel, or conform to the requirements of the new policy. This argument suggests that we should have found an increasing sense of influence over the new graduation requirements as we moved from the state level to the district level. Within districts, moreover, those charged with making decisions about course offerings and student selections—guidance counselors and, in many cases, teachers—should have expressed a greater role in shaping students' high school careers than principals or central office staff have.

Such was not the case. We found a generalized expression of little control over policy implementation and, hence, students' careers at all levels. We call this a *policy vacuum* where key actors see other actors (often higher up the system), events, and local context as powerfully constraining their actions. The discussion relies on interview data, focusing on perceptions of the mechanisms that support influence and the constraints on that influence in the policy implementation process. We discuss the views of state department staff, district administrators, high school administrators, and counselors. In the discussion, we move from the state's concerns for policy development and implementation to microanalyses of counselors' influence on students' course-taking patterns.

STATE STAFF PERSPECTIVES

Maryland State Department of Education (MSDE) staff identified mechanisms that supported their influence and constraints on that influence. The first way influence was exerted was through staff contributions to the development of the policy; the second was through technical assistance and support to local educators as they implemented the new policy. But MSDE staff also voiced several frustrations about their inability to make the new policy accomplish what they had originally hoped it would.

Policy Development

Key staff contributed to policy development by recommending various positions that the state board might take on a particular issue. For example, when the state board was ready to deliberate the awarding of diplomas to special education students under the new graduation requirements, state staff drafted language that eventually became the High School Certificate of Attendance.

State staff also acted as facilitators when the state board appointed commissions and task forces to address an issue. MSDE staff played a central role in the work of the Maryland Commission on Secondary Education. They helped coordinate meetings, find resources, bring in speakers, and draft sections of the commission's report. Although all of these tasks were in the background and were not visible to most outsiders, they were critical to building consensus at the state level about the shape of the new policy. And consensus is a key part of getting work done in Maryland education, as the political interaction model shows (see Chapter 2).

Technical Assistance and Support

"Technical assistance and support" is a general label for the major part of the work that state staff thought they were accomplishing. During

our interviews, staff offered many examples of what technical assistance and support entailed. One of their support functions was to provide a coordinated, planned perspective on policy implementation
drawn from across different divisions in MSDE. They accomplished this
by creating an informal team of staff from several divisions who met
periodically to review local concerns and build consensus for a departmental position. In the words of one participant, "I think it's been very
helpful; one of the best things we ever did was put that small committee together so we could talk these things out. At least we all knew
what the issues were."

One staff member offered an important historical perspective on
this support function. Reflecting on the state's changing influence at
the high school level, he commented:

> This past decade has moved ahead further in our high schools than pre-
> vious decades did. In previous decades, we [state] were a kind of laissez-
> faire organization, a good old boys' network. Whatever the locals
> wanted to do was okay. If you could help them in some way, do it. That
> all changed when David Hornbeck came in. The department took on a
> direction that provided leadership; it was a whole new exciting ball
> game.

The specific nature of technical assistance took many different
forms, ranging from providing leadership at meetings, convening special conferences (e.g., Maryland's Statewide Conference on the Maryland High School Toward and Beyond the Year 2000), or presenting
the state's position to local staff. As one state staff put it, "It's our job to
provide assistance as we can and support to ensure that the implementation [of state bylaws] comes about." Two other comments elaborate
further on the kind of implementation assistance that state staff provided with regard to the new graduation requirements:

> Technical assistance means we have regional meetings where we deal
> with specific recommendations, asking local people to go back and put
> them into place. Secondly, a major conference was held in which there
> were teams invited from every local school, over half the participants
> were teachers. . . . I've also been to well over half of the local school
> districts to make presentations. Many of these were done to follow up
> the first report of this research.

> I think the state has been giving information, technical assistance, and
> interpreting the bylaw. We have also offered some staff development

because we put a lot of money into one big high school conference. We also set up liaison communications to have ongoing meetings twice a year with high school directors to bring things to their attention. I have gone out and given inservices to guidance counselors. We also developed a brochure, *Graduation Requirements for Public High Schools in Maryland,* in 1988 that was small, handy, not cumbersome, with answers to questions that were most frequently asked.

Technical assistance also involved helping local districts to determine which courses qualified under different subject requirements. But assistance went far beyond merely responding to individual district requests. Indeed, state staff were involved in the development of "curricular frameworks"—broad statements that described the intent of a particular subject area requirement. These frameworks were used as guidelines to help districts in assigning courses to given disciplines (e.g., Is journalism a practical art or an English course?).

Constraints

State staff considered their technical assistance and support roles important but thought they had only limited ability to effectively assist local districts. An obvious but often overlooked constraint was their difficulty in remaining focused on a task. Once a bylaw was put into place, more often than not they went on to something new. One staff member commented:

I guess there are a number of factors that mitigate against things happening the way I would like. One is that the pendulum of education swings ever faster. No sooner had the five reports been out than we were trying to deal with other issues. Local school systems had just found it increasingly difficult to keep up with all of the new priorities, all the new reports.

Another staff member added that a lot of momentum was generated early in the process but that the state did not capitalize on it:

Initially, everyone had a lot of involvement; we had a commission with five task forces, and they involved key positions throughout the state. I think a lot of momentum went into the development of the high school study and the five task force reports, and everyone waited for the ball to be picked up further and it wasn't. I think we lost the momentum when the study was first released. When something is first released, there is

always a certain amount of attention because it's new. I think momentum capitalizes on momentum, and it's not that we shouldn't make
things better all the time, because we work to make things better all the
time via technical assistance and different types of programs and so
forth, but when you have a big study like that, you owe it to yourself to
continue the momentum and follow it through because people are pay-
ing attention and waiting and saying what does this mean.

Staff also acknowledged that the state gave little financial assistance to ensure that the recommendations took hold: "The state
never invested much money in helping at the school level to look at
the reports and try to do some planning to bring about some of the
recommendations."

Consequently, a pattern of confusion and eventually ambivalence
emerged around the state role. For their part, state staff were constrained by a larger institutional culture that dictated a hands-off position when dealing with local districts. One staff member described it
thus:

I am seeing a shift in roles. I'm a bit concerned that from one side of our
mouths we are saying there ought to be more local autonomy, there
ought to be fewer strictures (that's the key word in the report from the
recommendations) but from the other side of our mouths I see us moving toward increasing goal statements. . . . *We have never at the
state level gone into a school, except as invited by central office staff.
There has always been that line that divided what the state did and
where it acted. So, our real influence has been centrally, not at the
school level, unless in the few cases where we were asked to help at the
school level.* [emphasis added]

Another concern voiced by several state staff was the limited way
in which much of the Commission on Secondary Education's recommendations were being translated into practice. One staff member eloquently voiced his frustration over insufficient changes by stating:

I need to be positive about this because I think in the long run kids are
better served, but it's just that *I had hoped to see more movement in
certain directions than we had.* For example, we still have discrete subjects taught in isolated classrooms by faculty members who have very
little time to plan and be with teachers from other disciplines. Scheduling has eliminated much that we would like to have done. [emphasis
added]

That same person had a perceptive answer to why local educators did not respond to the requirements more creatively:

> The traditional approach to delivery that local boards have expected and the fact that they, by law, have to provide reasonably uniform approaches—"reasonably uniform" is a legal quote from the state law—so that individual schools and school staff until recently have not gone out on their own too far. I have a theory about that. There are two imaginary lines, and as long as you stay within those two imaginary lines, you have no problem. The minute you fall below expectations, there will be massive input from outside the school. The minute you go above the line, there will be massive pressure from your peers.

State staff indicated further concern about the potential impact of the requirements on the high school tracking system:

> The thing I was worried about and still worry about is: Are we making a bunch of "haves" and "have nots"? If I have an upwardly mobile family and I want my family to have the best that is offered in my school, I am going to work like heck to make sure my kid gets a Certificate of Merit. As I do that, as the school pushes toward that, how much energy will be left for those that do not have parents pushing at home, that don't have the inner discipline, or have not been trained to move on. Is there going to be enough energy in the school to give the time to work with those kids who need to be taught basic skills?

State staff also questioned whether a centrally defined policy could adequately account for the many local contextual features that determine a district's response to new mandates (see Chapter 3):

> I have a general disillusionment with the ability of the state in all areas. It is very difficult to put policy in place and have it go the way you envision it because *the locals are so different from one to the next.* . . . I don't believe the diploma you give to one school necessarily ought to be the same one you give to another. (emphasis added)

A final concern was whether the state was taking a strong enough position on key matters. Some staff feared that local districts had so much responsibility in deciding which courses qualified under which subject requirements that almost anything could qualify.

> It's been evenly split across the state. There are those local agencies that have administered the bylaw as it was written and have stood their

ground with it. There are other locals who have felt that many things should be counted—things that traditionally would not be in that area, such as the yearbook. In one local, ROTC was proposed as being a vocational area even though it doesn't fall in any vocational programs. . . . There are still mixed feelings across the state about the practical arts credit. Chairing a curricular framework committee was one of the most challenging things I had to do in my life. I literally felt like I was walking a tightrope between the two factions on the committee. . . . Every time I went to a meeting, we had a voice on one side saying we want all the flexibility and the voice on the other side saying you ought to abide by the law. One side wanted a very strict guideline about what alternatives should count, and the other wanted it very open so they could decide.

The state board added the practical arts requirement. Yet when it came time for the board to take a stand on saying what constituted an acceptable course in those four categories, the board refused, and that has continued to cause some problems.

This lack of momentum may be part of an age-old problem in policy implementation: Just because something was on the books did not mean that everyone would adhere to it. Follow-through was essential:

If there is a change I would love to see on the state level, it is the redefining of credits and the elimination of some of the hour requirements (I credit=132 clock hours) that exist—or at least providing some other alternatives and then marketing those alternatives. That's the problem that I've seen all along. There has really been very limited marketing of the five books of recommendations, and if you go back and read what those task forces and then the commission recommended, they are recommending the flexibility we are talking about. They're recommending changes in instruction. It's just that we have not marketed it well at all.

Or to sum up: "A bylaw and a report do not an implementation plan make."

In summary, we found state staff feeling that they had the potential to influence education in a constructive way. Indeed, they were quick to share concrete examples of activities they were engaged in that were having a positive effect on Maryland's students. Yet despite all that potential, there appeared to be significant impediments that often stood in the way of maximizing their roles.

DISTRICT ADMINISTRATORS' PERSPECTIVES

Administrators at the district level provided two different perspectives on their influence over policy. On one hand, they discussed local systems often moving beyond what the state required; on the other, they lamented the limitations of their control once an issue reached their level.

Proactive Stance

It should be clear by now that the five schools, each in a different district, responded differently to the new requirements. Several district administrators assumed a fairly proactive stance, with some going beyond what the letter of the law called for. In the words of one policy analyst, it's a game of one-upmanship, or "I'll see you and raise you five." For example, instead of just adding a course or two to the fine arts curriculum, one district used the opportunity to upgrade its entire fine arts curriculum:

> A decision was made at the county level not to fill requirements with just one course in fine arts. At the same time, we did not want to cause a crisis or problem in scheduling or dramatically alter curriculum/course offerings. What we did was to change the objectives of courses to match the four key objectives outlined by the state (performance, aesthetics, history, and criticism). Teachers had not really been teaching these even though it was in the curriculum. Most of the focus had been on performance. We then produced curriculum and instructional guides and trained the teachers to use them.

And administrators in this district did more than just alter the curriculum. To ensure that the new curriculum guides were being used, central office content specialists designed and delivered mini-training programs for building principals "so that they would know what to look for when they evaluated teachers of fine arts courses."

One district, which regards itself as one step ahead of the state, tried to anticipate changes in state policy and, in fact, began requiring 3 years of math a full year before the state did. Several districts had requirements that were more demanding than the state's (e.g., 22 credits, a third year of science, a foreign language, or additional certificates). As one supervisor commented, "We have our own advanced certificate. We've always had advanced courses; we are at the forefront in this area. . . . What these requirements call for, we already felt was important and had already."

Another example of district proactivity was the creation of a highly visible district steering committee to interpret and recommend local policy for dealing with the new requirements. The steering committee was divided into four groups: administration, local requirements, curriculum, and Certificate of Merit. "We identified problem areas to get smooth implementation," commented one administrator in that system.

All of the systems also reported developing and widely disseminating brochures or pamphlets that outlined the requirements. These brochures were given to students each year prior to course selection so that they at least theoretically knew what was expected of them.

A final example of districts responding in a proactive way was the record-keeping systems they developed to keep track of the requirements. These records were like alternative "report cards" for individual students. In one system, the "report card" displayed major subject areas down the left-hand side and four columns down the right: the credits required, credits earned, credits in progress, and credits needed. The Certificate of Merit courses had similar charts, with additional information about the student's grade point average. These report cards were designed to help students, counselors, and teachers to see quickly how students were progressing toward the requirements. In principle, such systems could also assist counselors, who invariably become responsible for any new record-keeping systems that affect students.

Concerns

Despite their often proactive response to the new policy initiative, district administrators also had their share of frustrations and concerns in trying to implement the requirements. Frequently, organizational constraints limited their response.

Communication was a common complaint. Although many school staff said they didn't know what was happening, central office staff said that they worked hard to get information to the building level but that often it fell on deaf ears. For example, one district administrator commented:

> The information has been given out to the principals and to the guidance counselors. But how much of this is clear to individuals is unclear. . . . I have gotten on the principals this year because *I have the feeling they aren't on this [the requirements] as much as they should be.* [emphasis added]

Central office staff acknowledged that they had limited control over instruction. Much of their contact with it was through the principal's observations of classroom teachers. There were so few curriculum specialists to go around that it was impossible for them to have significant contact with classroom teachers.

Administrators also talked about the problems of trying to fit everything into an already crowded school day. Some systems responded by adopting a seven-period day, but for others that simply wasn't economically feasible. One administrator pointed out that students in special programs are often hit the hardest:

> At one point in time, we had a seven-period day. The principal could reschedule requisite vocational courses so that students could get all the requirements in, but now we don't have room for that. There isn't room for failure for the youngsters in the vocational program. It's that tight. It's a six-period day now. We have to provide for at least fine arts for those youngsters. We have to be creative. Now it isn't easy to do. Before, we had Saturday schools or we could refer them to summer schools. A lot of things we do, we're not doing for the majority population. They are being penalized for reform aimed at a minority of students. For the vocational students, once they fail, there's no way to make it up. These extra requirements are superfluous to what the students want to do.

Although some administrators were proud of the fact that they often anticipated state actions and initiated their own requirements, simultaneous state- and local-level change created confusion:

> The state had its minimums; local systems have their own minimums. The counselors asked us to work with them at their inservice. It was utter confusion! Some counselors were working with an alpha basis (i.e., letter grades), while others were on a 0 to 100 scale. Some of the students entered in 1983/84 while others [entered in] 1984/85.

> I am bothered by the duplication of certificates. It's confusing for kids and everyone. The state needs to take a more active leadership role—I don't know how we could do that.

In a similar vein, although there was universal acknowledgment of the need for better record-keeping systems, in the larger scheme of things, a fully integrated system of records rarely moved up on the list of district priorities. As a consequence, many districts struggled with less than adequate records.

Record keeping is our weakest part. We've got records that I consider to
be in deplorable condition, and they're all kept by hand. . . . We have
not moved quickly enough to automate records management. The
counseling staff typically handle that, and they are dramatically under-
staffed.

In conclusion, like their state-level counterparts, school system
central office staff were upbeat about their potential to positively influence school improvement efforts. They were quick to credit their own
districts for outdoing the state in tightening standards. On the other
hand, the reality of constraints tempered much of that enthusiasm.
Poor communication, lack of direct control over instruction, poor
record-keeping systems, and inability to creatively schedule students
all converged and sapped much of the enthusiasm for reform.

SCHOOL ADMINISTRATORS' PERSPECTIVES

School administrators responded much the same way in their interviews. Although they were one step further removed from decision
making than their district counterparts, they were not shy about offering their views. Principals and vice principals in the five schools we
studied focused on the readiness of their districts and schools to deal
with the new requirements. At the same time, they were more than
willing to share their thoughts on how the state or their own district
had not taken full advantage of the opportunity that the policy change
presented.

System Readiness

There was a general consensus that school systems were ready for the
new policy when it took effect or were able to quickly make the necessary changes:

We were prepared at the onset for the new requirements. No major
reorganization was necessary.

The district did an excellent job preparing for the new requirements.
There were inservices and summer work examining courses to see if
they met high-level thinking skills necessary for qualification as a Certificate of Merit course.

The county has already gone to a seven-period day.

Administrators expressed some pleasure in the fact that the new requirements forced some of their teaching staff to rethink their approaches to instruction. One principal, in particular, applauded the competition that the policy encouraged: "The competition between departments is good. Anyone who sits back and tries to recruit students with the old curriculum will lose students. Each department has to make courses attractive for students."

A principal echoed district administrators by saying that little had to be done at the school because the county had already passed more stringent requirements: "The state requirements have had little impact because county requirements are either greater or more prescriptive in terms of the curriculum. . . . The requirements are not a big deal here because of high county standards."

In anticipation of the new requirements, one school decided to "semesterize electives" (the rest of the program was organized around full-year courses) to give students more options in fulfilling the fine arts and practical arts requirements. That school was also grappling with the issue of student scheduling. The principal commented, "We are looking at other schedule alternatives (e.g., modular). We are reading widely about scheduling techniques because we are so small and kids get blocked out of courses. The greater the requirements, the greater the scheduling pressure."

Failure to Take Advantage

Building administrators in the five high schools gave examples of how their systems had anticipated or were adapting to the new bylaws. Their language, however, indicated that they were primarily meeting the letter of the law. They did not mention creative responses to the mandate. Indeed, there was almost a feeling that schools had been given an opportunity to make some significant changes and that they were not taking advantage of it.

I would like to see the district build on the state requirements and require more of our students.

We have had a few state workshops and we spun around some ideas at the county, but we have not seriously addressed the problem [of adding more rigor]. We could start with Certificate of Merit and spin off to other areas. It is not too much to expect all kids to be analytic, critical problem solvers.

The regulations gave us an open door to be more flexible, but we artificially impose restrictions on kids [by using artificial tracking].

Time is the biggest disadvantage of the new requirements that can be overcome with creative changes in scheduling. This is still an untapped potential. We haven't taken advantage of this the way we should.

One administrator criticized the profession for failing to meet the needs of students: "We need to reevaluate the format of secondary education. It doesn't fit our clients. We are losing kids who are eager to be in the adult world."

The blame was not always placed on local schools. Administrators were quick to say that the state needed to be more involved in leadership:

The state hasn't done much. There's a lot of opportunity to foster critical thinking, analysis, and synthesis. It's a shame they can't be more prescriptive.

We need clarification. The state needs to say what the district is allowed to adjust and what is set. The booklet [forthcoming explanation of the requirements] will be good—a little bible to clarify some of this.

School administrators' sense of influence over changes in graduation requirements can best be summarized this way: They complied with the letter of the bylaw but fell far short of its spirit. Several were proud of the fact that their schools had weathered the storm without having to make too many accommodations. Yet whatever sense of accomplishment administrators felt was tempered by the realization that much more had to be done to strengthen instruction. Just requiring another math credit did nothing to indicate what the content for that third credit should be or the form that instruction should take.

COUNSELORS' ROLES IN SHAPING HIGH SCHOOL PATHWAYS

We now shift our focus to a level of schooling much closer to the targets of the new graduation policy: students. Our interest was in counselors' perceptions of their role in shaping students' courses and track assignments. Previous research (Cicourel & Kitsuse, 1963) has shown that counselors shape students' judgments about appropriate courses and appropriate levels of difficulty. They also shape students' expectations and aspirations in subtle and powerful ways. The analyses presented here examine how counselors viewed their work. Specifically, we asked counselors how their roles had changed with the new requirements and what they took into consideration when helping students to make course selections.

We also looked at students' perspectives on how counselors influenced their course selections. We were particularly interested in how students thought counselors would respond if students asked to undertake more difficult course work: Would they encourage, discourage, or subtly dissuade? We were also interested in how they ranked their counselors among influential people in the course-taking process: Who helped them decide what courses to take? How did they go about making those decisions? A series of questions probed this decision-making process.

Views of Counseling by Counselors

As stated earlier, we were interested in how counselors saw their roles in shaping students' high school careers, particularly in light of the stricter requirements. We asked them what role they played in interpreting the new requirements for students and whether that role had changed over the past 4 or 5 years. In response to the first question, overall, counselors described their roles as giving information and monitoring the requirements. While analyzing these data, we also uncovered two additional themes worth elaborating: The first was the notion of counselors as gatekeepers, and the second—a theme presented earlier in the chapter—was the limited influence that counselors thought they had.

Regarding the question about counselors' changing role with the new requirements, about one third of the counselors interviewed said their role had shifted so that now they do more information dissemination, one quarter mentioned increased emphasis on student record keeping, less than one third reported no change, and a small percentage pointed to increased accountability as a result of the new requirements.

THE ROLE OF INFORMATION GIVER. When describing their information-giver role, counselors emphasized the importance of the dissemination of proper information in a timely fashion. They wanted students to know about the requirements in sufficient time to meet them all, without placing undue pressure on their senior year. One remarked, "I try to get all the requirements out of the way so that the senior year can be flexible." Another described the counselor's role as "the front line—we make sure certain kids are aware of what they need from 8th through 12th grade." One counselor noted that as department chair, part of his role was articulation with middle school guidance counselors to ensure that students received full information. Several counselors also described meeting with teachers, parents, and students to disseminate information accurately. The counselor who listed these responsibilities was typical: "We review credits during registration time [and] give parents information. We spend time updating credit information. There are nighttime meetings with parents explaining the information, individual contact with students." Only one counselor thought that he had information dissemination down pat:

> Well, that has been a standard counseling role since I entered counseling. . . . My blueprint has become very firm. The kid has no margins, parents have no margins because the elite schools have additional requirements. *My blueprint is 90% done for me. I have to make sure the student follows that blueprint.* [emphasis added]

Practical arts and fine arts credits were an aspect of the new requirements that counselors indicated needed extra explaining. Several noted that students remained unsure which courses would satisfy those stipulations, often with good cause. For example, one counselor suggested:

> For the most part, kids understand the requirements. The confusion is in the practical and fine arts. The county changes the designation from time to time. Interpreting the practical arts requirement is the issue. Courses are counting as two or three things, so doing credits is difficult, for example, graphic arts is fine arts.

THE ROLE OF MONITOR AND RECORD KEEPER.   The role that counselors played in monitoring the requirements and in record keeping emerged as counselors described their responsibilities. In describing this role, one counselor said that he now spends "more time reviewing records, especially seniors. We are the keepers of the records. *Like it or not, it will be our fault if someone is halfway through the senior year and doesn't have fine arts or practical arts filled"* [emphasis added]. Others echoed his concern:

> Now we have more detail in keeping track of what students need. A lot more record keeping, but not as much as I thought it would be.

It's much more time consuming. More time with record keeping. We have to be much more careful when it comes to reviewing the records because there are so many more requirements. We need to make sure students are taking exactly what they need.

THE ROLE OF GATEKEEPER.   One aspect of the counselors' role that particularly interested us was gatekeeping. That is, if counselors influenced students' aspirations by sorting them into curricular programs or tracks, how would they describe the criteria or student characteristics they looked for in making those decisions? We asked counselors to describe what they considered when helping students to make course selections.

Several counselors mentioned ability or aptitude as a prime criterion in course selection. These were often defined as "past achievement," suggesting that the tracks into which students had already been sorted would by and large continue in their high school careers. Counselors mentioned:

Their past achievement, career goals, postsecondary educational plans, and personal interests.

Previous sibling, kid's goals, academic ability (CAT) scores, grades, teacher input, and parents.

Past academic record, future plans, likes/dislikes, teacher recommendations, and parental contact.

CAT scores, functional test scores, curriculum choices (academic, business, vocational), student interests, and special talents.

The notion of "career goal" is embedded in the criteria used to sort students into tracks. This confirms that one way students are sorted is by their vague aspirations for adult life, first expressed to high school counselors when they are age 13 or 14. One counselor placed full emphasis on this, telling us that she looked at "what they want to do when they leave high school, if we can convince them that there is a correlation, which is sometimes very difficult." Another emphasized "their abilities, aptitudes, motivation, career goals, most importantly what they need to make it in life," but tempered it with a strong academic orientation: "No matter what their goals are, I try to encourage them to take as many academic courses as possible."

Some counselors also listed considerations such as special talents, student interests, and parents' recommendations as the determiners of course placements. Usually, however, these were mentioned after ability-linked criteria and career goals.

LACK OF INFLUENCE.   One consistent theme we found in interviews with counselors was the lack of substantial influence over the decision-making process. Counselors often mentioned that students' paths were fixed already, that all they did was plug students into a prescribed set, or that others usurped their authority in truly advising students. This is most interesting in light of students' views of counselors as advisors and helpers (discussed next).

For example, in discussing his lack of influence over shaping students' learning experiences, one counselor noted that the "departments make lots of decisions. There's lots of pressure on teachers to get kids to succeed. Teachers try not to put kids in the wrong place." In fact, this counselor went on to assert, "We just put them where they [the teachers] say." Another counselor felt much the same, saying, "Now the teachers all make recommendations about what the student should take next year," and although parents had ultimate authority, "a teacher will intervene if he or she doesn't like what the student has signed up for." Still another bemoaned the lack of influence on the selection process: "The parents place kids in Certificate of Merit. They may hop around in the first 2 years, then move out. *It's been taken away from us as counselors* because people have taken it upon themselves to make decisions about the Certificate of Merit or not" (emphasis added). He then went on to describe how the process of articulation with the middle school further eroded counselors' professional judgments:

> We send a list back to eighth grade; we ask them if we've made the proper selections. We don't know those kids at all. Kids are picking and choosing—one Certificate of Merit in English, not in another. I don't like that. We give too many choices to kids. If the student is in Certificate of Merit in English, (s)he should be in Certificate of Merit in world geography. *The kids do all the selecting—we don't have any control over that.* [emphasis added]

The overall picture was two-dimensional. On one hand, some counselors reported having a great deal of influence (as the "first line" or the "most important") on students' course selections and, by implication, their high school careers and even beyond. On the other hand, counselors thought of themselves as "constrained decisionmakers" (Conley, 1988) in their work. That is, the requirements constrained student choices (the "blueprint" was not that flexible), students' past records constrained appropriate options, and the schedule constrained choice even further, suggesting counseling functions that were little more than scheduling, monitoring, and paper pushing.

We turn now to a discussion of how students viewed their counselors' role and of the influence that counselors had on shaping students' course selections and high school careers. Students tended to describe a more varied and rich set of roles for counselors than counselors presented to us.

Views of Counselors by Students

As mentioned earlier, academic grouping, or tracking, has been a persistent focus throughout our analysis. In Chapter 4, our analyses indicated that the notion of track is at times unstable and ambiguous—that is, many students have to be categorized as being in a "mixed" track, taking some general courses, some college preparatory, and some business, for example. Thus, assigning students to any particular track became difficult. Nevertheless, we asked school personnel to schedule interviews with students from all the major tracks (typically honors, college preparatory, general, and vocational/business; at United Nations, we added a "magnet" track) so that we could talk to a reasonable distribution of students. Given the vicissitudes of student inattention, absence, and reluctance to be interviewed, however, interview samples varied across the five high schools.

At Fast Track, we interviewed more college preparatory and general track students than either honors or vocational/business students. At United Nations, we spoke with more college preparatory and general students than with students from any other category. At Urban, most of the students we spoke with were in the vocational/business track; almost none were from the honors track. At Middle Class, we talked with more honors and general students than either college preparatory or special education students. And finally, at Rural, we interviewed more college preparatory students than students in any other category. Given these differences and given that our data do not lend themselves to quantitative analysis, we offer the following themes and patterns in students' views of their counselors. In some cases, academic track seemed to make a difference; where so, we indicate. In most cases, however, academic track made no difference.

We found three major themes in students' views of their counselors. These were (1) counselors who gave support, encouragement, or were particularly responsive to a variety of student needs; (2) counselors who were information givers who disseminated information about courses and requirements but served no other role; and (3) counselors who were functionaries who were unavailable, uninterested, or unknown. Students also described some counselors as discouraging, controlling, or inflexible, but this was not very common.

The weight given to each role was determined by a simple tally of student responses from each track in each school. Overall, students found their counselors to be good information givers or supportive much more than they found them to be uninterested or unavailable.

SUPPORTING AND ENCOURAGING ACADEMIC DECISIONS.   At times, students waxed eloquent in describing counselors who served as their advisors in the fullest sense of the word. These individuals were seen as supportive, helpful, and encouraging. They challenged students to take on more rigorous course work. Some students even likened their counselor to a parent—someone supportive who was always there for them. In discussing help and support in developing post–high school plans, one student told us, "He takes a lot of time. He doesn't make decisions for you—gives us alternatives. He's helped a lot, especially in the senior year with college searches, scholarship searches. I wouldn't know anything about these things if it weren't for him." Another referred not only to her counselor's assistance with college applications but also to help in overcoming barriers of being a non-native English speaker: "He helps me choose the courses I need, financial aid for college, scheduling. He helped me find someone who talked my language when I first came here and helped me learn English." Others talked about how their counselors encouraged them to take on more challenges, not to slack off, and to try for more:

> He pushed me—tried to keep me in Magnet. He didn't want me to get lazy.

> He's everything—advisor on academics, home life. He looks out for us— makes us put our nose to the grindstone, get our work done.

> He tells me what I need, and I tell him what I like. He encourages me to take the harder courses and not slack off.

One student told us that her counselor was "like a mother sometimes"; another said, "She's like a sister and a mother to me." Describing how important her counselor was in the decision-making process, yet another student told us, "She's right behind my mom. She called

me down about my credit check. She's caring and anxious for me."
Counselors were also characterized as helpful. One linked being moth-
erlike with being helpful, telling us, "[my counselor] is like a mother to
me. She is very helpful. She has helped me solve a problem." Others
corroborated their counselors' helpfulness:

> He has the biggest job, between the principal and vice principal. He's
> friendly—always around when you need someone to talk to.

> He helps, a good friend, and is honest to tell you if you should or
> shouldn't take the course you're planning on taking.

> When I have a problem, he is really helpful. He always seems like he has
> time for you.

Another way students characterized their counselors was as providing support of a more general kind with all sorts of problems. One
described how "he knows all the students personally. He's like a doc-
tor—you tell him what your problems are, and he gives you a prescription—what you need." Another described this general helping
role as follows:

> I will see her every now and then concerning an issue. If she thinks you
> are capable, she supports you. Even if you have your mind made up
> about something, she will still support you. She gives me information
> and tells me that she will always be there for me. She is the tiebreaker
> between me and my family on personal and school-related matters. I go
> to the counselor a lot, whenever I have a problem with anything.

Finally, the remarks of a young woman sum up this kind of counselor. She told us that her counselor was "kind of like an alarm clock,
a year-long alarm clock. My counselor is wonderful."

THE INFORMATION GIVER.   When we asked students who participated in
deciding which courses they should take, we specifically wanted to
know about the role that counselors played and how students saw that
role. We were also interested in whether information flowed in a
timely manner from the counselor regarding the new requirements
and the Certificate of Merit. Many students responded by describing
their counselors' role as being exclusively that of an information giver.
Typically, counselors would tell students what courses they needed
and what classes were available, check credits earned against credits

required, change courses for them, and generally oversee the administrative aspects of ensuring that all requirements were met. In some
cases, this was viewed as a good thing; in others, it was not. Typical
responses from students who thought it was all right were:

> She'd take care of the administrative tasks of setting up my courses and
> what teachers.

> He helped find courses by going through the credits, scheduling it all in.
> He was real helpful.

> She tells me what classes are available, what periods, what requirements
> are needed, adjusts schedules so I can get in the class.

> He helps make sure I'm taking all the classes I should to get the Certifi-
> cate of Merit and keeps an eye on my grades.

> She looks on the requirements sheet and lays out the options. She lets
> me decide first, and then she challenges me.

> If I don't like a class, he'll change it. He keeps track of credits. He asked
> what certificate I wanted and then reinforced that I was on track. He did
> not recommend any new classes.

Students who viewed this role with some concern said:

> Someone who recommends classes for me. Not a person who can really
> help me.

> She helps me with requirements. I don't come to her a lot. I don't need
> to.

> Scheduling, changes. I've never been to the counselor with a problem.

> The counselor told me what I needed, and I went from there.

Thus, nearly one third of the students whose interviews were cod-
able on these questions suggested that their counselor was there primarily to do record keeping. They described how the counselor kept
track, checked credits, advised about needed courses, ensured proper
sequences of classes, and performed similar administrative duties. For

many, this was all they expected; for others, there was disdain in their voice as they dismissed these administrative activities.

UNAVAILABLE AND UNINTERESTED.   Finally, some students saw their counselors as being unavailable and/or uninterested in them. One depicted his counselor as being a mere functionary but assured us that he really didn't mind: "She's merely a processor. She hasn't gotten involved with anything. I don't mind; I'm sort of glad." Others said, "They write on the board and tell you what to pick. They gave a list to students to carry around and turn in later. It makes you do whatever the person next to you does. Not one on one." Several attributed their counselor's inaccessibility to the lack of time:

I hardly ever talk to my counselor. They are always busy—you have to make an appointment, and it takes so long.

School counselors don't have a lot of time for their students. She's played very little role.

I don't see him much. They are [so] overwhelmed with paperwork that they don't have time for us.

Whether the fault of the counselor or the timidity of the student, many students appeared to have little contact with their counselors. Typical comments from these students were:

I don't see my counselor that much.

Up until last year, I did not know my counselor.

I haven't talked to the counselor more than three times since I've been here.

I've never really talked to him; I don't know.

To these students, the counselor was someone in the school who expedited certain administrative duties but had little interest in them or time to spend with them.

Quite naturally but disturbing nonetheless, some students described personal conflicts with their counselors: "My counselor gets on my nerves—good person, bad counselor." Somewhat more gentle was the student who told us, "Sometimes he's not the biggest help; there's nothing he can do sometimes. I've had some problems with him about getting into colleges." And one student hinted at conflict between the counselor, himself, and his parents when he described, "He helps with schedules and college. If you want something you have to ask him three or four times. My parents have complained." Another noted conflict over the value of course work: "She tries, but because I'm interested in business, she wasn't as interested. Business is second class to academics."

A young woman summed up this perspective of the counselor as an uninterested functionary, telling us: "I haven't had a good experience. I'm too far ahead of her. I like to be in control of my life. No one needs to change my diapers."

DISCOURAGING, INFLEXIBLE, OR CONTROLLING. We found that a small proportion of students saw their counselors as actively discouraging them from certain courses or as being inflexible or unnecessarily controlling. Several described having their course selections or preferences overruled, overridden, or disregarded by counselors. Again, they were eloquent:

> The counselor didn't give me any support. I failed pre-algebra in eighth grade—I knew I wouldn't pass Algebra I. She said, "I'm not taking you out; you can do it." I said I still wouldn't understand. There was a whole conflict, and I brought my parents in. I failed the first test in the course and finally got out to take applied math III.

> The counselor has no role. I saw the counselor only in the office; she doesn't provide any help. She doesn't help me at all. They lost my records when I came to the school and said I did not pass the writing test. They took me out of all honors classes because of this. I passed the test.

> I'm taking geometry for the second time. I wanted applied math 2, but they wouldn't let me take it because I passed the Maryland Functional Math test and applied math is only for people who didn't pass. Now I'm in danger of failing again. I talked to the counselor and head of the math department to get into applied math and both said no.

> I try to stay away from her. I don't get along with her at all. When I think a class is too hard for me and I put in a request, she left me in it. There was conflict.

He's not influenced me a lot. He gave me the graduation requirements and said, "Here—choose your courses." I chose them on my own. They really haven't helped me that much. As far as finding colleges, he said in my junior year that I was looking too early.

Others described their counselors as discouraging them from taking more rigorous or advanced classes. Sometimes this was linked to race. One student maintained: "They put blacks and Hispanics in stupid classes. There's a lack of expectations. The counselor is not good—he just signed off. I bother him almost every day."

CONCLUSION

In conclusion, students offered both positive and negative portraits of counselors. On the positive side, they saw their counselor as a supportive person who backed them up in academic decision areas and went out of his or her way to encourage students to stretch as far as they could. Positive counselors also offered useful information about future course and career options. The less flattering picture was of the counselor who showed little interest and was rarely available to assist students. In the rare case, this manifested itself in behavior that was discouraging and very controlling of students' options.

The perspectives of state department of education staff, district- and building-level administrators, and counselors and students suggest that shaping students' pathways through high school was a terribly complex process. Because of the institutional climate and competing demands on time, policies articulated at the state level received insufficient attention to be fully implemented. Likewise, district and school constraints inhibited full attention to policy requirements, except to conform to the letter of those requirements. Counselors, in turn, viewed themselves as becoming increasingly functionaries who process papers and record credits earned. The more substantive work of advising and challenging students often seemed lost in the press to ensure that the minimal number of credits was met. Students reflected these views, although some felt fully advised in selecting their courses.

It seems likely that this *influence vacuum* is typical of state policy-making and the implementation process. Each set of actors works within what we describe as a fragmented, fluid, and pressured policy arena. Demands for reform come and go, with little monitoring or oversight. The state's lack of sustained attention to a broader vision of educational reform promotes minimal compliance at the district and school levels. This is consistent with the effects of mandated reform, where laws and regulations promote a *pro forma* response by local agencies.

Within the influence vacuum, however, changes did occur. With increased exposure to certain courses, students would likely graduate from high school better prepared in those areas. The intent of the graduation requirements reform, although not fully realized, might be noticeable to those who receive students after graduation: colleges and universities and employers. We turn next to a discussion of the intentions of policymakers complemented by views about how fully those intents were achieved.

7

WHAT'S THE BOTTOM LINE?
POLICY INTENTIONS AND THE
PERCEPTIONS OF EFFECTS

The promulgation of policy is intended to mandate that an agency or individuals change their behavior or entice them to do so. These "intuitive causal models" are embedded in the specifics of a reform. In the case of graduation requirements reform, the causal model was that with increased course taking in required areas, students would be better prepared for their postsecondary experiences whether these were college, work, or service. As McDonnell (1988) found, however, there is little monitoring of either the implementation of the required reform or its outcomes. Scant attention is paid to whether the causal model works.

In this chapter, we explore the causal models operating when reform of the high school curriculum was debated. We describe policymakers' intent in altering the graduation requirements and discuss whether their intent was realized. The first section deals with the intent of the policy as expressed in interviews with members of the Maryland Commission on Secondary Education (the group charged with recommending policy changes) and in the commission's written materials. The second section describes local educators' views on whether the intended effects took place. The final section discusses the

extent to which the policy intent was realized, as perceived by consumers of the high school product: colleges and local employers.

POLICY INTENTIONS

State Superintendent David Hornbeck appointed the Maryland Commission on Secondary Education in June 1982. The 23-member commission was made up of Maryland school superintendents, deputy and
assistant superintendents, teachers, school board members, principals,
a director of secondary education, a university professor, and community leaders. The commission impaneled task forces and charged them
with preparing recommendations for graduation requirements and
alternative diploma options, as well as studying a variety of other
areas, including curriculum, student services and activities, instruc-
tion/instructional support services, school climate, and school administration. In November of 1983, the commission submitted *Recommendations of the Maryland Commission on Secondary Education. Volume I:
Graduation Requirements* (Maryland State Department of Education,
1983) to the superintendent. The commission produced four additional reports, but these had little to do with the bylaw that changed
the graduation requirements.

We interviewed five Maryland Commission on Secondary Education members and seven Maryland State Department of Education staff
to solicit their views on the intentions that drove the policy changes.
The five commission members were chosen as representative of the
diverse membership and as knowledgeable of policy-making in the
state.

We selected seven Maryland State Department of Education staff
because of their expertise in the areas affected by the requirements, as
well as their role in establishing the graduation requirements and facilitating their interpretation at the local level. The interviews lasted from
1 to 2 hours and explored the political climate at the time of the policy
change, the process by which changes were deliberated, and the history behind the recommendations.

Volume I, the first of five published reports submitted by the commission, outlined the mission of the public high school in Maryland as
one to "challenge and help students to grow intellectually, personally,
and socially." However, equally explicit in focusing that mission was:
"The primary responsibility of the public high school is to promote the
intellectual growth of its students" (emphasis added). A state department respondent reiterated that mission, stating, "Our primary goal

was the academic learning of kids. Personal or individual growth, we'll deal with, but that's not our main purpose." As defined in the commission's report, intellectual growth "includes the ability to reason, to imagine, to value, and to decide."

Of the 12 commission members and state department staff interviewed, 10 agreed that the purpose of the policy was to raise standards. Five interviewees used those words exactly, and five expressed it in various other ways: "increasing the quality of courses and raising the level of difficulty to make it more challenging"; "creating higher expectations and more incentives for exemplary work"; "squeezing the bullishness out of school"; and "getting students to choose a more strenuous high school academic program." One respondent did not address the issue of policy intent, and another (who did not mention higher standards) stated that the policy was aimed at creating "a more balanced curriculum." The remainder would most likely have concurred with the interviewee who told us, "Everybody from the outset was along the lines of higher expectations, higher standards, more requirements, and more incentives to exemplary work."

This dialogue about raising standards did not occur in a vacuum. "The raising of standards became a necessary agenda item and perhaps the highest agenda item. On that point, I think we were affected by the national attacks," pointed out a commission member. A state department employee echoed this, saying, "The reform movement hitting the nation at the time, the one in which accountability was being stressed" was the impetus for the change in requirements. We heard little about the third credit in mathematics and assumed that its value was universally accepted. General consensus about its efficacy in raising standards, along with the fact that many other states had a similar requirement, made this policy feature noncontroversial.

The desire to raise standards was most clearly the driving force behind the creation of the Certificate of Merit, but a second reason was to develop a mechanism by which to recognize student achievement. According to *Graduation Requirements for Public High Schools in Maryland* (Maryland State Department of Education, 1988), a booklet that summarized the new policy initiative, the Certificate of Merit was "designed to *encourage* as many high school students as possible to pursue more challenging programs and to *reward* students who successfully pursue more challenging programs." One respondent reiterated this by stating that the Certificate of Merit was intended "to recognize those kids who were going beyond those minimums that we identified." This respondent also alluded to the certificate as an incentive, calling it a "carrot."

In addition to the intent to raise standards, there was also a belief that students should be exposed to a broader range of course offerings. This was enacted through the addition of both a fine and practical arts credit, as well as the requirement that students enroll in at least four credits during their senior year. The issues of a practical arts credit and a four-credit senior year were fraught with political complications. Both commission members and state department staff criticized the original conceptualization and implementation of the practical arts credit. Although not recommended by the commission, this credit was included by the state board (the group with formal authority to make policy changes) because of "pressure from constituencies" and a board member with a vested interest in the subject. A commission member who was displeased with the addition of this requirement noted, "the only saving grace, though I think it's absolutely absurd, is computer work counts as a vocational education course. Now that sounds like a compromise if I've ever heard one." The political compromise finally struck placed a wide range of eligible courses under the label of practical arts, including business, vocational, home economics, and computer subjects. This diversity created real confusion in schools about what did or did not count as a practical arts credit. Indeed, the propriety of computer courses satisfying the practical arts requirement was different across districts and caused one state department staff member to comment that she receives "more questions about the practical arts than anything else." She is continually asked, "Can we count this course as a practical arts requirement?"

The stipulation that seniors enroll in at least four credits was also a political headache for those overseeing its implementation. The reason for this requirement, according to *Graduation Requirements for Public High Schools in Maryland* (Maryland State Department of Education, 1988), was "to ensure a strong senior year that prepares students well for the next step into work or study, citizenship or personal life." One respondent explained:

> Complaints were coming into the state department saying that the senior year was so weak and watered down that something needed to be done immediately. There was one system in the state where half of the senior class left at noon; most received waivers to go out and work. A number of students were approaching their senior year needing only one or two credits, and there have been increases in the numbers of students taking those courses in the summer of their junior year and skipping senior year altogether.

This four-credit senior year requirement created more difficulties for state department staff than any other requirement. The problem was with students who had met all the other requirements but could not receive a diploma. Take, for example, the high-achieving, highly motivated student who wanted to go on to college after her junior year. She had met all the college entrance requirements but could not afford to enroll without financial assistance. The dilemma was that scholarship assistance was predicated on a high school diploma and that the diploma could not be granted until she had completed 1 more year of high school.

Although commission members and state department staff talked about the state as a whole, throughout the interviews the message was clear that what applied in some school districts did not necessarily apply in others. There was a great deal of diversity across the state. "If there was anything I came away with, it was a realization of the great diversity of the state, for better or worse. Certain school districts have to cope with a hell of a lot less resources than others," commented one person interviewed.

These interviews and our review of the documents show that the commission and the state department had explicit intentions in establishing the new high school graduation requirements. These focused primarily on raising standards for students and exposing them to more diverse content. The purpose of the Certificate of Merit was to encourage more academic rigor and install a vehicle for recognizing students who earned it. The intent of the practical and fine arts credits, as well as the four credits during the senior year, was to increase students' exposure to a broader range of the curriculum, although in the case of the practical arts requirement, its inclusion in the policy was embedded in larger political issues such as the survival of specific content areas. In the next section, we explore where local educators believed those policy intents were met.

SCHOOL-LEVEL PERCEPTIONS OF POLICY EFFECTS

To determine whether these policy intents were being realized, we interviewed approximately 650 teachers, counselors, administrators, and students across the five schools on two separate occasions: 1988 and again in 1990. The interviews were based on open-ended questions about the graduation requirements and the Certificate of Merit and their effects. Overall, respondents talked about improvements in student outcomes as a result of the requirements. The improvements they described sort into four themes: higher standards, increased exposure to curriculum, a more well-rounded education, and more planful course selections. Each is discussed in the following.

Raised Standards

The primary benefits of the new policy, according to teachers, counselors, and administrators, were higher standards and higher expectations for students. Specifically, the new requirements were to "raise the expectations of students and motivate them" and "help let students know that education is serious business." One teacher at Urban told us, "I look at it [raised standards] as positive, because if you leave it up to kids they will take the path of least resistance." A teacher at Fast Track reinforced this: "It is forcing students to use their time in a more meaningful way. There is not as much of an opportunity for them to put in their time and be dead wood. They are going to learn in spite of themselves."

Students confirmed this assessment. When asked if they had received an adequate academic education at their schools and if the graduation requirements had contributed to this, higher standards reasserted themselves in a variety of ways:

> The requirements made me push myself further.

> If I didn't have to take the requirements, I would have taken all electives. If English was not required for 4 years, then people around here would be stupid.

> If it was not required, more people would take electives just to get them by.

> If not for the requirements, people would be taking seven periods of gym; they'd be playing around too much.

Although standards were raised for most students, they were not necessarily raised for all of them. We heard, "If kids could graduate with one subject failed, they'd fail that subject. Now we've raised the level, and they are working up to it. But the kids who *were* going down the tubes *are still* going down the tubes." Certain subgroups of students received the full benefits of the new requirements: "the 25% of the students at the top," "the 18% going on to college," and the "college-type kids." For other groups of students, the requirements were perceived as detrimental. As one United Nations teacher stated, "I approve of the new requirements, but they have had a negative effect on low-SES/broken-family students where more pressure brings lower motivation." And one school administrator said, "In the area of student activity and performance, the jury is still out. Some kids haven't made the adjustment well to higher expectations."

Although most teachers, counselors, and administrators agreed that students were better off as a result of the requirements, most also thought the requirements did not go far enough. Several respondents commented, "I'm all for it, but it's not enough. There are more things needed. This is not a panacea" and "We're on the right road to being better off. The country needs stricter requirements." Another stated, "I hope it doesn't stop where it is now. I can see realistic requirements in the future in computers, additional science, even a ninth-grade citizenship component."

Increased Exposure to Curriculum

Local educators consistently remarked that students were being exposed to a broader curriculum as a result of the new requirements. Mainly, this was accomplished by "more kids signing up for classes they wouldn't have before," mostly in the areas of practical arts and fine arts. For instance, one technical education teacher stated, "Kids have been exposed to our program who wouldn't have taken it otherwise" and "Kids are able to explore areas, such as practical arts, that they might have avoided. The academic kids never made time for it; now they need it." Another teacher personalized the experience: "I wish someone had made fine arts and practical arts required for me. I'm sure I would never have set foot in some places if I was not forced to do it."

Some felt that increasing students' exposure to fine arts was a particularly good idea: "Music is a big curriculum that kids wouldn't take unless they had to." And one art teacher said, "If they didn't have to take a fine arts course, I probably wouldn't ever see them in our classes." In short, teachers, administrators, and counselors supported the fine arts requirement because, as one of them said, "If we don't expose students to art in high school, I don't know where they are going to get it."

Students affirmed the value of this increased exposure to new curriculum areas. Commenting on the impact of the requirements on their education, they remarked, "They forced me to take classes I needed; I learned that science is fun" and "The requirements made me take classes I didn't want to take, but I knew they would be best for me."

A More Well-Rounded Education

One effect of increased exposure to curriculum is that students received a more well-rounded education. When teachers, counselors, and administrators were asked if they thought that students' awareness was more well rounded as a result of the new graduation requirements, most agreed strongly that it was. Only administrators were divided on the issue. Respondents attributed this improvement to the new requirements in general and to the fine arts requirement in particular. Several educators commented, "The graduation requirements have provided a little more rigor and better balance to the overall course of study" and "Kids in the end are better off if for no other reason than they are more well rounded." Regarding fine arts, they stated, "It will make students more well rounded" and "I'm glad art is a requirement because kids need a broader background."

Students concurred. In response to the question about the adequacy of their education and the contribution the graduation requirements made to this, they reflected on becoming more well rounded and balanced:

You're a little bit educated in every little thing when you leave here.

The requirements encouraged me to become more well rounded because I have had to take a variety of courses. I couldn't narrow my options. It opened my mind to a lot of opportunities.

It helps better suit you for society. Without them, I would have taken all science. It made me more well rounded.

Students did not become more well rounded simply with the onset of a new policy, however. Each school had to reassess its organizational practices to integrate the new requirements effectively. At Fast Track, for instance, a seven-period day was implemented to make room for the new requirements in student schedules. One Fast Track teacher hailed the seven-period day as the key to "students taking more of a variety of courses." Without the extra period, it would have been difficult for students to have taken the extra courses needed in order to graduate. The seventh period "allows students to take more of a variety, to take fun courses, to explore themselves in a different manner." This teacher continued: "I saw algebra students on stage singing; it was wonderful to see that side of them."

But respondents also had some concerns and reservations about the requirements, particularly as to whether they had become perfunctory. They wondered if students were internalizing the additional content or if they were just going through the motions and earning the credit. One teacher worried, "Students who take a course only for credit don't get anything out of it," and another affirmed the point, saying, "Students are taking these classes because they have to, so they're just passing. They are not learning as much."

More Planful Course Selections

About half of the teachers and counselors we interviewed believed that students had become more careful planners as a result of the new policy. There was little consensus among administrators, however, about whether this was so. Taking obvious pride in the centrality of their role, guidance counselors attributed most of students' increased planning to their own work. For example:

> We counselors are more planful. It may be a detriment to kids because we are forcing them to get the basics out of [the] way first.

> We've done some things—we start preplanning by having the counselor sit with them and plan out 4 years.

> Then they plan the next year. They used to say they'll sign up for anything and change it in the fall; we don't allow that anymore.

Several of the schools reportedly changed the guidance strategies used to help students plan, but there were instances in which guidance counselors were accused of doing all the planning for students. This suggests that it wasn't always that students were becoming better planners; it may well have been that they were becoming more planned for. One interviewee put it this way: "For a lot of students, guidance does it all for them."

This planning applied to parents as well, particularly at Fast Track. One teacher sought clarification to the question "Are students becoming more planful?" by asking, "Students or their parents? Both seem to be." And with reference to the Certificate of Merit, a Fast Track teacher stated, "Now when students come into grade 9, many have their 4-

year schedule all worked out. When eighth-grade parents come in, they have, along with students, everything figured out." Another teacher recounted how the parent of an eighth-grader solicited the teacher's advice about course taking for the student's senior year. He said, "My son has an opening his senior year—what course in your department should he take?" Students also might have become more careful in selecting courses merely because of the increased requirements and the attendant need to be sure they met them. With less freedom and leeway in selecting courses, they had to pay strict attention to their programs of study.

In conclusion, educators in Maryland viewed the graduation requirements policy as beneficial to students for several reasons. First, the higher standards satisfied one major policy intent. Students felt more challenged as a result of the new requirements, but not all students agreed. Several respondents suggested that the requirements were advantageous for those who were already succeeding and a hindrance to those who were not. And school-level personnel agreed that although the requirements were valuable in certain ways, they did not go far enough. These educators also believed that students were exposed to curriculum areas they might otherwise have bypassed. In particular, they singled out the fine arts and practical arts. Students were also becoming more well rounded, teachers and counselors maintained. Some schools reassessed various organizational practices, such as the number of periods in a day, to promote this process. There was general agreement that students were becoming more planful, largely attributed to revised guidance practices. In short, school-level educators and students perceived some positive changes; however, none of these changes was overwhelmingly powerful.

CONSUMER PERCEPTIONS OF EFFECTS

Although the new graduation requirements policy was intended to raise standards, this intent was not directly linked to post-high school outcomes: The policy did not specify what benefit higher standards would give students once they graduated. Although we learned that the policy affected students in several different ways while still in school, we also wanted to determine if these effects continued beyond graduation.

Because students' next steps after high school are usually employment or college, we conducted a series of interviews with admissions representatives from community colleges, 4-year colleges and universities, and employers in the vicinity of the five high schools in the study. We viewed employers and higher education institutions as the primary consumers of the "product" of this policy change—that product being an enhanced high school graduate. We focused our questions on the consumers' awareness of graduation requirements, knowledge and importance of the Certificate of Merit, and any differences noted in cohorts of students prior to and after implementation of the new graduation requirements. A complete description of those protocols can be found in the Appendix of the technical report on Maryland's graduation requirements (Wilson, Rossman, & Adduci, 1991).

Colleges and Universities

We conducted telephone interviews with admissions officials from 14 four-year colleges and universities and 9 community colleges in the state of Maryland. The institutions were chosen based on the following criteria: rate of attendance by graduates of the five schools in the study, percentage of students who were Maryland residents, geographical representation, and school academic competitiveness. The analysis focused on the level of respondents' knowledge about the new graduation requirements and their views on the impact and degree of importance of these new requirements.

CRITERIA USED IN ADMISSIONS. During the interviews, we determined the criteria used by 4-year colleges and universities to admit students, reasoning that these indicate the importance of various courses to the admissions process, whether in a particular curriculum area, such as fine arts, or at a certain academic level, such as Certificate of Merit or honors. The majority of college and university representatives indicated that grade point average (GPA) and Scholastic Aptitude Test (SAT) scores far surpassed any other criterion for admission. The high school record was the first priority: "We figure out a GPA for each student only in academic subjects [i.e., foreign language, English, science, math, and social studies]" and "We are interested in whether the courses the student is taking are Certificate of Merit, honors, or gifted and talented." The second priority was performance on the SAT, which was becoming increasingly important.

The practice of calculating an "academic GPA" excluded consideration of fine arts and practical arts courses by a large majority of 4-year colleges and universities. Most officials made a substantial distinction between the third-year math credit and the fine and practical arts when discussing the new graduation requirements. The extra credit in math took precedence over the credits in fine and practical arts in admissions decisions:

> The additional math credit helps because we look primarily at GPA and SAT scores. The fine arts and practical arts wouldn't really matter—we are looking for a well-rounded student so it *wouldn't hurt,* but our primary concern is the GPA, SAT, and core courses.

> The practical arts and fine arts don't matter because we never consider it. But the third year of math is important.

> The fine arts and practical arts unfortunately have no bearing. They aren't included in the academic GPA. But the math requirement has very much impacted on the applicant pool. It has helped us with raising admissions standards. Now we have more qualified students applying.

> Students are more prepared in math, definitely in math. The other two—fine arts and practical arts—wouldn't matter. When we evaluate transcripts, we only evaluate college prep courses so those courses [fine arts and practical arts] would be thrown out. They have no effect at all on any decisions we make.

> We were told [by college officials] that if a student is taking an arts class, *don't hold it against them* because it is a new requirement.

KNOWLEDGE OF THE REQUIREMENTS. Of the 14 four-year college and university officers, only 2 could list the new requirements specifically; 5 had no knowledge of them whatsoever. Seven were somewhat aware of these requirements. As one respondent stated, "The new requirements were brought up at a meeting, but we weren't given anything in detail."

The community college respondents were much more aware of the requirements. Eight knew what the graduation requirements in Maryland were, and none were unaware that they were new. Only one respondent did not know about the specifics of the requirements. This increased awareness by community college representatives may reflect the fact that minimum competencies are of greater importance in their admissions process.

IMPACT OF REQUIREMENTS ON APPLICANT POOL. Given the lack of detailed knowledge about the requirements, assessments of impact must be interpreted cautiously. However, this did not discourage those interviewed from passing judgment. When asked if the new requirements had any impact on the school's applicant pool over the past 2 years, one fifth of the 4-year institutions' respondents saw no difference. For some schools, other factors carried more weight than the new high school graduation requirements. For instance, six had recently entered the University of Maryland admissions system, which meant their own requirements had increased: Students were required to have three math credits (algebra I, algebra II, and geometry) in order to gain admittance into state colleges and universities. Admissions staff were therefore unable to tell if a school's applicant pool had been impacted by the high school graduation requirements or by the college's own new admission requirements.

Over half of the admissions officials from community colleges stated that the graduation requirements had no impact on their applicant pool. The remainder felt that their applicant pool had changed over the past few years; they could not, however, directly attribute the change to the new requirements. One official said the improved applicants were a result of increased excellence standards at that particular college. Another stated, "There has been an increase in those entering higher education over the past 12 years. This is due to an increase in socioeconomic status [of the applicant pool]."

One third of the 4-year institution representatives stated that the new requirements did make a difference in areas such as entrance exam scores (the math section of the SAT) and students' "well roundedness." This was most apparent in less competitive institutions, where all three officials stated that the requirements helped prepare high school students for college. Another third of the 4-year institution representatives stated that the requirements made somewhat of a difference. An extra math course couldn't hurt, they said, but the practical and fine arts courses did not matter.

About a third of the 4-year college and university representatives believed that the new requirements made no difference in student preparedness. Two of these officials represented schools ranked as most competitive and said they saw no difference because their applicants usually take these classes (particularly math) anyway; practical arts and fine arts were not an important consideration in their admissions decision. In contrast, at the community colleges, none of the admissions representatives thought that students were better prepared academically as a result of the new graduation requirements.

KNOWLEDGE OF THE CERTIFICATE OF MERIT. Nearly half of the 4-year college and university representatives knew something about the Certificate of Merit; none, however, knew its specifics. One said, "If students do well in high school, they have a strong GPA, and [their] SAT scores are good, they receive a certificate at the end of the year." Revealing a lack of information about the Certificate of Merit, another noted, "a student brought it up in the interview, and I had never heard of it before. I wanted to put it in the category of honors or AP [advanced placement], and she kept saying no, that's not what it is. I came back and asked the dean of admissions if he had heard about it. He had, but just in vague terms." Still another official thought students earned the Certificate of Merit for excellent or perfect attendance. Although all of these respondents stated that they knew what the Certificate of Merit was, they were vague as to the specifics.

Of the nine community college respondents, five had heard of the Certificate of Merit, but they, too, were vague about the specifics, referring to it as "an honors program for high school students" and a "new system whereby students can graduate by taking a certain number of advanced courses." Like their colleagues in 4-year colleges, none of the community college respondents had detailed knowledge of the Certificate of Merit.

Respondents frequently attributed their lack of knowledge about the Certificate of Merit to the fact that it was not always marked on student transcripts. One admissions officer commented, "In certain counties, the Certificate of Merit was listed right on the transcript; in others, no. It doesn't make any difference in admissions decisions because we never knew what it was." Similarly, another college representative stated, "I can't tell [when looking at the transcript]; if I could, we would try to take that into consideration." For community colleges, often the final transcript goes to the records department and is not even seen by the admissions representative. One community college representative said, "Many times, the way the transcript is printed, it is difficult to tell what level the student is in."

The majority of admissions officials from both 4-year and community colleges who were somewhat familiar with the Certificate of Merit learned of it from sources other than the Maryland State Department of Education. Four officials heard about it from high school administrators, at meetings, and through personal relationships. Another four became aware of it by processing transcripts. One stated, "I found out through processing the transcripts and asking what the Certificate of Merit designation was as it showed up on the transcript." Two officials became aware of it through high school profiles sent to the college, another two had been notified of it by their own children's schools, and one heard of it during an interview with a student.

USE OF THE CERTIFICATE OF MERIT IN ADMISSIONS DECISIONS.   Over three fourths of the 4-year college and university representatives said they did not consider the Certificate of Merit when admitting students. One admissions official commented: "We expect all students to follow a college prep course of study anyway, and that's what the Certificate of Merit would encompass." Those who did consider the Certificate of Merit (one fifth) stressed that it would be viewed as any other honors program. Thus, the Certificate of Merit was important only insofar as it signaled a particular level of course work; the actual attainment of the certificate itself was not important: "While it's not the same level of consideration as some other honors programs, we do consider it. It comes in the middle area of our consideration—it's not the most or least important, but it does make a difference."

At the 4-year institutions that interview students, all of the officials stated that they personally do not bring up the Certificate of Merit in interviews with students, and three quarters reported that neither do students. Three fourths reported that the Certificate of Merit never gets mentioned in letters of recommendation; when it does, it is usually the guidance counselor who mentions it.

Several officials from 4-year colleges and universities mentioned that the Certificate of Merit was difficult to consider because of the timing of admissions decisions. Admissions decisions were often made early in the spring, but Certificate of Merit eligibility was not determined until just a few days before graduation. One university representative stated that he likes "students to have everything in by March 1. By the time they have the Certificate of Merit, most admissions decisions are pretty much done. Only a few people are waiting to hear about admission by the time they graduate from high school."

The admissions procedure across the nine community colleges in the sample was similar. Admission was open to all students. A personal interview was not a requirement or criterion for admission, but a face-to-face meeting was used as an information or advising session, usually to discuss student placement. Again, the Certificate of Merit was never brought up in interviews, either by admissions officers or by students. All students who enrolled were required to take a placement test and fill out an application. All the admissions officials stated that evidence of the Certificate of Merit was not located anywhere on the application, and respondents who looked at transcripts stated that the Certificate of Merit was never indicated or that they were not aware that it was indicated anywhere on the transcript.

Generally, for the community college staff we interviewed, the Certificate of Merit did not come into play at any time during the admissions process. It is not used as an admissions criterion, as all Maryland community colleges have open admissions. A few of the respondents stated that a Certificate of Merit could help a student if he or she were applying for a scholarship or trying to get into a specific program (e.g., nursing). However, none of the respondents had, in their experience, ever processed a student who had earned a Certificate of Merit. One community college representative stated, "It's not the type of thing we look for. It's not a criterion we'll go out of the way to look for. If we get a student who is good, we know. We won't hunt for the Certificate of Merit."

IMPACT OF THE REQUIREMENTS AND THE CERTIFICATE OF MERIT.   Overall, these interviews suggest that the effects of the graduation requirements and the Certificate of Merit on college admissions have been minimal at best. Almost 90% of the admissions officials from 4-year colleges and universities in the study had minimal or no knowledge of the new requirements. Although some officials stated that the extra academic course (math) couldn't hurt, no one seemed too impressed or concerned about the practical or fine arts requirements. Most stated that these courses had no effect on admissions decisions.

None of the representatives from 4-year institutions had a clear idea of what the Certificate of Merit entailed and what purpose it served. Colleges that actually came across the Certificate of Merit in the admissions process viewed it as they would any honors program, suggesting that the Certificate of Merit has not had any noticeable effect either way on the college admissions process.

The new graduation requirements and the Certificate of Merit had very little impact at the community college level as well. This was more true about the Certificate of Merit, however. Community college administrators seemed ill informed as to what the Certificate of Merit actually was and as to how it could be used in admissions and placement processes.

Although less competitive colleges and universities stated that their applicants seemed to be better prepared academically, respondents from community colleges (which would be categorized as less competitive as well) did not notice that to be true on the whole. According to one official, although her particular college was admitting more students who had taken advanced placement courses, it was also admitting more students with academic deficiencies. Also, any changes in applicant pools and student success could not be attributed to the new requirements alone, but to a combination of other outside factors, such as a rise in socioeconomic status in some applicant pools, fine-tuning of remedial programs, and stricter standards in many community colleges. All this suggests that if there were students who seemed more academically prepared for community college than before, the new high school graduation requirements were not the cause.

Employers

We also interviewed 13 employers located in the general vicinity of the five high schools. Those interviewed were chosen for proximity to the schools, employment of graduates of the high school under study, and type of industry (health, manufacturing, government, restaurant, hotel, security, and publishing). Interviews were open-ended but followed a general outline, focusing on qualities that employers looked for when hiring, their use of high school transcripts, their knowledge of graduation requirements and the Certificate of Merit, and the impact of these on the hiring process.

HIRING CRITERIA.   Employers most often mentioned work experience as the primary criterion they used to make hiring decisions. Five of them mentioned dress or appearance, four mentioned presentation or way of talking, and two mentioned prior skills and high school diploma. The criterion mentioned varied by the type of job and the skill level: The two respondents who mentioned skills and the one respondent who mentioned types of courses were all hiring employees for technical work in government and manufacturing.

When asked directly if the type of courses that prospective employees had taken mattered, equal numbers of employers replied that it did and did not matter or that it depended on the situation. Employers who judged student course taking to be important were hiring for positions that required technical expertise, such as computer operators or secretaries. Overall, employers were interested in the relevance of particular courses to the positions for which they were hiring; little importance was placed on the well-rounded student. Employers made the following comments, which illustrate their focus on the type of courses needed for specialized work within their industry:

> When hiring security guards, it's good if they are specializing in security-type courses, i.e., communications, criminal justice.

> If they are looking for a job in machining, they should have taken a machines class, and business courses are preferred for office workers.

> To be placed in certain jobs, they must have had certain classes, i.e., to

be a computer aide, they must have at least one computer course; same for accounting aide; for clerical work, they should be in the office technology program and have typing.

For engineering aides at the GS2 level, we look for different courses, not like general business but science, algebra, trigonometry—Certificate of Merit courses, I believe they now call them.

Other employers reiterated that it wasn't the course that was important, but the skill that the student had. If students learned a skill outside of the classroom, it did not matter as long as the skill level was appropriate for the job. For instance, one respondent stated, "If they have no work experience, what they took at school is important, what classes. Just the skill is important, not the course title, weight, or level." The unimportance of course taking or even of earning a high school diploma and the concomitant importance of skill were reflected in the view expressed by one employer:

We prefer experience—they don't need a high school diploma. Welders and machinists usually do have a diploma, but they may have been trained at ARCO—trained but not necessarily in a high school setting. The same goes for clerical work—they don't need a diploma, just the skills needed for the job.

This varied, however, by the type of job and industry. The restaurant industry, unlike manufacturing, publishing, and government, could not afford to be too particular about the skills of the people it hired. As one restaurant owner stated:

We are in a tight job market right now. In hiring employees, we do something called a pulse test—if they have one pulse a minute, they're hired. I have five waitresses right now; 5 years ago, I wouldn't have considered any of them.

Ten of the 13 employers interviewed said they did not look at potential employees' high school transcripts when making hiring decisions. In contrast, three employers who assessed transcripts looked at grades or overall GPA. But generally, there was a lack of interest in grades. As one employer stated, "Grades are the least of our concern, given the number of other factors that are looked at, such as the aptitude test." And another, who offered a training program to all new employees, said, "Grades are not important, as long as they have the desire to learn." Even the one employer who conceded that certain grades are important did not consider them, because it was too time consuming to do so.

KNOWLEDGE OF THE REQUIREMENTS.   Only two respondents had any knowledge of high school graduation requirements, new or old. One was a parent of a Fast Track student, and another was a work study coordinator at Middle Class. These were exceptions, however. Only one employer noticed any differences in students who graduated since the new graduation requirements went into effect. Students, she said, had better word processing and computer skills, but she wasn't sure if they had learned them at home or at school. Her comment made the effects of the increased practical arts requirement difficult to assess but indicated they were negligible at best.

When told about the new requirements, most employers reacted favorably and felt it was a good idea. One employer, typical of the respondents, told us that "the more credits needed to graduate, the better. There will be a smarter pool of people to choose from." Several respondents were selective about which credits should be increased. For instance, one employer stated:

> It depends on the job they're looking for. Vocational courses are important to us—we recruit from vocational schools. Practical arts is good because certain jobs require that (e.g., computer jobs). For computer operators, a third year of math would be attractive as well.

Eight of the employers had never heard of the Certificate of Merit, three had heard of it, and two weren't sure. The three employers who were aware of it quickly attributed their knowledge to the fact that they had children in high school. One, an employer who was also the parent of a Fast Track student, stated, "When my daughter just started ninth grade, we took her into school the first day for her registration, and all we heard was Certificate of Merit this and Certificate of Merit that. The Certificate of Merit is the academic courses." None of these employers, however, had any specific knowledge about the Certificate of Merit.

SPECULATION ON IMPACT.   After telling employers precisely what the Certificate of Merit entailed, we asked if it would make a difference in their hiring of a student. Seven agreed that it would be an advantage, calling it "a good recommendation" and "important because it reveals high motivation and excelling," signifies a "more career-minded student," and "shows that the person has potential, drive, and wasn't a screwup in school, which could reflect upon his work." Many employers figured they would not receive information about the Certificate of Merit because students earned it after interviewing for a job. For instance, said one employer, "I've never had a student mention it because we interview them in October of their junior year." Similarly, we heard that "it will be too late; they will already be hired before we know if they are getting it. They get security clearance by February, and we don't know about the Certificate of Merit until June."

Overall, only a few respondents mentioned the types of courses that students took and their skill levels in these courses as important hiring criteria. When asked specifically if these were important, some respondents said that they were, although the importance varied by type of job. The more specialized the job, the more certain skills (and therefore certain courses) became valuable. Typically, employers looking to fill computer, clerical, and some mechanical jobs placed more emphasis on high school courses and student skills than did others. This lends support to the value of the practical arts requirement. Students who took computer or vocationally oriented courses were more likely to have an advantage in obtaining employment should that be their post–high school choice. Students looking for highly technical positions upon graduation, however, would most likely have taken practical arts courses anyway and would therefore be unaffected by the practical arts requirement.

Most employers agreed that in principle, having a Certificate of Merit would be an advantage to students in the hiring process. In practice, however, they had never heard about the Certificate of Merit. It was usually awarded after students had been hired, and employers rarely looked at school transcripts. Even if they did consult transcripts, seldom was the Certificate of Merit clearly indicated.

CONCLUSION

The graduation requirements were designed to raise standards and to broaden course experiences for students. We found that this was largely achieved, according to teachers, counselors, administrators, and students themselves. Positive effects of the new requirements included increasing students' exposure to particular curricula and thus helping them to become more well rounded and more planful in their course selections. Although these effects may have had intrinsic benefits for students, they did not significantly benefit their admissions to college or employment directly upon graduation from high school. Even though the policy changes were regarded as beneficial and positive within high schools, their effects were not particularly powerful outside that setting.

ACKNOWLEDGMENT

Acknowledgment is gratefully extended to Lynn Adduci for the assistance in collecting and analyzing the data and preparing an earlier draft of this chapter.

8

EDUCATIONAL REFORM: RETROSPECT AND PROSPECT

P art of the first wave of educational reform that emanated from the federal bully pulpit and state capitols in the early- to mid-1980s, high school graduation requirements reform was a frequent hallmark of omnibus state legislation. The 4-year investigation reported here has documented the changes that five high schools made in response to that reform in the commonwealth of Maryland.

The purpose of this chapter is twofold. The first is to summarize the key findings from our research and to review how those findings match up to the lofty intentions of state-initiated reform. The second is to extrapolate some learnings from this research and fit them into the current dialogue about educational reform in the decade of the 1990s. How do these learnings fit into a discussion that is substantially different from the policy discussions and debates of the 1980s? We strive to tease out some implications for individuals charged with designing and implementing reform that will affect schools into the 21st century. To do this, we espouse a position that holds great promise for current reform efforts, initiatives that stand in stark contrast to the standards-raising efforts implemented in the mid-1980s. In our opinion, the current emphasis on systemic changes with its focus on integrating the efforts at multiple levels for the benefit of diverse learners (Barth, 1990; Elmore, 1990; Fullan & Miles, 1992; Jacobson & Conway, 1990;

Schlechty, 1990) represents nothing less that a "new" philosophy of education. We place new in quotation marks because its fundamental assumptions are not new—they have been with us for a long time. It seems that, at least in part, their time has come.

In urging forward many of today's ideas, we move well beyond the data and offer some challenges to both practitioners and policymakers. Premised on the notion that significant changes are necessary to ensure that all students are successful learners, our experiences in the five high schools generalize to a set of important messages targeted at schools and state decision makers.

THE FIRST WAVE OF REFORM: MUCH ADO ABOUT NOTHING?

From the vantage point of near-perfect hindsight, critics and observers of the educational scene have criticized reform measures of the early- and mid-1980s as excessively bureaucratic in approach ("more is better" thinking), insufficiently far-reaching in potential effects, and driven by a hyperrationalistic (Wise, 1979) view of reform. Critics also note that the reform measures were relatively easily installed in schools and districts and did little to disturb the technical core. They are thus viewed as ceremonialized reform efforts, ones that tinkered at the edges of the classroom but did not pass through the doorway. As largely symbolic initiatives, they served to pacify a public disenchanted with educational outcomes, signaling that something was being done. The demand for far-reaching change inside classrooms was reserved for a decade later.

The results of our research from intensive data collection in one state suggest that this was largely true. To the extent that the changes documented here are in part attributable to the policy reform, we must conclude that there have been only modest effects on local school organization, student course-taking patterns, and hence (we extrapolate), student outcomes. Four broad themes capture the essence of our findings. First, the reform of graduation requirements increased some students' participation in academic courses and altered a few high school department course offerings. However, those modest changes are more a function of local context than they are of state changes. Second, any changes associated with the graduation requirements reform did little to alter either the exclusionary effects of tracking systems or other labels used to identify at-risk populations. Third, the key actors in the educational reform arena identified a *policy vacuum*. They felt they had little influence in helping improve local educational practice.

Finally, changes have been systematically unremarkable to what we call the *consumers* of high school graduates: 2- and 4-year colleges and local employers. We address each point in turn.

Course-Taking Patterns

Studies of high school curricular and graduation requirements reform (discussed in Chapter 2) have identified some trends that our research supports. First is the increase of course taking in mathematics, science, and in some cases, computer education and foreign languages. Paralleling these increases were declines in the vocational education areas, notably home economics, industrial arts, and business education. In states that stipulated a fine arts requirement, increases in art and music enrollments were noted.

The second trend found in these studies is that in most cases, the increases in mathematics and science were found at the basic and remedial levels. This internal redistribution of course offerings suggests a need on the part of local educators to move students through the system, even at the expense of "watered down" courses (McDonnell, 1988). Thus, more students are taking more basic academic courses but are not being exposed to the most rigorous and challenging offerings that stress higher-order thinking skills (Clune, White, & Patterson, 1989).

Our research both supports and challenges these two trends. Moreover, because of the fine-grained, school-specific analyses, we are able to link variations in these trends to local school context. In terms of academic course taking, in the five high schools we found that although most students already took close to the newly required three courses in mathematics, there were still increases after the new policy went into effect. Not surprisingly, the urban high school revealed the most substantial increases.

In terms of nonacademic course taking, our results suggest that stipulating requirements in the fine arts and vocational areas has a positive and balancing effect on students' overall programs of study. Thus, for the five high schools, the fine arts enrollments increased, as they did in Florida, with the biggest increase at Rural. These increases were tempered by reductions in practical arts course enrollments at all five high schools but most significantly at Urban and Rural, suggesting a more balanced profile of courses for those students.

Finally, we comment on advanced course taking, one concern of the critics of the reform. As was the case in California, for four of the five high schools in the study, we noted substantial increases in advanced course taking; the exception was the rural high school, where no increases were found. These increases are attributable to the Certificate of Merit option. However, it should be noted that important differences exist by race and academic performance, with white students and high performers earning more advanced credits than racial minority students and low performers.

What is most remarkable about these comparisons of our study with previous research is not so much the similarities and differences, but the fact that we are able to link these results to the local school context. We believe that this local variation is a function of a complex mix of local school and district capacity, will, and attention. *Capacity* reflects both fiscal and psychic resources—that is, the monetary and psychological resources available in the school and community to commit to a reform effort. *Will* is the focused desire to respond to mandated changes in a timely and substantive manner. Finally, *attention* captures the energy available in the school to listen to the larger policy arena and pay it some mind. We found that educators at the large urban high school were so consumed with the issues of poverty, disintegrating family structures, abusive relationships, and violence that they had little energy left to pay attention to policy demands emanating from the state.

Tracks and Track Rigidity

As discussed in Chapter 2 and corroborated in Chapter 4, the evidence suggests that tracks and tracking systems allocate opportunities differentially to students. Students tracked into college-bound programs of study have access to more challenging course work and more varied instructional strategies than do students slotted into general or vocational programs of study. These sorting systems, moreover, cast students of poverty and color and often young women into lower-level or remedial courses; these students frequently take fewer courses overall. Disproportionate numbers of these students are often found in the lower tracks, a situation that denies them the full educational resources available in high schools.

Strong evidence for this last assertion comes from our analysis of the breakdown of track data by race. Only two schools, United Nations and Urban, both with significant racial diversity, permit such a complicated breakdown. In Table 8.1, we present the proportion of students by race who are enrolled in college preparatory courses.[1] In addition to illustrating different experiences by race, the data also reinforce the first theme of important contextual differences by school. That is, pat-

TABLE 8.1.

PERCENTAGE IN COLLEGE PREP COURSES—BY RACE AND SCHOOL

	United Nations		Urban	
	White	Black	White	Black
Pre-policy	58	19	19	13
Post-policy[1]	81	44	45	17

[1]These figures represent an average of the calculations for the two post-policy years,
1989 (Post$_1$) and 1990 (Post$_2$).

terns by race are not consistent between the two schools. For example, although white students (58%) were three times more likely to be exposed to college prep courses prior to the policy change than were African-American students (19%) at United Nations, the difference at Urban was considerably smaller. There was little opportunity for any students at Urban to be exposed to college prep courses prior to the change in graduation requirements; percentages from both groups were only in the teens.

After the new requirements were in effect, both whites and African-Americans at United Nations were able to take advantage of increased college prep classes. Although the African-American student gain (from 19% to 44%) was greater than that of whites, they still were only half as likely as whites to be represented in this track. On the other hand, at Urban, the only winners were white students; their exposure to college prep classes more than doubled (from 19% to 45%) while African-American students made almost no progress.

Our analyses revealed that students in the general track earn fewer credits and fail more courses than students in the more challenging tracks. These students, moreover, enroll in fewer mathematics courses and more practical arts courses. With the exception of mathematics enrollments, the graduation policy did little to correct discrepancies by track.

Student perspectives on tracks suggested that tracks still represent substantially inflexible structures in the daily lives of students. Repeatedly, we heard of denied opportunities, rigid course entrance requirements, and inflexible scheduling. These students spoke to us of low expectations and lack of encouragement on the part of school personnel. When balanced against the transcript data, the overall portrait is a gloomy one for many students.

If tracks are relatively impermeable or permeable only in a downward direction, the opportunities for students to move up and have access to richer educational resources seem scant. If, however, tracks are not as rigid as most previous research has suggested, some flexibility exists within tracking systems to alter the inequitable allocation of resources.

Consistent with the research reported in Chapter 2 by Garet and DeLany (1984), our results also suggest some movement across tracks, especially in mathematics and science (often considered the most lockstep of the disciplines). In fact, in both math and science, fewer than half of the students stayed in the same track, and the least likely pattern was downward. That is, more students moved up to a more challenging and academically oriented course than moved down into a remedial or general one in those disciplines. This suggests that tracks are less clearly bounded phenomena than previous research asserts. These findings suggest the need for more detailed empirical derivations of the track concept and for more fine-grained analyses of student experiences.

The Policy Vacuum

Policy researchers and analysts assume one perspective or another in their interpretations of research. For example, Smith and O'Day (1990) call for a substantial state role in promoting systemic school reform. Calling the state "a critical actor" (p. 245) in educational reform, the authors note the states' considerable authority for education (grown over the past decade) and their "unique position to provide coherent leadership" (p. 246) in reform initiatives. The states should develop (1) a system of curriculum and instruction that is grounded in curriculum frameworks that grant latitude to local schools, professional development, and accountability assessment; (2) a restructured governance system that fosters school-based management through a "rationalize[d] and legitimate state authority" (p. 257); and (3) educational equity through closely overseen choice programs and teacher professionalism initiatives.

Although their proposals seem comprehensive, the bias is clearly in favor of an expanded state role, largely one of constructing parameters for local reform efforts through consultation, training, and technical assistance. Precisely what stance the states would take regarding their considerable authority in compliance issues remains unclear.

Our findings suggest a much less clear "claim to influence" for any of the key actors in the policy arena. The various individuals and agencies within the policy domain—specifically the graduation requirements reform policy area—talked about having little influence on the policy process, whether of policy formation, implementation, or evaluation. As an aside, little monitoring of the policy change took place, a phenomenon also noted by Clune, White, & Patterson (1989). This is quite remarkable, given the calls for an increased but altered state role in educational reform. If, in fact, the key state actors feel they have little capacity to shape policy-making or implementation, what use are calls for their increased role? Moreover, if local educators feel powerless to shape how policies are integrated into complex and multifaceted systems, what becomes of their role? We call this situation a policy vacuum where key actor groups deny influence and focus on the constraints within their particular spheres.

Consumers

The major intent of the policy reform, as discussed in Chapter 7, was to raise standards and thereby expose students to more challenging and rigorous course work, promote their intellectual growth, and presumably better prepare them for experiences after high school. Our results indicate that the major consumers (if you will) of high school graduates—local employers and 2- and 4-year colleges and universities—were singularly unimpressed with any changes in students over the years of the reform. They were largely unaware of the tighter graduation requirements and noted no particular increase in student preparedness.

These results must be interpreted cautiously. Although it seems unlikely that students would show dramatic increases in intellectual skill in a few short years, it also seems possible that employers and colleges would note the more full academic preparation signaled by increased courses in several subject matter areas. This might well have been most apparent in mathematics, an area often identified by both employers and colleges as necessary for improvement and one in which students overall showed a full course increase.

We find it quite a commentary on the reform effort that these consumers remained unaware that new requirements were in effect. Although the intent was to increase students' intellectual skills through more rigorous and challenging course work, from the consumers' perspective, these skills have changed little.

EDUCATIONAL REFORM IN THE 1990s

Concern about inequitable access to educational resources shares center stage with persistent concern about excellence and high standards.

Although many individuals couch the debate as either/or (we can have equity *or* we can have excellence, but we can't have both), others take the stance that we cannot have excellence *without* equity. Much of this debate plays out in discussions about school restructuring, currently the most visible and least clearly defined reform initiative. Although this definitional ambiguity is frustrating for researchers and practitioners alike, it is nevertheless useful as a "rallying point for reformers" (Elmore, 1990, p. 4).

At least four definitions of restructuring exist in the literature, emerging in roughly the following order. These definitions focus on governance structures, efforts to professionalize teachers, accountability, and profound alterations in how we organize children for learning at the classroom level. Each definition of restructuring has moved successively closer to the "technical core" of the educational enterprise—where interactions between teacher and student, as well as between student and student, take place.

Restructuring was originally defined as "redesigning governance structures (the formal arrangement for making and administering public policy on education)" (Swanson, 1989, p. 268) to include more key actors in important educational decision making. Early definitions focused on devolving decision-making authority and creating more participatory structures. Reformers called for new structures that would bring parents, teachers, community members, and local administrators into important decisions. Today's reform discourse refers to this aspect of restructuring as school-based management. In school-based management, authority for decisions rests with a team at the local school level rather than with the district office or the state.

A second emphasis in the restructuring movement has been to professionalize teaching (one might well call this an effort to reprofessionalize teaching)—to develop in teachers the knowledge and skills they need to enact their new roles in educational governance. Darling-Hammond (1990) pushes these ideas further, demanding that the entire educational bureaucracy be restructured to foster greater investment in human capital—primarily teachers but also school administrators—responsible for educational services. She notes:

> Unless major reallocations of resources and authority are made from regulatory offices to schools and classrooms, we cannot expect schools to find either the financial means or the organizational momentum needed to make significant changes. School restructuring not only needs to decentralize decisionmaking, so that parents, students, teachers, and administrators have a greater voice; it also needs to decentralize resources, so that investments can be made where they are needed. (p. 294)

Increased accountability has been a third focus of the restructuring movement. Although accountability in education has been around for a long time, linking it to system improvement is new. As McDonnell (1989) commented, the link was tightened when the National Governor's Association (1986) suggested an "old-fashioned horse trade," where state governments would loosen their reins on schools and school districts in exchange for local educators producing better student results. Although it is widely acknowledged that accountability systems are powerful levers for changing local behavior, there is widespread concern about the appropriateness of the measures being used to achieve results (Corbett & Wilson, 1991). For accountability to be an effective component of restructuring requires more attention to both the quality and range of indicators included in the assessments.

The final focus of restructuring is on ways to bring children together for learning more equitably in classrooms and schools. The structures of tracking and ability grouping and the perverse effects they have on at-risk learners have been important themes in educational reform. Reformers have called tracking and ability grouping discriminatory in their allocative function and unjustifiable in a democratic society. Recently, concerns about the inequities of tracking and ability grouping have been brought into the discussion about children with special needs and other at-risk children and youth.

The federal government's policy to more fully integrate children with special needs into regular classrooms (the Regular Education Initiative [REI]) stands as a hallmark of this aspect of the restructuring movement. First articulated in the mid-1980s and driven by both financial and equity concerns, REI has fostered state-initiated local experiments that place all types of children in the classroom. This initiative has the potential to profoundly change how we bring children together for learning. The implications for curriculum, pedagogy, school culture, and the purposes of education, as well as for the roles of teachers and administrators, are enormous.

In fact, all four aspects of the restructuring movement work in concert to alter formal decision-making structures, the knowledge and skills of professionals in schools, accountability at the local community and state levels, and the structure of learning environments. This "transformation" (Elmore, 1990) of the schools, however, must be grounded in a vision—a sense of purpose for American schools very different from that of the past. The vague, ambiguous, multiple, and conflicting purposes of the American high school have led to schools that increasingly serve well only a small minority of students. Systemic change offers a powerful avenue to rethink high schools' purpose and aims.

One can view the current calls for systemic reform as constituting a "new" philosophy of education. As noted before, we place "new" in quotation marks because many of the assumptions that undergird today's calls for reform are not new; they have historically been a part of educational discourse. Five assumptions underlie this evolution of the reform movement and can be viewed as constituting a philosophy of education.

First are the changing conceptions of change. Historically, educational researchers and reformers thought of change as innovation— something discrete, definable, and relatively easily installed in schools. This technical or "engineering" model of planned change was built on the assumptions that experts could best understand the needs of those in the targeted system and that implementation depended on persuasion (Benne, Bennis, & Chin, 1976, p. 17). Innovations were elements of education, and most often, new curricula were developed with the help of experts in colleges and universities and were intended to be implemented as designed in classrooms. Designers sought to "teacher-proof" the curricula, thereby avoiding the nasty problems of context. In fact, the power of context to shape the installation of such innovations remained obscure.

Today, however, conceptions of change are neither linear nor context free. Instead, they focus on the centrality of local context and value the talents of the individual teacher to modify, adapt, and individualize new ideas to better suit the diversity of the students present in the classroom, as well as his or her own predilections and professional skills. Change is viewed as complex, multifaceted, messy, and systemic: In today's view, altering the curriculum has profound implications for teaching strategies, organizational structures and supports, and professional relations, as well as for a host of other elements of schools (Cohen, 1983).

Second, today's calls for systemic change are grounded in a different view of the learner than those of a decade ago. Constructivist assumptions, which view the learner as a creator of knowledge, are embedded in such reforms as those called for by the National Council of Teachers of Mathematics (1989), as well as in whole language approaches to reading, process writing models, and experiential approaches to science, to mention a few. These ideas challenge the assumptions of the first wave of reform, in which, it can be argued, the learner was still viewed as a receiver of knowledge. With this assumption's focus on the creation of knowledge and the role of direct, hands-on experience in the construction of that knowledge, we are reminded of the ideas of John Dewey (1916), Jean Piaget (Piaget & Inhelder, 1969), and Jean Jacques Rousseau (1979).

Third, these conceptions of the learner have direct and immediate implications for instructional practice. Rather than a giver of information, the teacher becomes the architect of an environment in which students can engage in meaningful learning experiences, carefully monitored and guided by the teacher. The teacher becomes a resource, a colearner along with the students, and an active participant in the construction of knowledge. These ideas harken back to Rousseau's emphasis on the "structured environment" for learning, one that is crafted by the tutor/teacher to elicit learnings from the student. These views are radically different from those embedded in reforms that focused on standards and outcomes, which at times called for the assessment of teachers by student achievement.

Fourth, the notion of outcomes is changing. At least one camp calling for systemic change places on center stage a more holistic view of the "product" of our schools (Corbett & Blum, in press). This position assumes that students should be independent, complex thinkers who can also work effectively in groups of their peers. Rather than having mastered an identifiable, discrete "body of knowledge" (one determined by the teacher and/or the curriculum), students display complex knowledge and skills in areas largely of their own choosing (ones that best suit their own particular talents and challenges). But this broadened conception of learning is more than just the development of individual qualities. It also requires the construction of positive social relationships. As Corbett and Blum suggest, a successful learner must also focus on the common good—that is, model the ability to discern *and* act in the best interest of others.

This notion of the "what" of education demands more supple and complex means of assessment. Authentic assessment is a more variegated, complex, and multifaceted form of evaluating student performance than simple reliance on standardized testing. Portfolios and exhibitions, such as those developing at the Central Park East School, are seen as more natural and respectful of the whole individual than narrower forms of testing. This position represents an entirely different set of assumptions about evaluation and performance than previous ones.

Finally, today's calls for systemic change are inclusive and caring rather than exclusionary and tracked. Driven by concerns about distributive justice and equality of access to educational resources, this perspective argues that our educational system has become more separatist and egalitarian and that, over the past two decades, we have responded to differences in students by "creating new and separate" programs for the gifted, the disadvantaged, and the at risk, as well as for students with disabilities (Kane, 1991, p. 2). These programs create segregated systems in which both students and teachers have become increasingly specialized. Arguing that this is inherently undemocratic, this final assumption calls for schools and classrooms where empowered and caring people work through flexible and democratic structures that are responsive to the diversity of the students they serve.

This constellation of assumptions that underlies much of the current calls for reform is substantially different from those of a decade ago but has strong intellectual roots in the writings of educational thinkers of the past. But what are the implications of this discourse of the 1990s for reform initiated in the early 1980s? How can we place the findings of this 4-year study into that context? One useful way is to identify challenges that key educational actors confront as they enter the 1990s. These challenges or issues, articulated in the following section, are based on the previous seven chapters of this report. They do not flow directly from specific findings or recommendations; they are instead a discussion of the implications of Maryland's ongoing educational reform effort. That is, we move beyond the data to speculate about the challenges involved in making all youth more successful learners and more productive citizens of the 21st century.

CHALLENGES FOR EDUCATION IN THE 1990s

Challenges facing the nation and the 50 states—the latter becoming increasingly important actors in the delivery of human services and education—center on the changing composition of the U.S. population over the next several decades. Made up of growing numbers of minority students, children born and raised in poverty, and children whose native language is not English, school populations and ultimately the work force are becoming significantly more diverse (Hodgkinson, 1991). The evidence is strong that schools and schooling systems do not serve these children well (Darling-Hammond, 1990). The "large and persistent achievement gaps" (Cohen, 1990, p. 256) between whites and minorities, between the affluent and the poor, and between those whose native language is English and those whose primary language is another demand profound changes in the way we serve those persistently excluded from educational resources. Clearly, restructuring schools has the potential to alter those patterns.

Challenges for Schools

Schools carry enormous responsibility to effect change. They are sites for the delivery of educational services and places where the state requires students to come for a minimum of 12 years. We see seven major restructuring challenges that emanate from this research:

1. Create a vision of inclusive, caring schools
2. Reorganize how students are brought together to learn
3. Build flexible time schedules
4. Alter the role of the counselor
5. Infuse the curriculum, especially remedial or general courses, with challenges to higher-order thinking and problem-solving skills
6. Increase the comprehensiveness and diversity of data bases to inform decision making
7. Enhance communication structures within districts and between schools

These seven challenges must become part of a more complex restructuring agenda. They do not in and of themselves constitute restructuring.

One of the most pressing problems that our schools face today is the barrage of competing and often conflicting demands to do all things for all people. Schools not only get blamed for many of society's ills, but they are also viewed as the primary solution. However, all these different expectations make it difficult for schools to be truly successful at anything. What is missing from this complex mix of divergent pressures is any coherent vision at the local level about what schools should be accomplishing. The challenge is to structure a coherent vision around students and what it means for them to become successful learners. Although a climate for this can be encouraged at the national and state levels, the specifics must be left to the teachers and communities who best know the needs of their own students.

The perverse effects of tracking in high schools have been well documented. As the demographics of the school-age population shift, those whom schools historically fail—students at risk—will increasingly become the students that schools will be called on to serve. As a society, we cannot "continue to write off this segment of the population; the future well-being of this country depends fundamentally upon their educational success" (Cohen, 1990, p. 257). The challenge for local schools is to restructure student grouping arrangements to make them more flexible and to create environments where students learn from one another in teams, where the teacher is not the only person who claims knowledge, and where at-risk students can become active participants in learning. Altering learning structures to better serve all students, but especially those poorly served in the past, seems imperative.

Time is a powerful structure within schools. Time determines the pacing and content of learning over the day and the year, students' progression from one learning experience to another, social interactions outside of the classroom, and even the language used to communicate within a school building. As such, time profoundly influences students' educational experiences. How often do we hear of a student being denied access because of the schedule? The challenge that local schools face is that of using time to better meet important educational purposes rather than to constrain goals and expectations. Building flexible temporal organizations where students can engage in a subject for long periods and where creative scheduling and groupings foster engagement and problem solving would be an immeasurable contribution to student learning.

The role of the counselor is related to school organization and the use of time. School counselors have the potential to deeply influence students' expectations, hopes, and beliefs about themselves. The challenge is for schools to redefine counselors' roles so that they have more time to work with students. Counselors should help students, either individually or in small groups, to understand their options in successfully navigating through high school, coach and cajole students into fully engaging in available learning opportunities, and negotiate with teachers and administrators on students' behalf when appropriate. Although counselors claim modest influence over students, we believe they have enormous potential to serve all students better—at-risk students particularly.

Another challenge for schools is to infuse the curriculum with rigorous, thought-provoking inquiry into the topics at hand. Although enriched curricula and instruction for a few students at the top may have sufficed for an earlier manufacturing society, today's technologically based information society requires everyone in the labor market to have complex skills (Darling-Hammond, 1990). Thus, human resource development, as influenced by high school curricula and instructional practices, weighs even heavier on educators. This is especially crucial in remedial, general, or lower-track courses, which tend to suffer from impoverished curricula and pedagogical practices. Because at-risk students are disproportionately found in those classes, the twin demands are to regroup these students into more diverse classes and to ensure that they are exposed to a curriculum that will engage them in the learning process. Altering teaching strategies, ensuring a challenging curriculum, and bringing diverse students together may well create "opportunities for all students to become meaningfully engaged in reasonably complex and demanding learning tasks and gain practice working cooperatively with others" (Cohen, 1990, p. 261).

Another challenge for schools is to create and maintain useful, comprehensive sources of information—data bases—about their own practices. If the goals of restructuring and the devolution of authority to the school building are to be fully realized, schools must become their own best sources of information. They will need to monitor practices, spot trends that are divergent from their goals, clarify the impact of initiatives, and so on. To build and use complex sources of information is a challenge, but one that needs to be met if schools are to assume responsibility and accountability for their own operations.

This is particularly true in the current climate of criticism of the performance of our educational systems. Schools are struggling to balance the demands for restructuring and increased accountability. If they rely on traditional measures (e.g., test scores), they will fail to capture the complexity of the structural changes that need to take place. By adopting a more comprehensive information system, schools and districts will be in a better position to communicate what they are doing and the progress they are making.

The final challenge is to create better communication channels within schools (from teacher to teacher), within districts (from school to school), and across districts (from system to system). Education is a complex organizational enterprise that requires the integration of many different components. An optimal communication system provides organizational members with the tools necessary to do their work (Hall, 1982). This is particularly true when significant changes are taking place. Schools are generally regarded as isolating environments with little opportunity to discuss one's work and learn from others (Dreeben, 1973). The challenge is to create formal and informal channels that encourage a timely, full, and open flow of information.

Although these seven challenges do not encompass all of the challenges that schools and school districts face in the 1990s, they do represent the conclusions of our investigation. Children at risk are certain to be underserved by schools if current structures and practices continue. Strategies to better meet these students' needs should touch on curriculum, instructional practices, grouping for learning, the use of time, and the use of staff. Up-to-date data bases and open communication among all participants are also needed to support these efforts.

The challenges to the state are to clarify its role as authority devolves to the local district, to clarify educational goals, and to develop a more complex mix of strategies to encourage educational reform. These are discussed next.

Challenges for the State

The primary challenge for the state is to devise ways to encourage and support local districts as they restructure. To accomplish this, states can:

1. Articulate a broad vision for its educational systems
2. Ensure a redistribution of state funds so that investment is increasingly in human capital that serves children directly
3. Devise mechanisms for policy implementation so that creative and flexible time schedules, learning environments, and teaching strategies can be tried
4. Build greater capacity to assist districts in timely and comprehensive information systems
5. Build communication structures that ensure the accurate and thorough flow of information between districts and the state

A task for state boards of education is to formulate a clear vision that shapes education within each state. Historically, both national and state educational goals have been too broad to guide specific policy (Cohen, 1990). More effort is needed to articulate that vision to stakeholders and to ensure that a consistent course is followed in carrying out that vision. Specific policies should emanate from that vision and define the arena for state activity. The policies should incorporate concerns for equity and for the at-risk children who will increasingly make up the school-age population. This direction, moreover, should help shape local districts' and schools' vision. Great latitude, however, should be granted local districts in framing their own vision, so that the opportunity to build site-based authority and responsibility for important decision making will not be lost.

The achievement of locally generated goals (consistent with the state vision) will not be possible unless the investment in human capital—teachers—increases dramatically. As Darling-Hammond (1990) points out:

> The supply of qualified teachers, the nature of the preparation they receive, and the extent to which their talents are available to schoolchil-

> dren in different communities are the critical factors that will make or break education reform efforts across the country. (p. 291)

Reform will flounder if training, retraining, supporting, and revitalizing educators do not become state priorities. Such training, technical assistance, and support must also move beyond the individual. Schools are important units of change. It is essential to build capacity in them to problem solve creatively, plan, implement, and sustain change. Support means more than assistance. The state can also play an important "cheerleading" role. After capacity has been developed, it is important to acknowledge and reward that effort. More aggressive promotion of successful programs and practices needs to take place. Educators are most receptive of innovations initiated by their peers. The state might well play a more active role in identifying successful role models and in disseminating them widely.

Another role of the state in the 1990s will be to develop and implement policies that will foster achievement of the broad educational vision while encouraging local districts and schools to experiment and create their own visions and goals. In so doing, the state may find it valuable to build a long-term internal commitment to holistic policy initiatives such as restructuring. Such commitment signals the seriousness of the effort to local districts and builds internal expertise in training and technical assistance.

Several mechanisms are available to the state to foster policy implementation: mandates, inducements, capacity building, and system changing (McDonnell & Elmore, 1987). Policies developed in the first wave of reform were typically enforced through mandates and accountability measures. Thus, they carried the weight of legislation and were "intended to produce compliance" (McDonnell & Elmore, 1987, p. 134). With mandates, there is at least an implied threat of legal sanctions should the agency not comply. Mandates are the "stick" of the "carrot or stick" style of motivation.

The other mechanisms—incentives, capacity building, and system changing—are more complex and typically take longer to implement and to produce results. Because of their complexity, they foster a wide range of responses, encourage experimentation and innovation at the local level, and in the case of system changing, provide legitimate areas in which to experiment with restructuring. In sum, the choice of policy instrument or mechanism to implement policy has a profound influence on whether there will be a sense of shared responsibility between state and local actors or whether that relationship will be one of oversight and authority (Firestone & Rossman, 1986).

Fostering experimentation and innovation at the local level has long been a concern of state policymakers. Much of the success of any new initiative, however, rests in understanding variation in local capacity and will. Our research clearly shows the influence of local capacity, of organizational constraints and resources, and of the culture of the local school and district on the implementation of state initiatives. Success in the future will not occur simply because mandates evoke compliance (Cohen, 1990) but rather because a complex mix of strategies shapes district and school cultures in creative and innovative ways. Such strategies, if they are effective, will restructure relationships among those who have decision-making authority and will foster equity for at-risk students while maintaining high expectations for everyone's learning. As the five schools in this study showed, mandates seldom take the local context into consideration. A mixture of strategies is more useful for addressing local contextual conditions and meeting the state's aims.

Devising multiple implementation strategies signals a fundamental shift in the state's authority relations and in how it defines local accountability. The state is moving away from a regulatory role, and local districts are becoming self-regulatory. Not only is the state asking districts to transform themselves, but it is also transforming itself.

The state also needs to help local districts and schools to construct and actively use comprehensive and efficient information systems. Maryland has already acknowledged this need with its implementation of the School Performance Program (Maryland State Department of Education, 1990a). Through the use of well-designed data bases, districts have the potential to become their own best "monitors." They can take the pulse of learning within the district and adjust their practices to ensure progress is being made toward their vision and goals. However, comprehensive information systems are more than internal barometers. They also offer educators and policymakers the opportunity to communicate more effectively with the outside world about what schools are trying to accomplish. Current testing tools distort the larger purpose and may even get in the way of significant reform (Corbett & Wilson, 1991). Broad-based, well-conceptualized information systems offer legitimacy and increased accountability to policymakers and the public.

A final challenge for the state is to articulate more fully and openly with all key elements in the educational system. This includes other state agencies that provide services for children and families, state-level associations, and local districts. It is also important to ensure full communication with institutions of higher education and employers in designing a vision and set of goals for high schools. Often, these agencies and institutions work in ignorance of one another or at cross-purposes. To ensure close articulation between the secondary educational system and postsecondary systems or the workplace, regular, timely, and open communication is necessary.

These challenges posed at both the state and local levels should not, however, be met in isolation. They cannot be regarded as discrete elements to be installed in a state's strategy to shape local districts or as independent features of a school's restructuring initiative. They must be incorporated into a larger, comprehensive vision of educational reform. A framework that includes a set of perspectives on educational reform is required to foster multifaceted thinking about the policy decisions that will lead to an improved education system.

A FRAMEWORK FOR REFORM

In thinking about the education policy domain and its potential to effect reform, we find it useful to view any initiative (whether it is a policy decision, implementation of a specific new practice, or the general change process) through four frames: the technical, the political, the cultural, and the moral. Such an approach is not new. The first three frames have been offered by others to interpret organizational change (Tichy, 1983), innovation in schools (House, 1981), and tracking in schools (Oakes, 1992). What has not been offered is incorporation of the moral dimension.

Viewing education as a moral enterprise has a long-standing tradition in educational thinking. Dewey (1916) made a strong case for grounding education in moral principles. That perspective has seen a revival in recent educational literature, with a critique of organizing high school studies around academic disciplines (Noddings, 1992), an account of the moral imperative in leadership (Sergiovanni, 1992), a discussion of the need for caring in the teaching profession (Goodlad, Soder, & Sirotnik, 1990; Noblit & Rogers, 1992), and an analysis of how ethical principles are transmitted in the 20th century (Sichel, 1988).

Any call for systemic reform, such as that outlined by Smith and O'Day (1990), could fruitfully incorporate all four frames. To assess a policy reform from just one or two frames offers an incomplete and often misleading picture of the potential for that reform. In this section, we define each of the four frames through which policy decisions and their concomitant reforms might be viewed. We also apply the framework to one challenge that cuts across both state and local responsibility—the challenge of articulating and supporting a coherent vision—and discuss how the four frames provide different yet complementary ways to approach policy reform.

The Technical Dimension

The *technical dimension* of policy reform focuses attention on the knowledge and skills required to accomplish certain objectives—the "rules" governing the transformation of resources into some product or outcome. In schools, quite often this entails managing and transmitting information, learning new skills, or mastering new practices. When seen through the technical lens, policy reform should ensure that practitioners have the skills necessary to accomplish what the initiative demands.

The development of a shared vision for education requires that educators, parents, and community members—those with a legitimate voice in that process—have the knowledge and skills to articulate various aims of education, discuss competing views rationally, consider alternatives, and reach consensus. These skills are prerequisite to the reasoned, sensitive, and respectful deliberations necessary to develop a vision for education.

The Political Dimension

The *political dimension* embraces questions of influence, power, and authority, as well as conflict and negotiation within the organization. Under conditions of scarce resources, conflict will necessarily arise as factional groups compete for those resources. The political frame highlights how conflict is managed and compromise or integrative solutions reached. The essence of this frame is that multiple perspectives—and demands—are always brought to bear in the decision-making process and that different forms of negotiation are used to produce a decision. A focus on the political sharpens awareness of the equitable distribution of resources and decision-making processes that ensure fairness.

The political frame draws attention to the various and sometimes conflicting views on the aims of education that are found in any district or school and its constituencies. When a vision is shaped, conflict is likely as groups and individuals offer alternatives. Claims and counterclaims as to the "best" education for children will pepper the discussion. The political frame acknowledges the legitimacy of these claims and provides an orderly process for discussion and agreement. It further sensitizes actors to the dangers of the "power of position" overwhelming the discussion. Alternative visions should be given a forum for open discussion and resolution—they must be heard and considered.

The Cultural Dimension

The *cultural dimension* captures the values, beliefs, and norms of the organization—the rules, roles, and relationships that shape daily life and determine what is and ought to be for organizational members. Embedded in daily life and often unspoken, cultural values both shape and reflect a group's sense of itself. In schools, a generalized ethos may be apparent; however, often competing definitions exist. These beliefs and values shape daily behavior and decisions in profound ways.

Creating a shared vision for education directly implicates a school's or district's cultural values. It draws out the tacit and forces individuals and groups to grapple with what matters to them. The cultural frame draws attention to these underlying, often deeply held values and beliefs and, just as with the political frame, admits the possibility for conflict in competing definitions of what the school or district should be.

The Moral Dimension

Finally, the *moral dimension* draws out the principles of justice and fairness embedded in policy reform. Reasoning that when we make decisions that shape other people's lives we are making moral choices, this perspective challenges educators to think morally and to make decisions in a principled manner. There is a growing call for educators, as well as other social institutions, to develop more deliberately "an adequate foundation of acceptable social behavior and a basis for more mature moral life" (Sichel, 1988, p. 5). Reform policies need to reflect that concern. Noddings (1992) put it succinctly when she said that schooling focuses too much on the head and too little on the heart and soul. That is clearly reflected by the behavior of some of the more successful products of our schooling systems, who led us into the savings and loan crisis and the breast implant cover-up.

From the moral perspective, shaping a vision for education considers what is best for *all* children. Acknowledging that what is fair for the individual child may be unjust for the larger group, this frame identifies dilemmas of fairness and justice that are embedded in the process of developing a coherent vision for education. The vision also needs to acknowledge explicitly that schools teach more than knowledge in the content areas and that we should do more to celebrate competence in caring for others.

These four frames draw attention to various implications of reform policies. The technical frame focuses on the knowledge and skills necessary to enact policy; the political addresses how power, influence, and conflict are inherent in policy reform; the cultural evokes deeply held and often tacit beliefs and values; and the moral gently turns to consider the rightness of decisions. We argue that considering each—looking through its lens—will enhance policymakers' and implementors' understanding of the complexity of policy reform.

A FINAL WORD

This investigation clearly took us beyond narrow counts of courses to more complex issues of equity; curriculum and pedagogical practices; and relations of authority within schools, between schools and districts, and between schools, districts, and the state. Our broad brush also touched on the complex processes of reconceptualizing school reform and on the state's role in framing and encouraging experimentation and innovation at the local level.

The study began with five questions about the reform of high school graduation requirements: What is the variation in implementation by school and how can we account for that? How are tracks and tracking systems affected? What is happening to students and teachers at risk? How is influence played out in the policy arena? And what was the intent of the policy and has it been realized? Answers to these questions are complex and multifaceted. Schools are complex organizations in which reform of one aspect reverberates throughout. We end our discussion with a call for the state to move away from the mandated change of the first wave of reform and to embrace a strategy of capacity building and system changing that makes the state, local districts, and schools partners in experimentation and innovation. This strategy also calls for policy reforms to be viewed simultaneously through four frames: the technical, the political, the cultural, and the moral. In such a model, the state's role would be no less crucial than it is in a top-down, mandate model; in fact, its role becomes even more crucial. The state would provide resources, train and offer technical assistance, encourage and facilitate innovation at the local level, and lead the way to restructured schools. In short, the state would lead the way in meeting the challenges that all our students face in the 21st century.

Appendix A

RESEARCH METHODS

This appendix details the methods used to conduct the research. It is organized into six sections. The first section reviews the overall approach employed to collect research data and discusses how the literature influenced the research methods chosen. The second section gives a chronology of events that both preceded and accompanied the research activities. The third section explains the six data collection strategies. In it, we also detail the specialized training that helped us to prepare for the work. Fourth, we discuss site selection and sampling of participants in the study. A fifth section describes the analysis strategies involved in each data collection effort, along with discussion of efforts to ensure the reliability and validity of data. In the sixth and final section, we describe our feedback to research participants about what we learned from the research. This is particularly important for policy research such as this because the real value of the research is in the lessons that policymakers learn for new efforts to improve our schools.

OVERALL APPROACH

The overall approach in this study was to use several methods in multiple sites (five schools) to investigate the effects of a state policy initiative over a 4-year time span. The research included both quantitative and qualitative methods. Quantitative data consisted primarily of student transcript records with detailed accountings of which courses students took in each subject, the degree of difficulty of the courses, the grades that students received, and the number of credits they earned.

In addition, the research documented students' attendance, test data, and involvement in extracurricular activities. Qualitative data consisted primarily of field notes from interviews with state and local educators. Interviews were designed to solicit these individuals' knowledge of the new requirements and their perspectives on local implementation. Interviews were frequently supplemented with printed documents (memos, catalogs, brochures, and so on) from each school. Although quantitative and qualitative data addressed some unique issues, the research was also designed so that both could inform other questions. A concerted effort was made to triangulate findings across the two basic types of data.

Two concurrent emphases guided the research: (1) a general interest in policy implementation and (2) a focused inquiry into the effects of the new high school graduation policy on students' opportunity structure. The first emphasis—policy implementation—is based on the concept of backward mapping (Elmore, 1980). This approach assumes that the most complete knowledge can be gained through understanding implementation at the local level, where it must be put into practice. Focusing on those who implement the policy and their interpretation of the policy yields a more complex picture of the policy's effects and provides more meaning than if one were to track the policy from the top down. The design invests heavily in looking at individual school responses to the new policy, with particular attention paid to perspectives of classroom teachers. This bottom-up focus, however, did not neglect the other end. An important part of the research involved coming to understand the historic intent of the reform as seen by the original framers of the policy. We sought the perspectives of those at both the top and the bottom, as well as the middle, at district and state levels. Descriptions of important local-level differences in responding to policy changes offer important but incomplete insights into the policy. It is equally important to explore the bottom-line question of what impact these changes had on students' high school careers. We rely on the concept of opportunity structure to help focus that emphasis. Of interest are both the immediate and more distant forces that influence students as they make decisions about their high school careers, running the gamut from friends, family, printed materials, teachers, and counselors to school-wide, district, and even state policies. Additional internal pressures—individual hopes and aspirations, fears and doubts, and expectations and beliefs about what the student ought to be doing—rounded out the concepts that guided the research questions.

CHRONOLOGY OF EVENTS

The impetus for this research grew from one state department staff's conviction that important insights could be gained from studying the implementation of the state's new policy on altering high school graduation requirements. This employee had been appointed as staff liaison to the Maryland Commission on Secondary Education and was responsible for overseeing their work and production of the commission's final report. Initial meetings between the research team and this state department staff member took place while the commission was still formulating its recommendations. The timing of these meetings coincided with a new focus for the research team on more applied policy studies (Research for Better Schools, 1985).

Once the new bylaw (Maryland State Board of Education, 1985) was in place, the research team worked collaboratively with the state department staff member to develop a research proposal for the study on the implementation of this policy initiative. This proposal eventually became part of the work scope for the Curriculum and Instruction Division at the state department, the group formally charged with implementing the new requirements. Thus, the state bureaucracy acknowledged that this was a valued activity. The state agreed to contribute some resources—mostly staff time—to assist in collecting data, gaining entry into the schools, and maintaining a positive relationship with the research sites.

Once the state approved the research, the first order of business was to seek approval from the five district superintendents to conduct research in their respective high schools. The state superintendent drafted a letter requesting support from each of the superintendents. These approvals were reconfirmed midway through the research after there was a change in state superintendents, as well as several local superintendents.

Training each of the state facilitators (Department of Education staff assigned to each district) occurred next. The research team spent a day briefing the facilitators on the specifics of the study and their role in it. This was particularly useful in getting everyone to talk the same language and promoting a common understanding of what was happening. Once the initial training had taken place, future changes were easily dealt with either over the telephone or in short meetings with everyone assembling at a research site. On the evening prior to the first site visit in 1986, all the researchers, the state department staff, and the state/local facilitators reconvened to review specific assignments and to go over details for coding the transcript records. In preparation for these meetings, the researchers had developed coding forms and manuals to help guide the work of the state staff.

The research team also needed to be trained in conducting interviews. Approximately 10 experienced researchers conducted interviews over the course of the project. Two of the researchers were involved during the entire process and were responsible for development of the research design and overall coordination of the project. They, in turn, provided other interviewers with background on the study and with specifics about the kinds of information sought during the interviews with students, teachers, counselors, and administrators. The two senior researchers were present at all sites during the three rounds of data collection; the other eight were involved in either some visits on each round or in only one round of visits for all of the schools.

After the first round of data collection in 1986, the research team issued a report to the Maryland State Department of Education (MSDE) (Rossman, Wilson, D'Amico, & Fernandez, 1987). This report documented initial insights into the implementation process and spelled out eight recommendations, one of which was that the research continue.

In an effort to make the research as comprehensive and useful as possible, we also sought input from consultants. Shortly after the first report was issued and plans for continuation of the research had been drafted, we made formal arrangements with three nationally recognized scholars for their input on the design of the research. Based on their recommendations, we broadened the scope of the work by expanding the transcript data sets to include substantial minority student representation and equal sets of pre– and post–policy implementation samples. In addition, we added components that focused on the state perspective and an analysis of school-level changes (i.e., analysis of school course and scheduling records).

During the three data collection phases (1986, 1988, and 1990), regular communication took place between the researchers and both the schools and state department staff. Regular meetings were scheduled with the state department to keep them apprised of progress and to seek their assistance in facilitating data collection.

Near the middle of the research effort, the state initiated a new review process for research conducted in the state. The bureaucracy required that our research activity also be reviewed. After several delays, approval was finally obtained for continuation of the effort.

Staff turnover is one of the many trials of keeping a longitudinal research effort on track. This was particularly true for this research because we depended on the cooperation of a wide range of state and local staff. During the 4 years of our research, we experienced a number of key staff changes, including a new state superintendent, several new district superintendents, two new building principals, one new key school liaison person, and two changes in state/local liaison staff. These changes had the potential to create new obstacles in the data collection efforts. Two examples of staff turnover at different levels are described in more detail in the following. They illustrate some of the potential pitfalls and how we worked to prevent or minimize them.

The first example involves the change in state superintendents. As mentioned earlier, the impetus for this research came from state department staff who were working with the Maryland Commission on Secondary Education in developing new graduation requirements. There was a concern that the state be able to document the impact of this policy change.

In July of 1988, halfway through data collection, the state superintendent resigned and a new superintendent was appointed. State department staff informed the new superintendent of the research effort, and he approved continuation of the work. To assist in that information-sharing process, we summarized the work to date and attended two meetings with the new superintendent. The first meeting was just with the superintendent, and the second meeting was with his leadership council. These meetings gave the policymakers an opportunity to hear what we were attempting; we also discussed preliminary findings. The superintendent, in turn, reinforced his support for the research by writing to the local superintendents of the five high school research sites to ask for their continued cooperation in the effort.

The second example involves turnover of key staff at the school level. Cooperation between the researchers and staff at the five high schools was critical to the success of the research. In all five cases, cooperation was superb. In the initial stages of the research, the five local/state facilitators served as key contacts. When materials were needed or visits to the high schools had to be scheduled, we communicated through these facilitators, who, in turn, worked with school staff. Although we continued to rely on these facilitators throughout the research, after the first visits to the schools, much of the communication flowed directly between the schools and the research team. Each site had a different contact person. In two cases, it was the principal; in the third, it was the vice principal; in the fourth, it was the chair of the guidance department; and in the fifth, it was both the principal and the guidance counselor.

During the last year of research, just prior to the final round of interviews, the chair of the guidance department retired from one school. This person had been responsible for coordinating the assembly of transcript records for our visits but, more important, had also set up elaborate interviewing schedules. In this last round of data collection, we had planned to conduct more than 150 interviews in this school alone. With the guidance chair's retirement just 4 short weeks before our scheduled visit, we worried that the replacement would either be too busy learning the new job or simply not be interested in the research. Fortunately, neither was the case. The new guidance chair was a counselor already in the school who knew about the earlier research (she was one of the interviewees). She was very willing to take on the additional administrative task of sampling staff and students according to the criteria outlined for her and then ensuring that interviewees showed up for interviews. That kind of cooperation was invaluable to the project.

DATA COLLECTION STRATEGIES

This research involved several data collection methods, including interviews, document reviews, and student transcript record review. Data collection was conceptualized around six components:

1. A qualitative, in-depth set of interviews with *key state actors* who made recommendations for state bylaws outlining the new requirements. This historical perspective contributed to an understanding of assumptions, values, and purposes of the new requirements.
2. A quantitative review of *master schedules and course catalogs* to document on a school level the changes in the quantity and character of the courses being offered.
3. *Interviews and document reviews at the district level* to assess the degree to which the new requirements produced significant changes in local practice. This was necessary because several districts already had in place requirements stricter than those required by the state.
4. A qualitative, in-depth set of *interviews with students, teachers, counselors, and building administrators* to document the effects of the new requirements.
5. A quantitative, student records–based analysis of *student transcripts* to document course-taking patterns on an individual student level.

6. A semistructured set of *interviews with state college (2-year and 4-year) and university admissions officers,* as well as *local employers,* near the five schools to assess their views about the effects of the new requirements on the quality of recruits.

Each of these components is described in more detail below.

State Interviews

The new graduation requirements are derived from a report prepared by the Maryland Commission on Secondary Education, a group assembled by the State Secretary of Education in 1982 to reassess the high school program in Maryland. Chapter 1 of this report outlines the details that led to the formation and deliberation of this group. This group of 23 educators and citizens prepared a series of six reports, the first of which was *Recommendations of the Maryland Commission on Secondary Education. Volume I: Graduation Requirements* (Maryland State Department of Education, 1983). These recommendations were then forwarded to the State Board of Education and, after considerable debate, the state board enacted a revised set of requirements into bylaw in July 1985. A complete text of the bylaw is reproduced as part of the technical report (Wilson, Rossman, & Adduci, 1991).

To better understand the commission's values and assumptions as it carried out its charge, we interviewed five members. The five were chosen to represent the diversity of roles (state staff, local district staff, business staff, and university faculty) on the commission. All five were known to be critical and thoughtful participants in commission deliberations. The five members were interviewed using an open-ended interview guide with a series of predetermined questions. The open-ended format encouraged flexibility and allowed the interviewer to probe interesting tangents. The interviews were conducted several years after the commission's work had been completed but just at the time that the new requirements were beginning to be felt by local school districts. The same senior researcher conducted all the interviews. Interviews were tape-recorded and transcribed for further analysis. The lengths of the interviews varied from 1 to 2 hours. Six broad themes guided the interviews:

1. What was the background that brought the commission member his or her appointment?
2. What was the state and national political climate at the time of the commission's deliberations, and how did that affect the deliberations?

3. What was the process that the commission employed to accomplish its work?
4. What was behind the set of recommendations that the commission forwarded to the state board?
5. What happened between the time the commission report was made public and the state board passed the new bylaws?
6. What has been the impact of the new requirements?

Commission members were also asked to share with us any documentation they had kept on the work and deliberations of their team. The research team reviewed these documents to look for further clues about the values and assumptions underlying the commission's efforts.

The work of implementing these new requirements at the state level fell to a small group of MSDE staff. Seven key state staff were interviewed for their perspectives on the process of implementing this policy. These staff were selected because their expertise correlated well with the areas affected by the requirements. Three of the seven staff were from instruction and one each was from support services, vocational-technical education, special education, and communications. Four broad categories of questions guided these open-ended interviews, which lasted from 1 to 1-1/2 hours each. These interviews were also tape-recorded and later transcribed for further analysis. The categories included:

1. What has been the nature of your involvement in the state implementation team?
2. What was the intent of the requirements and what has helped/hindered in the implementation of the initial intent?
3. What has been the state's role in the implementation process?
4. What has been the impact of the new requirements?

A complete description of this interview guide and of all other data collection tools is presented in the technical report (Wilson, Rossman, & Adduci, 1991).

School-Level Course and Schedule Effects

The master schedule and course catalog analyses gave a detailed accounting of school-level effects of the new policy. This component shifted the unit of analysis from the state to the school. Here we were concerned with how the new requirements affected the kinds and number of courses offered and the scheduling of those courses. Perhaps the single biggest impact on the operation of the American high school is the schedule of courses. Most school schedules operate under *zero-sum* principles. That is, if additions are made in one area, they necessitate deletions in another. For example, if five new sections of mathematics are scheduled to accommodate the additional math requirement, five sections of something else will probably have to be eliminated. This would not necessarily be the case if additional funds were available to hire staff to teach these sections. The new requirements, however, made no such provision for that. Thus, important tradeoffs typically had to be made in adjusting the schedule.

To empirically test these changes, we reviewed 6 years' worth of master schedules (1985 to 1990). The number of course sections taught in each department was tallied and compared across years. One complicating factor was enrollments in each section. A longitudinal comparison of the number of sections offered would be appropriate only if the number of students in those sections did not change from 1 year to the next. Unfortunately, those data were not available to us for all five schools. For two of the five schools, master schedules documented courses without indicating the number of students in them. In these schools, any conclusions we draw about changes over time must necessarily be more suspect than findings in schools in which we were able to verify the number of students per section. Thus, this analysis compares only the three schools in which enrollments per section were known.

District Staff Perceptions of Effects

The typical flow of communication about the new requirements was from the state department to central office staff in the 24 Maryland school districts. A new linkage was established with regular meetings between state department staff and the district directors of secondary education (or their role equivalents). These directors, in turn, were responsible for disseminating information to individual schools. Consequently, it was important for us to find out central office administrators' views of the new requirements.

The fact that many districts in the state had graduation requirements that exceeded those of the state also made it necessary to collect district-level data. Indeed, some of the more aggressive districts regarded themselves as more enlightened than the state and prided themselves on being one step ahead. They mandated increased requirements that both preceded and exceeded those required by the state. Understanding that district context was important in understanding the school response. Consequently, a handful of central office administrators in each of the five districts in the study were interviewed to get their views on the new state requirements and to learn more about specific requirements of their own school systems. Researchers conducted open-ended interviews, between half an hour and an hour in length, writing responses by hand directly on the interview guide. Questions concerned specific district requirements that exceeded state requirements; the process of communicating the requirements to individual schools; the impacts the requirements had on schools; the purpose of the Certificate of Merit; and the strategies, if any, that districts employed to monitor the effects of the requirements.

School Interviews

We conducted interviews in the five schools with four different role groups: students, teachers, department chairs, counselors, and building administrators. Three rounds of interviews were conducted over the duration of the project, with the first set in the fall of 1986. These were held just after the new requirements had been enacted into bylaw but before the schools had much opportunity to accommodate the changes. Consequently, responses were very speculative in this first round, with staff and students hypothesizing about changes that might happen in the future.

The second round of interviews was completed in the spring of 1988. By that time, many of the changes were already in place (e.g., changes in course offerings, changes in scheduling, and teacher reassignments), and individuals interviewed could offer more direct anecdotal insights into how the requirements had affected them and their school.

The third round of interviews was completed in the spring of 1990. Because the first class to graduate under the new requirements was the class of 1989, these interviews gave us our first information after implementation had occurred, including data on any last-minute adjustments made to accommodate seniors who may have been missed in 1988 and on the stability of effects first documented in 1988.

These three rounds of school interviews provided an important longitudinal perspective on the implementation of the policy. Whenever possible, we interviewed the same people so we could document their perceptions of effects over time. Important interview protocol changes were made between the 1986 and 1988 interviews, with only minor changes made between 1988 and 1990. Furthermore, researchers' regular visits to the schools to conduct interviews and collect transcript records offered important insights into the culture of each school and how that culture was or was not changing over time.

In all three rounds, interviews were conducted in 2-day visits to each high school. Anywhere from three to five trained field researchers conducted the interviews. Interviews were open-ended, and the interviewers were given license to probe and seek more information on interesting responses. Responses were handwritten onto an interview protocol. Researchers then coded responses that lent themselves to frequency counts (yes/no or how often something occurred) and entered them into a computer for further analysis. (See the "Analysis Plan" section later in this appendix for details on this.)

The overall intent of the interviews was to get local reactions to the implementation process and to solicit interviewees' perceptions of the effects of the state-mandated policy change. Although the purpose was the same for all four role groups, there were important differences in the types of questions asked each group.

STUDENT INTERVIEWS. Student interviews began with questions that elicited descriptive information about the students (e.g., courses taken, activities, and postschool plans). Specific questions addressed their knowledge of the requirements; the Certificate of Merit option; and the importance that students placed on the additional math, fine arts, and practical arts credits. Questions about tracks in the school were also asked, along with inquiries about who influenced student course selections. The interview concluded with students' views about the quality of education they had received and the impact of the new requirements on that quality.

TEACHER INTERVIEWS. Teachers and department chairs were asked the same questions. Questions in this guide focused on changes in the curriculum in the subject area, staff adjustments, and other organizational adjustments. Interviewers also probed for the differential effects of the policy on different student groups (e.g., dropouts, minorities, and vocational students). Several questions addressed the Certificate of Merit options, focusing on what interviewees thought the purpose was, what courses their department offered, and what the effect of this option was on students. Another topic was how tracking had changed. The interview concluded with a set of questions about whether teachers thought students were better off as a result of the new requirements.

COUNSELOR INTERVIEWS. The bulk of the responsibility for monitoring the requirements fell to high school guidance staff. Interviews with counselors were designed to learn more about the role that counselors played in student course selection and about the counselors' responsibilities in implementing the new requirements (e.g., as record keepers and information providers). As in the teacher interviews, counselors' opinions were also sought on the differential effect of the policy on various student groups, the Certificate of Merit option, tracking in the school, and whether the students and school were better off having implemented the new requirements.

BUILDING ADMINISTRATOR INTERVIEWS. The final set of school interviews was with school principals and assistant principals. In addition to the same questions asked of teachers and counselors about the effects of the requirements on various student groups, the Certificate of Merit option, tracking in the school, and the overall effect on students and the school, building administrators were asked several unique questions. Because these were the people most likely to have an overall perspective on the school, they were asked more global questions about curricular, organizational, and staff changes.

College and Business Perceptions of Effects

To understand the effects of the requirements on students' postsecondary plans, we conducted a series of telephone interviews with 2- and 4-year college admissions officials in the state of Maryland and with employers from local businesses in the communities where the five high schools were located.

College admissions officers from nine Maryland community colleges and 14 4-year colleges, both public and private, participated in short (10 to 20 minutes long) telephone interviews. Interviews were open-ended so that if college staff wanted to elaborate on a point, they were able to do so. A major focus of these interviews was the Certificate of Merit, as that is the program of studies that emphasizes a more rigorous academic program, something colleges are presumably looking for in student transcripts. The questions focused on admissions officers' knowledge of the certificate and how they used it in making admissions decisions. There were also several questions about the other graduation requirements and about whether the requirements had made an impact on their applicant pool. Interviews concluded with a question about whether students were more academically prepared as a result of the new requirements.

Thirteen interviews were conducted with local area employers. These interviews were also conducted by telephone and usually took between 10 and 20 minutes. They were open-ended but followed a general outline. In these interviews, we focused on the qualities that employers looked for in screening prospective employees, whether they reviewed student transcripts as part of the process, whether they knew about the new requirements and what impact those had on graduates, and finally, whether they had any knowledge of the Certificate of Merit and whether it held any value for them as employers.

Student Transcript Record Analysis

This part of the data collection was by far the most time consuming and complicated. The new requirements affected a wide range of subject areas: math, fine arts, and practical arts for a basic diploma, but potentially all subject areas for a Certificate of Merit. The research staff also recognized that when changes were made in one subject area (e.g., adding a math course), areas not directly mentioned in the new requirements felt the impact (e.g., less flexibility for elective courses). Consequently, we thought it necessary to look at students' complete course-taking patterns (i.e., all courses).

This data collection effort began by constructing a portrait of course-taking patterns for a baseline group of students (class of 1986) from the five high schools. Initially, we regarded this as a pilot effort. We selected a small sample and conducted analyses to see if it would be worthwhile to expand the sample to include more students, as well as another cohort of students affected by the requirements. With this latter group, the research team would then be able to compare and contrast a group of students who completed high school before the requirements took effect (class of 1986) and another group who planned their studies after the new requirements were in place (class of 1989). Initial analyses (Rossman, Wilson, D'Amico, & Fernandez, 1987) documented interesting variations in course-taking patterns and suggested the usefulness of this component for more detailed analyses.

We visited each of the five schools in the fall of 1986 to collect transcript data on the class of 1986. School staff made available to us permanent record files for that class. The logistics of such an effort required close coordination between the schools and the research team. In the initial phases of the work, state facilitators coordinated the effort. Each facilitator worked with the school before our research team arrived to assemble the material for coders. The following information was recorded from each transcript: title of the course taken, the course's level of difficulty, number of Carnegie credits associated with the course, and grade earned in the course. Each course's degree of difficulty was scored on a five-point scale: (1) advanced placement or honors, (2) academic or certificate of merit eligible, (3) general, (4) business/vocational, and (5) special education. A single person assigned these values to all the transcripts, while teams of researchers recorded the rest of the information. A review of course descriptions and consultation with counselors or department chairs guided the assignment of degree of difficulty. Once the subject and level of difficulty codes were assigned, another researcher double-checked all the codes to ensure they were accurate.

Information on each student was transcribed by hand onto coding sheets, which were then used to keypunch the data into a computer for further analysis. The process of transcribing these data was very labor intensive and required careful attention on the part of the transcribers. Typically, a group of 5 to 10 staff (usually a combination of research and state department staff) worked on this. All of these staff were trained in what to look for. More details about that training are presented in the following section.

However, it should be noted here that what appeared to be a fairly straightforward transcription process rarely turned out to be so. Often data were missing or were not located in the place on the form where they should have been. Summer school credits are an example of the care we had to take. Often students would make up courses in summer school that they had failed or done poorly in earlier, and that course would be recorded elsewhere on the transcript without any cross-referencing to the original course. Only careful attention to detail enabled researchers to pick up important idiosyncrasies of individual school record-keeping practices that had an impact on students' transcripts.

Each school had a different system for recording and reporting data. Another example of how varied local conditions complicated the data collection effort comes from the small rural site. At this school, the guidance counselor entered all the courses that students took and their grades into a local computer. Although the computer screen accepted up to a 20-character description of a course, unbeknownst to the counselor, the computer saved only the first 11 characters. He entered all the course titles and at the end of the course title entered the track (at this school, there are three tracks: general, business, and college prep). These track distinctions were important to the researchers' coding, but when the district computer truncated course labels to 11 characters, those track distinctions were often not included. Fortunately, the small size of the school proved advantageous for us. There was usually only one section of each course in each track, and those sections were offered at different periods during the school day. Because the transcript records were arranged chronologically by period of the day, it was possible to know that second-period American literature was college prep track while third-period American literature was general track. This is just one illustration of the difficulties encountered in working with transcripts from multiple school sites.

Another complication arose with reporting grades for each course. Four of the five schools used letter grades (A, B, C, D, or F), but one school used a numerical system (0 to 100). Fortunately, the district publishes a translation code that it sends with transcripts to colleges and employers. Thus, the research team was able to convert all the course grades (e.g., 93 to 100 = A).

The cumbersome process of recording transcripts by hand led the research team to explore getting computerized student records from district computer files. We attempted this in two of the larger, more sophisticated districts for the first 2 years of data for the class of 1989, meeting with only limited success. Several stumbling blocks prevented us from using the computerized records with the rest of the data collection effort. First, not all the information was available on a single file. Often, different departments within the district had responsibility for different pieces of the data puzzle, and the system was designed so that these pieces could not be integrated. Second, computer tapes were not in a format that could be easily moved to files for statistical analysis. They all had to be manipulated and reformatted to make them compatible with other files. That process took several months and canceled out any gains obtained by not doing the work by hand. Third, not all of the districts had computerized records. Only two of the five districts were fully computerized in 1988, when this approach was piloted. Finally, there were often inconsistencies (some more serious than others) between the district records and the school records. Several careful checks revealed that school records were often more accurate than district records. Consequently, we decided to transcribe all student data by hand.

SITE SELECTION AND SAMPLING

Sampling required two levels of decisions. The first concerned which schools would be in the school sample; the second involved which students and staff within the sampled schools would be involved in the research.

School Selection

MSDE selected the five school sites for the research. When the original commission was formed in 1982, five schools were designated as field site schools. The intent was that any data collection efforts that were part of the larger high school reform initiative or any new innovations could be piloted in these schools. The five schools were chosen because of their diversity and because they represented the full range of high schools that Maryland's students might attend. The student populations from these schools came from urban, suburban, and rural settings and reflected a mix of social and ethnic groups. The size of the student populations also varied markedly. In addition, the five sites represented the full range of economic health in the region and a diverse set of family socioeconomic levels. Chapter 1 of this book provides a discussion of each site.

Student and Staff Selection

An initial sample of 50 students was randomly selected from each school for the review of student transcript records. The purpose of this initial sample was to test whether the process of transcript record analysis was viable and whether the results would yield any consistent, interpretable patterns. This initial sample simply consisted of a random selection of graduates from the class of 1986 (e.g., every ninth student from an alphabetical list). After a successful initial analysis, samples from each school were significantly increased. The guiding principle in sample size was that there be an adequate sample of students ($n = 100$) from each significantly represented racial group. In the small rural school, all graduates were included because fewer than 100 students graduated each year. In the two suburban schools with predominantly white populations, approximately 100 white students were randomly selected (i.e., an additional 50 were added to the original 50). For the two urban schools with racially diverse populations, we tried to obtain data from as large a sample as possible (preferably 100) from each group. In one school where the population was almost equally split between whites and blacks, approximately 100 students from each group were randomly selected. In the final school, which had a significant proportion of whites, blacks, Asians, and Hispanics, as many students in each group as possible (with a maximum of 100) were selected.

This sampling process was complicated by the fact that realistic comparisons require that data be available for students across all 4 years of their high school careers. Furthermore, the ideal situation would be for students to have experienced their entire 4-year program in the same school. Given transience rates in urban settings, obtaining that ideal was not always possible. As a compromise, only students who were enrolled for a minimum of 3 years at the one school were included in the sample. Separate analyses were performed to compare students who were enrolled in the same school all 4 years with those who were enrolled for only 3 years. No significant differences were noted in course-taking patterns. Table A.1 summarizes the number of student transcripts collected at each school site for both prepolicy (1986 graduates) and postpolicy (1989 and 1990 graduates) changes.

Samples were also drawn when the three rounds of interviews were conducted with school staff and students in 1986, 1988, and 1990 (see Table A.2). In all cases, scheduling and final selection of interviewees was made by the liaison person in each of the schools. The research staff worked with that liaison person to define the guidelines for selecting interviewees.

Every attempt was made to interview all of the counselors and administrators (principals and assistant principals with instructional responsibilities) in each building. Selection criteria for teachers included diversity in teaching experience, content area, and perspective. Also, priority was given to interviewing teachers in departments that were more directly affected by the requirements (e.g., math, fine arts, and practical arts). A balance was sought when interviewing students. The goal was to interview a representative group of students with varied ability, race, track, and enthusiasm for school. The sample was increased during the last round because this was the first group of students who had seen the full effects of the requirements. Table A.2 summarizes the number of interviews conducted for each role group by year and by school.

TABLE A.1.
STUDENT TRANSCRIPT SAMPLE SIZE—BY SCHOOL

	Pre (1986)	Post$_1$ (1989)	Post$_2$ (1990)
Fast Track	100	102	122
United Nations	201	291	214
Urban	191	143	146
Middle Class	101	106	100
Rural	60	35	36
Total	653	677	618

TABLE A.2.
STUDENT AND STAFF INTERVIEW SAMPLES—BY SCHOOL

	Year	Fast Track	United Nations	Urban	Suburban	Rural	Total
Students	1986	12	14	9	12	12	59
	1988	17	16	15	19	18	85
	1990	36	95	58	30	44	263
Teachers	1986	11	17	14	27	26	95
	1988	15	16	14	17	12	74
	1990	38	38	31	52	15	174
Counselors	1986	3	3	3	2	1	12
	1988	3	3	5	4	1	16
	1990	3	7	3	4	1	18
Administrators	1986	3	3	4	4	2	16
	1988	3	2	2	2	1	10
	1990	3	4	2	3	1	13
Total		147	218	160	176	134	835

A sampling strategy was also employed to elicit local college and business response to the requirements. For 2-year colleges, priority was given to selecting schools that students in the study would attend, but keeping in mind the need for some geographic balance around the state. We interviewed nine community college admissions officers.

Criteria for selecting 4-year colleges included whether students in the study attended the institution, the geographic balance, and the level of competitiveness (most competitive, competitive, and less competitive). We interviewed 14 admissions officers from 4-year colleges.

Nominations for local businesses to be included in the sample were solicited from the five schools' guidance departments. We sought sites that hired the largest number of students for permanent positions upon graduation. During the interviews, researchers asked employers to nominate other places of business that employed high school graduates.

ANALYSIS PLAN

Although there were six different components to the data collection effort, there were basically two kinds of data: (1) quantitative data represented by individual student transcript records and school course schedules and (2) qualitative data collected through interviews with various role groups.

Quantitative Data Analysis

Student transcript records provide a portrait of course-taking patterns for a large sample of students in each of the five schools over the entire 4 years of enrollment. By using the computer to scan characteristics of individual courses, we were able to create a composite picture. A series of broad questions helped guide these analyses.

1. Are students enrolling in more courses? Are there differential effects by school, race, track, gender, or academic performance?
2. Are students enrolling in more rigorous courses? That is, are they earning more advanced credits, both in total and as a proportion of total credits? Are there differential effects by school, race, track, gender, or academic performance?
3. Are students struggling more with their courses? (For example, are their grade point averages lower? Are more students failing courses?) Are there differential impacts by school, race, track, gender, or academic performance?

4. Have the number of credits earned been affected in areas influenced by the requirements (e.g., math, science, foreign language, fine arts, practical arts, business, vocational, social studies)? Are there differences by school, race, track, gender, or academic performance?
5. Has the tracking system tightened or loosened as a result of the requirements? Are there differences by school, race, track, gender, or academic performance?
6. Has the proportion of students enrolling in each track changed?
7. Has the distribution of courses across subject areas changed as a result of the requirements? Are there differences by school, race, or track? As a corollary, are students enrolling in proportionately fewer academic courses (i.e., English, math, science, social studies)?

Comparisons were made between students in the pre-implementation class (class of 1986) and two postimplementation classes (classes of 1989 and 1990). The general strategy was to compute mean scores (e.g., number of credits earned, as defined by Carnegie units) and then employ statistical analyses (e.g., analyses of variance) to explore whether significant differences existed across groups. We often found it necessary to go through several steps before data across the five schools were comparable. For example, some of the schools offered only full-year courses (i.e., courses measured in single Carnegie unit credits), while other schools offered only semester courses (half a Carnegie unit credit). Yet others had combinations of full-year and semester credits. Moreover, many vocational course offerings were multiple-credit courses, further confounding analysis. The value of these different credits all had to be standardized before comparisons could be made across schools.

Similarly, with the school master schedules, the number of sections of each course offered each year was hand tallied and compared across the years during which the policy was being implemented.

Qualitative Data Analysis

Analysis of interview data took several forms. When there were small numbers of interviews (e.g., commission members and district administrators), one researcher read all the interviews and summarized the basic tone of comments with appropriate quotes. When the number of interviews was larger (e.g., teachers, counselors, administrators, and students), a case analysis strategy was adopted. That is, the data were summarized by role group and by school according to the five broad questions guiding this inquiry. Within those five questions, a set of categories helped define key points. Some examples included:

Information:	Level and sources
Departmental effects:	Staffing, recruiting, electives, and working conditions
Organizational effects:	Scheduling, record keeping, changes in the tracking system, and working conditions
Special programs:	Special education, vocational students, non-native English speakers, dropouts, and minorities
Curricular effects:	Changes in content, shifts in track, and addition/deletion of courses

Coding of data and analyses were conducted by several researchers to ensure systematic conclusions. In addition, preliminary findings were shared with participants in each of the five school sites and with state department staff, thereby ensuring the credibility and usefulness of the findings.

FEEDBACK

Regular communication between the research team and state department staff was maintained throughout the process. Because state department staff also participated in much of the data collection, natural opportunities arose while in the field to discuss and react to what we were learning. In addition, regular meetings between the research staff and state department staff kept the state up-to-date on progress and enabled state staff to provide important support when needed.

After the first round of data collection in 1986, when student transcripts from the baseline year were collected and analyzed and interviews were completed in the schools, a formal progress report was presented to the state (Rossman, Wilson, D'Amico, & Fernandez, 1987). This report documented preliminary findings and offered a series of policy recommendations. The report was circulated widely throughout the state department and in local districts across the state. Three presentations based on the report were part of the dissemination plan: a presentation at a major state convention on school reform; a presentation to a national research annual meeting, the American Educational

Research Association; and a briefing for the 24 local district high school liaison staff. This latter group was created especially to help keep high school staff informed of state reforms.

In addition to the initial presentation at the American Educational Research Association, the research team made annual presentations at the association's meetings on various pieces of the research (Rossman, D'Amico, & Wilson, 1987; Wilson & Rossman, 1988; Wilson & Rossman, 1992; Wilson, Rossman, & Adduci, 1989; Wilson, Rossman, & Adduci, 1991).

As noted earlier, the state superintendent was also kept informed of the research progress. His leadership council also had the opportunity to review some of the preliminary findings and to discuss the implications for future policy initiatives.

By serendipity, in 1990, the state superintendent initiated a plan for improving Maryland's schools by the year 2000. This plan has 10 major goals and 15 strategies necessary to accomplish those goals (Schilling, 1990). The 10 goals adopted by the state board on May 22, 1990, reflected the national goals for education (U.S. Department of Education, 1990); recommendations in major state reports on school performance (Maryland State Department of Education, 1990a), vocational education (Maryland State Department of Education, 1989a), middle learning years (Maryland State Department of Education, 1989b), and students at risk (Maryland State Department of Education, 1990b); and issues identified through the state's strategic planning initiative.

The 15 strategies were elaborated over 1990 and 1991. One of the strategies was to revisit high school graduation requirements. The state board empowered a group of educators and business leaders to be part of this process and to make recommendations. Their deliberations were informed by the research reported here.

Appendix B

TABLES OF SAMPLE SIZES

TABLE B.1.
SAMPLE SIZE OF TRACK DATA—BY SCHOOL

	CP	CP/Gen	CP/Gen/ Voc	Gen/ Voc	Gen	Total
Fast Track						
1986 (Pre)	—	24	8	—	67	99
1989 (Post$_1$)	7	70	9	—	16	102
1990 (Post$_2$)	5	46	35	—	34	120
United Nations						
1986 (Pre)	12	59	28	6	96	201
1989 (Post$_1$)	110	87	34	—	58	289
1990 (Post$_2$)	86	55	20	—	49	210
Urban						
1986 (Pre)	—	9	21	43	118	191
1989 (Post$_1$)	—	17	14	15	97	143
1990 (Post$_2$)	—	34	18	11	83	146
Middle Class						
1986 (Pre)	—	36	10	6	49	101
1989 (Post$_1$)	35	31	6	—	34	106
1990 (Post$_2$)	36	30	7	—	26	99
Rural						
1986 (Pre)	14	12	9	8	17	60
1989 (Post$_1$)	—	16	—	5	11	32
1990 (Post$_2$)	—	17	8	8	—	33
Total	305	543	227	102	755	

CP, college preparatory; Gen, general; Voc, vocational.
Note: Some minor differences from totals presented in Table A.1 are due to missing data or very small cell sizes.

TABLE B.2.
SAMPLE SIZE OF RACE DATA—BY SCHOOL

	Asian	White	Black	Hispanic	Total
Fast Track					
1986 (Pre)	—	99	—	—	99
1989 (Post$_1$)	—	92	—	—	92
1990 (Post$_2$)	—	118	—	—	118
United Nations					
1986 (Pre)	22	74	83	22	201
1989 (Post$_1$)	40	143	76	27	286
1990 (Post$_2$)	37	104	55	16	212
Urban					
1986 (Pre)	—	93	93	—	186
1989 (Post$_1$)	—	89	43	—	132
1990 (Post$_2$)	—	105	38	—	143
Middle Class					
1986 (Pre)	—	92	6	—	98
1989 (Post$_1$)	—	97	7	—	104
1990 (Post$_2$)	—	92	8	—	100
Rural					
1986 (Pre)	—	51	9	—	60
1989 (Post$_1$)	—	28	7	—	35
1990 (Post$_2$)	—	28	8	—	36
Total	99	1,305	433	65	

Note: Some minor differences from totals presented in Table A.1 are due to missing data or very small cell sizes.

TABLE B.3.
SAMPLE SIZE OF ACADEMIC PERFORMANCE DATA—BY SCHOOL

	Low	Medium	High	Total
Fast Track				
1986 (Pre)	9	43	48	100
1989 (Post$_1$)	27	33	42	102
1990 (Post$_2$)	34	50	38	122
United Nations				
1986 (Pre)	45	76	80	201
1989 (Post$_1$)	60	114	117	291
1990 (Post$_2$)	45	68	101	214
Urban				
1986 (Pre)	146	41	4	191
1989 (Post$_1$)	107	25	11	143
1990 (Post$_2$)	98	41	7	146
Middle Class				
1986 (Pre)	25	36	40	101
1989 (Post$_1$)	19	51	36	106
1990 (Post$_2$)	21	39	40	100
Rural				
1986 (Pre)	9	20	31	60
1989 (Post$_1$)	7	10	18	35
1990 (Post$_2$)	8	12	16	36
Total	660	659	629	

Note: Some minor differences from totals presented in Table A.1 are due to missing data or very small cell sizes.

TABLE B.4.
SAMPLE SIZE OF GENDER DATA—BY SCHOOL

	Male	Female	Total
Fast Track			
1986 (Pre)	39	60	99
1989 (Post$_1$)	50	52	102
1990 (Post$_2$)	57	65	122
United Nations			
1986 (Pre)	101	100	201
1989 (Post$_1$)	152	139	291
1990 (Post$_2$)	109	105	214
Urban			
1986 (Pre)	91	100	191
1989 (Post$_1$)	56	81	137
1990 (Post$_2$)	52	94	146
Middle Class			
1986 (Pre)	60	41	101
1989 (Post$_1$)	54	51	105
1990 (Post$_2$)	51	49	100
Rural			
1986 (Pre)	25	35	60
1989 (Post$_1$)	19	16	35
1990 (Post$_2$)	16	20	36
Total	932	1,008	

Note: Some minor differences from totals presented in Table A.1 are due to missing data or very small cell sizes.

Notes

Chapter 4

[1]A similar analysis was also completed for the other two academic subject areas, English and social studies. Again, students showed significant movement across tracks. In the vast majority of cases (17 of 20), half or less than half of the students stayed in the same track. The rest of the students moved across tracks when making course selections. It was also apparent that there was no consistent pattern of movement.

Chapter 5

[1]Our intent was to test a fourth category, social class, but very early in the data collection, we discovered the difficulty of collecting reliable and valid indicators of student social class. School records listed parents' occupations, but the information was so outdated and incomplete that it was not meaningful. We also surveyed counselors about individual students' social class and found that with case loads of 250 to 300 students, counselors knew very little about individual students. The only other option was to survey students themselves, but the logistics of doing this made it impractical.

[2]Although the overall enrollment was equally balanced, the proportion of students with 4 years of transcript records—a necessary prerequisite for analysis of graduation requirements reform effects—was not. Thus, the transcript samples by race at Urban were imbalanced. The trend was for African-American students to be less likely to have complete transcript records and thus to be excluded from the analysis.

[3]The FTE was obtained by counting the number of sections taught and dividing it by the number of sections a full-time teacher would teach during the school day. FTEs were used rather than the number of sections each teacher taught because each school had different numbers of periods in the school day (two had six, and three had seven). This procedure also allowed us to disregard any teacher assignments that were not directly involved with delivering subject matter content. Time allocated to department chair duties, discipline, or other administrative/planning activities was excluded from the computations.

[4]For example, to say that the number of sections of math went up 20% without taking into consideration changes in overall enrollment gives a mis-

leading picture of real change. If enrollments increase by 20% at the same time that the number of math sections increase by 20%, then the two changes essentially cancel each other out. Thus, an adjustment was made to compensate for the overall enrollment shift from 1984–1985 to 1989–1990. In the first example, math FTE changed at Fast Track from 7.0 to 8.8. The actual change was 26%, but the adjusted change, when taking into account enrollment increases of 14%, was only 12% (26% minus 14%).

Chapter 8

[1]The variable for this analysis was obtained by collapsing the track categories described in Chapter 4. Because of the vastly different contexts in the two schools, we defined the "college prep" label differently. At United Nations, college prep was defined as students who were pure college prep or mixed college prep/general. Because there were no students at Urban who fell into the pure type, for purposes of this table, college prep included the two mixed types with some college prep courses: college prep/general and college prep/general/vocational.

References

Alexander, K. L., & Cook, M. A. (1982). Curricula and coursework: A surprise ending to a familiar story. *American Sociological Review, 47,* 626–640.

Alexander, K. L., Cook, M. A., & McDill, E. L. (1978). Curriculum tracking and educational stratification. *American Sociological Review, 43,* 47–66.

Alexander, K. L., & Eckland, B. K. (1975). Contextual effects in the high school attainment process. *American Sociological Review, 40,* 402–416.

Alexander, K., & Pallas, A. (1984). Curriculum reform and school performance: An evaluation of the new basics. *American Journal of Education, 92,* 391–420.

Allison, G. T. (1971). *Essence of decision: Explaining the Cuban missile crisis.* Boston: Little, Brown.

Apple, M. W. (1988). What reform talk does: Creating new inequalities in education. *Educational Administration Quarterly, 24,* 272–281.

Atkin, J. M., & House, E. R. (1981). The federal role in curriculum development, 1950–1980. *Educational Evaluation and Policy Analysis, 3*(5), 5–36.

Banks, J. A. (1987). Ethnic diversity, the social responsibility of educators, and school reform. In A. Molnar (Ed.), *Social issues and education: Challenge and responsibility* (pp. 59–77). Alexandria, VA: Association for Supervision and Curriculum Development.

Barth, R. S. (1990). *Improving schools from within: Teachers, parents, and principals can make the difference.* San Francisco: Jossey-Bass.

Benne, K. D., Bennis, W. G., & Chin, R. (1976). Planned change in America. In W. G. Bennis, K. D. Benne, R. Chin, & K. E. Corey (Eds.), *The planning of change* (3rd ed., pp. 13–22). New York: Holt, Rinehart, & Winston.

Berman, P., & McLaughlin, M. W. (1975). *Federal programs supporting educational change: The findings in review* (Vol. 4). Santa Monica, CA: Rand Corporation.

Berman, P., & McLaughlin, M. W. (1977). *Federal programs supporting educational change: Factors affecting implementation* (Vol. 7). Santa Monica, CA: Rand Corporation.

Bickel, R. (1986). Consequences of the extended school day and upgraded curriculum. *Planning and Changing, 17,* 31–44.

Carnegie Council on Adolescent Development. (1989). *Turning points: Preparing American youth for the 21st century.* Washington, DC: Carnegie Corporation of New York.

Cicourel, A. V., & Kitsuse, J. I. (1963). *Educational decision-makers.* Indianapolis, IN: Bobbs Merrill.

235

Clune, W. H., White, P., & Patterson, J. (1989). *The implementation and effects of high school graduation requirements: First steps toward curricular reform* (Research Report Series RR-011). New Brunswick, NJ: Center for Policy Research in Education.

Cohen, D. K., & Spillane, J. P. (1992). Policy and practice: The relations between governance and instruction. In G. Grant (Ed.), *Review of research in education* (Vol. 18, pp. 3–50). Washington, DC: American Educational Research Association.

Cohen, M. (1983). Instructional management and social conditions in effective schools. In A. Odden & L. D. Webb (Eds.), *School finance and school improvement: Linkages in the 1980s: Fourth annual yearbook of the American Educational Finance Association* (pp. 17–50). Cambridge, MA: Ballinger.

Cohen, M. (1990). Key issues confronting state policymakers. In R. F. Elmore and associates (Eds.), *Restructuring schools* (pp. 251–288). San Francisco: Jossey-Bass.

Coleman, J., Campbell, E., Hobson, C., McPartland, J., Mood, A., Weinfield, F., & York, R. (1966). *Equality of educational opportunity.* Washington, DC: U.S. Government Printing Office.

Commission on the Reorganization of Secondary Education. (1918). *Cardinal principles of secondary education* (Bulletin 1918, No. 35). Washington, DC: U.S. Government Printing Office.

Committee on Secondary School Studies. (1893). *Report of the committee on secondary school studies.* Washington, DC: U.S. Government Printing Office.

Conley, S. C. (1988). Reforming paper pushers and avoiding free agents: The teacher as a constrained decisionmaker. *Educational Administration Quarterly, 24,* 393–404.

Corbett, D., & Blum, R. (in press). Thinking backwards to move forward. *Phi Delta Kappan.*

Corbett, H. D., & Rossman, G. B. (1989). Three paths to implementing change: A research note. *Curriculum Inquiry, 19,* 163–190.

Corbett, H. D., Rossman, G. B., & Dawson, J. A. (1984). The meaning of funding cuts: Local context and coping with Chapter 2 of ECIA. *Educational Evaluation and Policy Analysis, 6*(4), 341–354.

Corbett, H. D., & Wilson, B. L. (1991). *Testing, reform, and rebellion.* Norwood, NJ: Ablex.

Cross, K. P. (1987). The adventures of education in wonderland: Implementing education reform. *Phi Delta Kappan, 68,* 496–502.

Cuban, L. (1990). Reforming again, again, and again. *Educational Researcher, 19,* 3–13.

Cusick, P. (1983). *The egalitarian ideal and the American high school: Studies of three schools.* New York: Longman.

Darling-Hammond, L. (1990). Achieving our goals: Superficial or structural reforms? *Phi Delta Kappan, 72,* 286–295.

Darling-Hammond, L., & Berry, B. (1988). *The evolution of teacher policy: Report prepared for the Center for Policy Research in Education.* Santa Monica, CA: Rand Corporation.

Dawson, M. M. (1987). Beyond ability grouping: A review of the effectiveness of ability grouping and its alternatives. *School Psychology Review, 16,* 348–369.

DeLany, S. (1991). Allocation, choice, and stratification within high schools: How the sorting machine copes. *American Journal of Education, 99,* 181–207.

Dewey, J. (l916). *Democracy and education.* New York: Macmillan.

DiMaggio, P. J. (1977). Introduction. In *Education and life chances* (Reprint Series No. 12). Cambridge, MA: Harvard Educational Review.

Dreeben, R. (1973). The school as a workplace. In R. M. W. Travers (Ed.), *Second handbook of research on teaching: A project of the American Educational Research Association* (pp. 450–473). Chicago: Rand McNally.

Education Commission of the States. (1990). *Clearinghouse notes: Minimum graduation requirements.* Denver, CO: Author.

Ekstrom, R. B., Goertz, M. E., & Rock, D. A. (1988). *Education and American youth: The impact of the high school experience.* Philadelphia: Falmer Press.

Elmore, R. (1980). Backward mapping: Implementation research and policy decisions. *Political Science Quarterly, 94,* 601–616.

Elmore, R. F. (1990). Introduction: On changing the structure of public schools. In R. F. Elmore and associates (Eds.), *Restructuring schools* (pp. 1–28). San Francisco: Jossey-Bass.

Fine, M. (1991). *Framing dropouts: Notes on the politics of an urban high school.* Albany, NY: SUNY Press.

Finley, M. K. (1984). Teachers and tracking in a comprehensive high school. *Sociology of Education, 57,* 233–243.

Finn, C. E. (1988). Education policy and the Reagan administration: A large but incomplete success. *Educational Policy, 2,* 343–360.

Finn, J. D. (1989). Withdrawing from school. *Review of Educational Research, 59,* 117–142.

Firestone, W. A. (1989a). Educational policy as an ecology of games. *Educational Researcher, 18*(7), 18–24.

Firestone, W. A. (1989b). Using reform: Conceptualizing district initiative. *Educational Evaluation and Policy Analysis, 11*(2), 151–164.

Firestone, W. A., & Rossman, G. B. (l986). Exploring organizational approaches to dissemination and training. *Knowledge: Creation, Diffusion, and Utilization, 7,* 303–330.

Fuhrman, S. H., & Elmore, R. F. (l990). Understanding local control in the wake of state education reform. *Educational Evaluation and Policy Analysis, 12*(1), 82–96.

Gamoran, A. (1987). The stratification of high school learning opportunities. *Sociology of Education, 60,* 135–155.

Gamoran, A., & Berends, M. (1987). The effects of stratification in secondary schools: Synthesis of survey and ethnographic research. *Review of Educational Research, 57,* 415–435.

Garet, M. S., Agnew, J., & DeLany, B. (1987). *Moving through the system: Curriculum decision making in high schools.* Stanford, CA: Stanford University.

Garet, M. S., & DeLany, B. (1984). *Course choice in science: Case studies of six high schools: Technical report for the Study of Stanford and the Schools.* San Francisco: Far West Laboratory for Educational Research and Development.

Garet, M. S., & DeLany, B. (1988). Students, courses, and stratification. *Sociology of Education, 61,* 61–77.

Geertz, C. (l983). *Local knowledge: Further essays in interpretive anthropology.* New York: Basic Books.

Ginsberg, R., & Wimpelberg, R. K. (l987). Educational change by commission: Attempting "trickle down" reform. *Educational Evaluation and Policy Analysis, 9*(4), 344–360.

Glatthorn, A. A. (1986). What about youth at risk? In H. J. Walberg & J. W. Keefe (Eds.), *Rethinking reform: The principal's dilemma* (pp. 39–45). Reston, VA: National Association of Secondary School Principals.

Goertz, M. E. (1989). *Course-taking patterns in the 1980s* (Research Report Series RR-013). New Brunswick, NJ: Center for Policy Research in Education.

Goodlad, J. I. (1984). *A place called school.* New York: McGraw-Hill.

Goodlad, J. I., Soder, R., & Sirotnik, K. A. (Eds.). (l990). *The moral dimensions of teaching.* San Francisco: Jossey-Bass.

Grant, C. A., & Sleeter, C. E. (1988). Race, class, and gender and abandoned dreams. *Teachers College Record, 90,* 19–60.

Grossman, P., Kirst, M., Negash, W., Schmidt-Posner, J., & Garet, M. (1985). *Curricular change in California comprehensive high schools: 1982–83 to 1986–87* (Policy Paper No. 85-7-4). Berkeley, CA: Policy Analysis for California Education.

Guthrie, J., Kirst, M., Hayward, G., Odden, A., Adams, J., Cagampang, H., Emmet, T., Evans, J., Geranios, J., Koppich, J., & Merchant, B. (1988). *Conditions of education in California: 1988.* Berkeley, CA: Policy Analysis for California Education.

Hall, R. (1982). *Organizations: Structure and process* (3rd ed.). Englewood Cliffs, NJ: Prentice-Hall.

Hamilton, S. F. (1986). Raising standards and reducing dropout rates. *Teachers College Record, 87,* 410–429.

Hansen, T. (1989). *Curricular change in Dade County: 1982–83 to 1986–87: A replication of the PACE study.* New Brunswick, NJ: Center for Policy Research in Education.

Hargreaves, D. H. (1967). *Social relations in a secondary school.* London: Tinling.

Hargreaves, D. H. (1982). *The challenge for the comprehensive high school: Culture, curriculum, and community.* London: Routledge & Kegan Paul.

Hawley, W. D. (1988). Missing pieces in the educational reform agenda: Or why the first and second waves may miss the boat. *Educational Administration Quarterly, 24,* 416–437.

Hodgkinson, H. (l991). Reform versus reality. *Phi Delta Kappan, 73,* 9–16.

Hotchkiss, L., & Dorsten, L. (1987). Curriculum effects on early post high school outcomes. In R. G. Corwin (Ed.), *Research in sociology of education and socialization* (pp. 191–219). Greenwich, CT: JAI Press.

House, E. R. (l981). Three perspectives on innovation: Technological, political and cultural. In R. Lehming & M. Kane (Eds.), *Improving schools: Using what we know* (pp. 17–41). Beverly Hills, CA: Sage.

Jacobson, S. L., & Conway, J. A. (Eds.) (1990). *Educational leadership in an age of reform*. White Plains, NY: Longman.

Jencks, C. L., & Brown, M. (1975). The effects of high schools on their students. *Harvard Educational Review, 45,* 273–324.

Kane, D. (1991). *Act 230: Regulation or revolution?* Vermont Education, Montpelier, VT: Vermont Department of Education

Kerckhoff, A. C. (1986). Effects of ability grouping in British secondary schools. *American Sociological Review, 51,* 842–858.

Lipsky, M. (1983). *Street-level bureaucracy: Dilemmas of the individual in public services*. New York: Russell Sage.

Maryland State Board of Education. (1985). *Graduation requirements for public high schools in Maryland* (Title 13A, Subtitle 03, Chap. 02).Baltimore, MD.

Maryland State Department of Education. (1983). *Recommendations of the Maryland Commission on Secondary Education: Graduation requirements* (Vol. I). Baltimore: Author.

Maryland State Department of Education. (1988). *Graduation requirements for public high schools in Maryland*. Baltimore: Author.

Maryland State Department of Education. (1989a). *Fulfilling the promise: A new education model for Maryland's changing workplace*. Baltimore: Author.

Maryland State Department of Education. (1989b). *What matters in the middle grades: Recommendations for Maryland middle grades education*. Baltimore: Author.

Maryland State Department of Education. (1990a). *Guide for implementation of the local school systems' Maryland school performance program plan*. Baltimore: Author.

Maryland State Department of Education. (1990b). *Maryland's challenge: A report of the Commission for Students at Risk*. Baltimore: Author.

Massachusetts Board of Education. (n.d.). *Structuring schools for student success: A focus on ability grouping*. Quincy, MA: Author.

McDill, E. L., Natriello, G., & Pallas, A. (1986). *The high costs of high standards: School reform and dropouts*. Paper presented at the annual meeting of the American Educational Research Assocation, San Francisco, CA.

McDonnell, L. M. (1988). *Coursework policy in five states and its implications for indicator development: Working paper*. New Brunswick, NJ: Center for Policy Research in Education.

McDonnell, L. M. (1989). *Restructuring American schools: The promise and the pitfalls*. New York: Institute for Education and the Economy, Columbia University.

McDonnell, L. M., & Elmore, R. F. (1987). Getting the job done: Alternative policy instruments. *Educational Evaluation and Policy Analysis, 9*(2), 133–152.

McLaughlin, M. (1987). Learning from experience: Lessons from policy implementation. *Educational Evaluation and Policy Analysis, 9*(2), 171–178.

McNeil, L. M. (1988). *Contradictions of control: School structure and school knowledge*. New York: Routledge.

Merton, R. K. (1968). *Social theory and social structure.* New York: Free Press.

Metz, M. H. (1978). *Classrooms and corridors: The crisis of authority in desegregated schools.* Berkeley, CA: University of California Press.

Metz, M. H. (1988). Some missing elements in the educational reform movement. *Educational Administration Quarterly, 24,* 446–460.

Meyer, J. W., & Rowan, B. (1977). Institutionalized organizations: Formalized structure as myth and ceremony. *American Journal of Sociology, 83,* 340–363.

Murphy, J. T. (1980). The state role in education: Past research and future directions. *Educational Evaluation and Policy Analysis, 2*(4), 39–52.

Murphy, J. T. (1989). Educational reform in the 1980s: Explaining some surprising success. *Educational Evaluation and Policy Analysis, 11*(3), 209–221.

Naisbitt, J. (1984). *Megatrends: Ten new directions transforming our lives.* New York: Warner Books.

National Commission on Excellence in Education. (1983). *A nation at risk: The imperative for educational reform.* Washington, DC: U.S. Government Printing Office.

National Council of Teachers of Mathematics. (1989). *Curriculum and evaluation standards for school mathematics.* Reston, VA: Author.

National Governors' Association. (1986). *Time for results: The governors' 1991 report on education.* Washington, DC: Author.

National Governors' Association. (1990). *Educating America: State strategies for achieving the national educational goals.* Washington, DC: Author.

New England League of Middle Schools. (n.d.). *Quality education for early adolescents.* Rowley, MA: Author.

Noblit, G. W., & Rogers, D. L. (1992). *Creating caring in schools.* Paper presented at the Lilly Endowment Research Grants Program on Youth and Caring Conference, Key Biscayne, FL.

Noddings, N. (1992). *The challenge to care in schools.* New York: Teachers College Press.

Oakes, J. H. (1985). *Keeping track: How schools structure inequality.* New Haven, CT: Yale University Press.

Oakes, J. H. (1990). *Multiplying inequalities: The effects of race, social class, and tracking on opportunities to learn mathematics and science.* Santa Monica, CA: Rand Corporation.

Oakes, J. (1992). Can tracking research inform practice? Technical, normative, and political considerations. *Educational Researcher, 21*(4), 12–21.

Page, R. N. (1984). *Perspectives and processes: The negotiation of educational meaning in high school classes for academically unsuccessful students.* Unpublished Ph.D. dissertation, University of Wisconsin, Madison, WI.

Page, R. N. (1987). Teachers' perceptions of students: A link between classrooms, school cultures, and the social order. *Anthropology and Education Quarterly, 18,* 77–99.

Passow, H. H. (1984). *Reforming schools in the 1980s: A critical review of the national reports.* New York: Clearinghouse on Urban Education, Columbia University.

Perrone, V. (1987). Promoting equity: The forgotten responsibility. In A. Molnar (Ed.), *Social issues and education: Challenge and responsibility* (pp. 125–132). Alexandria, VA: Association for Supervision and Curriculum Development.

Piaget, J., & Inhelder, B. (1969). *The psychology of the child.* New York: Basic Books.

Powell, A. G., Farrar, E., & Cohen, D. K. (1985). *The shopping mall high school: Winners and losers in the educational marketplace.* Boston: Houghton-Mifflin.

Randall, S. M. (1990). *Restructuring schools through participatory decision-making.* Unpublished comprehensive examination, University of Massachusetts at Amherst, Amherst, MA.

Research for Better Schools (1985). *Mid-Atlantic Regional Educational Laboratory technical proposal.* Philadelphia: Author.

Resnick, D. P., & Resnick, L. (1985). Standards, curriculum, and performance: A historical and comparative perspective. *Educational Researcher, 14*(4), 5–20.

Rist, R. (1978). *The invisible children: School integration in American society.* Cambridge, MA: Harvard University Press.

Rosenbaum, J. E. (1976). *Making inequality.* New York: Wiley.

Rosenbaum, J. E. (1978). The structure of opportunity in school. *Social Forces, 57,* 236–256.

Rosenbaum, J. E. (1980). Track misperceptions and frustrated college plans: An analysis of the effects of tracks and track perceptions in the National Longitudinal Survey. *Sociology of Education, 53,* 74–88.

Rossman, G. B., Corbett, H. D., & Dawson, J. A. (1986). Intentions and impacts: A comparison of sources of influence on local school systems. *Urban Education, 21,* 86–106.

Rossman, G. B., Corbett, H. D., & Firestone, W. A. (1988). *Change and effectiveness in schools: A cultural perspective.* Albany, NY: SUNY Press.

Rossman, G. B., D'Amico, J. J., & Wilson, B. L. (1987). *Pathways through high school: Tracking the effects of new graduation requirements.* Paper presented at the annual meeting of the American Educational Research Association, Washington, DC.

Rossman, G. B., Wilson, B. L., D'Amico, J. J., & Fernandez, N. T. (1987). *Pathways through high school: Translating the effects of new graduation requirements.* Philadelphia: Research for Better Schools.

Rousseau, J. J. (1979). *Emile: Or on education.* New York: Basic Books. (Original work published 1962.)

Schlechty, P. C. (1990). *Schools for the 21st century: Leadership imperatives for educational reform.* San Francisco: Jossey-Bass.

Schmidt, W. H. (1983). High school course-taking: Its relationship to achievement. *Journal of Curriculum Studies, 15,* 311–332.

Schwille, J., Porter, A., Alford, L., Floden, R., Freeman, D., Irwin, S., & Schmidt, W. (1988). State policy and the control of curriculum decisions. *Educational Policy, 2,* 29–50.

Sebring, P. A. (1987). Consequences of differential amounts of high school coursework: Will the new graduation requirements help? *Educational Eval-*

uation and Policy Analysis, 9(3), 257–273.

Sedlak, M. W., Wheeler, C. W., Pullin, D. C. , & Cusick, P. A. (1986). *Selling students short: Classroom bargains and academic reform in the American high school.* New York: Teachers College Press.

Sergiovanni, T. J. (l992). *Moral leadership: Getting to the heart of school improvement.* San Francisco: Jossey-Bass.

Serow, R. C. (1986). Credentialism and academic standards: The evolution of high school graduation requirements. *Issues in Education, 4,* 19–41.

Shanker, A. (l990). A proposal for using incentives to restructure our public schools. *Phi Delta Kappan, 71,* 344–357.

Shilling, J. L. (1990). *Forecasting success for all students: A vision for public education in Maryland.* Baltimore: Maryland State Department of Education.

Sichel, B. A. (l988). *Moral education: Character, community, and ideals.* Philadelphia: Temple University Press.

Sizer, T. R. (1984). *Horace's compromise: The dilemma of the American high school.* Boston: Houghton Mifflin.

Smith, M. S., & O'Day, J. (l990). Systemic school reform. In S. H. Fuhrman & B. Malen (Eds.), *The politics of curriculum and testing* (pp. 233–267). London: Falmer Press.

Stanlaw, J., & Peshkin, A. (1988). Black visibility in a multi-ethnic high school. In L. Weiss (Ed.), *Class, race, and gender in American education* (pp. 209–229). Buffalo, NY: SUNY Press.

Swanson, A. D. (1989). Restructuring educational governance: A challenge of the 1990s. *Educational Administration Quarterly, 25,* 268–293.

Tichy, N. M. (l983). *Managing strategic change: Technical, political, and cultural.* New York: Wiley.

Timar, T. B. (1989). A theoretical framework for local responses to state policy: Implementing Utah's career ladder program. *Educational Evaluation and Policy Analysis, 11*(4), 329–341.

Timar, T. B., & Kirp, D. L. (1988). State efforts to reform schools: Trading between a regulatory swamp and an English garden. *Educational Evaluation and Policy Analysis, 10*(2), 75–88.

Timar, T. B., & Kirp, D. L. (1989). Education reform in the 1980s: Lessons from the states. *Phi Delta Kappan, 70,* 26–32.

Toch, T. (1984). The dark side of the excellence movement. *Phi Delta Kappan, 66,* 173–176.

U. S. Department of Education. (1990). *National goals for education.* Washington, DC: Author.

Valli, L. (1988). Gender identity and the technology of office education. In L. Weiss (Ed.), *Class, race, and gender in American education.* Buffalo, NY: SUNY Press.

Veldman, D. J., & Sanford, J. P. (1984). The influence of class ability level on student achievement and classroom behavior. *American Educational Research Journal, 21,* 629–644.

Weiss, L. (1988). High school girls in a de-industrializing economy. In L. Weiss (Ed.), *Class, race, and gender in American education.* Buffalo, NY: SUNY Press.

West, J., Miller, W., & Diodata, L. (1985a). *An analysis of course offerings and enrollments as related to school characteristics* (NCES 85-207). Washington, DC: National Center for Education Statistics.

West, J., Miller, W., & Diodata, L. (1985b). *An analysis of course offerings and enrollments as related to student characteristics* (NCES 85-206). Washington, DC: National Center for Education Statistics.

West, P. (1992, April 8). "Common core" high school math curriculum offered. *Education Week*, p. 8.

Westat, Inc. (1988). *Tabulations: Nation at risk update study as part of the 1987 high school transcript study*. Washington, DC: National Center for Education Statistics.

Willis, P. (1981). *Learning to labor: How working class kids get working class jobs*. New York: Columbia University Press.

Wilson, B. L., & Rossman, G. B. (1988). *Local effects of state mandated high school graduation requirements*. Paper presented at the annual meeting of the American Educational Research Association, New Orleans, LA.

Wilson, B. L., Rossman, G. B., & Adduci, L. A. (1989). *Local response to state legislation of high school graduation requirements*. Paper presented at the annual meeting of the American Educational Research Association, San Francisco, CA.

Wilson, B. L., Rossman, G. B., & Adduci, L. A. (1991). *Maryland's graduation requirements: Local effects of policy reform*. Philadelphia: Research for Better Schools.

Wise, A. E. (1979). *Legislated learning: The bureaucratization of the American classroom*. Berkeley, CA: University of California Press.

Wise, A. E. (1988). The two conflicting trends in school reform: Legislated learning revisited. *Phi Delta Kappan, 69*, 328–333.

Wolfle, L. (1985). Postsecondary educational attainment among whites and blacks. *American Educational Research Journal, 22*, 501–525.

Index

About the Authors

BRUCE WILSON is co-director of the Applied Research Project at Research for Better Schools. He received his Ph.D. in sociology of education from Stanford University in 1979. His research interests focus on the relationship between school context and the implementation of educational programs, policies, and practices at the local and state levels. Currently he is investigating the effects of restructuring efforts on students' learning opportunities. Previous books include *Testing, Reform, and Rebellion,* with H. Dickson Corbett (Ablex, 1991) and *Successful Secondary Schools: Visions of Excellence in American Public Education,* with Thomas B. Corcoran (Falmer Press, 1988).

GRETCHEN ROSSMAN is an associate professor of education at the University of Massachusetts at Amherst. She received her Ph.D. in education from the University of Pennsylvania in 1983. Her research interests include policy studies and qualitative research methods. Her current research is examining the local implementation of state policy that encourages the integration into the regular classroom of children with disabilities and those receiving Chapter 1 and bilingual services. Previous books include *Change and Effectiveness: A Cultural Perspective,* with H. Dickson Corbett and William A. Firestone (SUNY Press, 1988) and *Designing Qualitative Research,* with Catherine Marshall (Sage, 1989). A second edition of the Sage book will appear in 1994.